D0580605

BEST *of the* BEST
from
WASHINGTON
COOKBOOK

🍎🍎🍎🍎🍎🍎🍎🍎🍎🍎

Selected Recipes from
WASHINGTON'S
FAVORITE COOKBOOKS

Mount Rainier, highest (14,410 feet) and third-most voluminous volcano in the Cascades after Mounts Shasta and Adams, dominates the Seattle-Tacoma area, where it is known fondly as "The Mountain."

BEST *of the* BEST
from
WASHINGTON
COOKBOOK

● ● ● ● ● ● ● ● ● ●

Selected Recipes from
WASHINGTON'S
FAVORITE COOKBOOKS

EDITED BY

GWEN McKEE

AND

BARBARA MOSELEY

Illustrated by Tupper England

QUAIL RIDGE PRESS
Preserving America's Food Heritage

Recipe Collection©2002 Quail Ridge Press, Inc.

Reprinted with permission and all rights reserved under the name
of the cookbooks, organizations or individuals listed below.

Allrecipes Tried & True Favorites ©2001 by Allrecipes; *Another Taste of Washington State* ©2000 Tracy Winters; *The Best of The Ark and More!* ©2000 Nanci Main and Jimella Lucas; *Bounteous Blessings* ©2001 by Frances A. Gillette; *The Chicken Cookbook* ©1994 Washington Fryer Commission; *Christmas in Washington Cook Book* ©1995 by Golden West Publishers; *The Colophon Cafe Best Recipes* ©1995 by Mama Colophon Inc.; *The Colophon Cafe Best Soups* ©1996 by Mama Colophon Cafe Inc.; *The Colophon Cafe Best Vegetarian Recipes* ©1998 by Mama Colophon Inc.; *Duck Soup and Other Fowl Recipes* ©1994 Lyndia Vold; *Extraordinary Cuisine for Sea & Shore* ©1990 Seattle Yacht Club; *Food for Tots* ©2001 Janice Woolley and Jennifer Pugmire; *Gold'n Delicious* ©1995 The Junior League of Spokane; *Good Food for (Mostly) Good People* ©2001 by Marla Emde; *Good Times at Green Lake* ©2000 Board of Regents of Washington State University; *Heaven on the Half Shell* ©2001 University of Washington; *The Ingredients* © 1996 Iron Athlete, Inc.; *LaConner Palates* ©1998 Patricia Flynn and Patricia McClane; *The 99¢ a Meal Cookbook* ©1996 Loompanics Unlimited; *Our Best Home Cooking* ©1993 Pend Oreille County Historical Society; *The Overlake School Cookbook* ©1984 The Overlake School; *Pig Out* ©2001 Skamania County Law Enforcement Association; *Recipes from Our Friends* ©2001 Friends of Whitman County Library; *Recipes to Remember* ©1992 by Cookbook Publishers, Inc.; *San Juan Classics II* ©1998 Dawn Ashbach and Janice Veal; *The Shoalwater's Finest Dinners* ©1991 Harris & Friedrich; *Simply Whidbey* ©1991 Laura Moore and Deborah Skinner; *Six Ingredients or Less* ©2001 by Carlean Johnson; *Six Ingredients or Less: Cooking Light & Healthy* ©1992 by Carlean Johnson; *Six Ingredients or Less: Pasta & Casseroles* ©1996 by Carlean Johnson; *Skagit Valley Fare* ©1996 Lavone Newell; *Sleigh Bells and Sugarplums* ©1992 by Frances A. Gillette and Daughters; *Tastes of Country* ©1987 by Frances A. Gillette; *20,000 Gallons of Chowder* ©1999 by Ray Dunn; *Wandering & Feasting* ©1996 Board of Regents of Washington State University; *Washington Cook Book* ©1994 by Golden West Publishers; *Washington Farmers' Markets Cookbook and Guide* ©2000 by Kris Wetherbee; *The Wild and Free Cookbook* ©1996 Tom Squier

Library of Congress Cataloging-in-Publication Data

Best of the best from Washington : selected recipes from Washington's favorite cookbooks /
    edited by Gwen McKee and Barbara Moseley ; illustrated by Tupper England.
    p. cm.
    ISBN 1-893062-35-X
      1. Cookery, American 2. Cookery—Washington. I. McKee, Gwen. II. Moseley, Barbara.

    TX715.B485654 2002
    641.59797—dc21   2002017880

Front cover photo of Mt. Rainier © Keith Lazelle Nature Photography.
Back cover photo by Greg Campbell. Design by Cynthia Clark. Printed in Canada.

QUAIL RIDGE PRESS
P. O. Box 123 • Brandon, MS 39043 • 1-800-343-1583
e-mail: info@quailridge.com • www.quailridge.com

CONTENTS

More than half of all apples grown in the United States for fresh eating come from orchards in Washington state.

PREFACE

When you think of Washington food, perhaps you envision delicious, juicy apples. And with good reason—more than half of all apples grown in the United States for fresh eating come from the seemingly endless acres of orchards nestled in the foothills of the Cascade Mountains in Washington.

As expected, apples do influence the cuisine of the Evergreen State; however, Washington is also known for its cherries, plums, grapes, huckleberries and blackberries, to name but a few of its wonderful fruit resources. The diversity of the land and climate contributes greatly to the many natural ingredients that bring a unique blend of flavors to the dinner table.

To the east of the Cascades lie the apple orchards along with rolling fields of wheat and barley; bountiful crops such as potatoes, corn, hops, mint, peaches, and apricots; and livestock, including hogs, cattle and sheep. Here, too, you'll find a booming wine industry. Farther west to the coast, seafood and fish abound.

You'll be transported all over the Evergreen State via your tastebuds as Washington's fantastic flavor unfolds within the pages of this book. You'll find sea-inspired recipes such as easy-to-prepare Puget Sound Oyster Bisque (page 62), Skagit Bay Crab and Havarti Omelet (page 54), calling for just a tad of Dungeness crab made colorful and delicious by chopped tomatoes and green onions, and Prawns Genovese (page 28), an appetizer that will impress your guests long after the evening is over. Sink your teeth into flavorful Garlic Grenadine Pork Roast (page 141) that calls on dried cranberries and orange juice to enhance its slow-cooked goodness, or a Walla Walla Steak Sandwich with Horseradish Sauce (page 130) that says, "Move over Philly Cheese Steak Sandwich!" There are plenty of recipes to expand your cooking horizons like Thai Chicken Pasta (page 123), one of many oriental dishes that are so healthful and delicious, and

The Original African Peanut Soup (page 69) that has such a distinctive taste, some people think it is addictive! What's for dessert?
How about a wild and creamy Huckleberry Cream Torte (page 237)
or Cranberry Whirl Cheesecake (page 198) that is nothing short of
a culinary masterpiece! And don't the best recipes usually get passed
down from one generation to the next . . . like Aunt Lulu's Chocolate
Cake (page 202) and Grandma's Lizzie's Ginger Cookies (page 222)
. . . goodness, gracious, delicious!

You'll also discover photographs and facts about Washington
(did you realize it was the only state named after a President?) that
give you an enhanced sense of all the state has to offer. Following
each recipe is the name of the contributing cookbook. A special
Catalog of Contributing Cookbooks Section (see page 259) in the
back of this book displays each book's cover, along with a descrip-
tion and ordering information. This section is particularly popular
with cookbook collectors.

We wish to thank every person who contributed to this book,
especially the people who so unselfishly offered recipes. We appreciate the food editors and the bookstore and gift shop managers who
guided us to the state's most popular cookbooks. Thanks also to
Washington's tourism department and many Chambers of
Commerce for providing historic and informative data. Thank you,
too, Tupper England, for your charming illustrations that capture the
true spirit of the state.

Enjoy your delicious journey through the state of Washington as
each sumptuous recipe takes you there . . . *tastefully.*

Gwen McKee and Barbara Moseley

CONTRIBUTING COOKBOOKS

Allrecipes Tried & True Favorites
Another Taste of Washington State
The Best of The Ark and More!
Bounteous Blessings
The Chicken Cookbook
Christmas in Washington Cook Book
The Colophon Cafe Best Recipes
The Colophon Cafe Best Soups
The Colophon Cafe Best Vegetarian Recipes
Cooking with Irene!
Costco Wholesale Employee Association Cookbook
Crime Stoppers: A Community Cookbook
Duck Soup & Other Fowl Recipes
Extraordinary Cuisine for Sea & Shore
Family Favorites Recipes
Favorite Recipes from Our Best Cooks
Favorite Recipes from the Employees, Family, and Friends of
Numerica Credit Union
Food for Tots
From My Heart For Yours
From Our Kitchen to Yours
Gold'n Delicious
Good Food for (Mostly) Good People Cookbook
Good Times at Green Lake
Harvest Feast
Heaven on the Half Shell
Heavenly Fare
The Historic Mid-1900's Cookbook
Home Plates
The Ingredients: Fresh Pacific Northwest Cuisine
LaConner Palates
Liberty Lake Community Cookbook
Mariners Mix'n and Fix'n Grand Slam Style

CONTRIBUTING COOKBOOKS

McNamee Family & Friends Cookbook
Nautical Niceaty's from Spokane Yacht Club
The 99¢ a Meal Cookbook
Northwest Garlic Festival Cookbook, Volume 3
Our Best Home Cooking
Our Burnt Offerings
The Overlake School Cookbook
Pig Out
Recipes from Our Friends
Recipes to Remember
San Juan Classics II Cookbook
Sharing Our Best
The Shoalwater's Finest Dinners
Simply Whidbey
Six Ingredients or Less
Six Ingredients or Less: Cooking Light & Healthy
Six Ingredients or Less: Pasta & Casseroles
Skagit Valley Fare
Sleigh Bells and Sugarplums
Starters & Closers
Taste of Balboa
A Taste of Heaven
Taste of the Methow
Tastes of Country
20,000 Gallons of Chowder
Unser Tagelich Brot (The Staff of Life III)
Wandering & Feasting
Washington Cook Book
Washington Farmers' Markets Cookbook and Guide
Western Washington Oncology Cook Book
The Wild and Free Cookbook
Your Favorite Recipes

BEVERAGES *and* APPETIZERS

Grand Coulee Dam, positioned deep in the Columbia River Gorge of Central Washington, is one of the world's largest producers of hydroelectric power and one of the largest concrete structures in the world.

PHOTO © CHARLES HUBBARD.

Bailey's Irish Cream

$^3/_4$ cup whiskey (brandy, rum, bourbon, scotch)
1 (14-ounce) can sweetened condensed milk
1 cup whipping cream
4 eggs

2 tablespoons chocolate-flavored syrup
2 tablespoons instant coffee
1 teaspoon vanilla
$^1/_2$ teaspoon almond extract

Blend till smooth. Store in a tightly sealed container in the refrigerator for up to 1 month.

Recipes to Remember

Creamy Hot Chocolate

Delicious! This is deluxe!

1 (14-ounce) can sweetened condensed milk
$^1/_2$ cup unsweetened cocoa
$1^1/_2$ teaspoons vanilla extract

$^1/_8$ teaspoon salt
$6^1/_2$ cups hot water
Marshmallows (optional)

In large saucepan, combine sweetened condensed milk, cocoa, vanilla, and salt; mix well. Over medium heat, slowly stir in water; heat through, stirring occasionally. Top with marshmallows, if desired. Makes about 2 quarts.

Sleigh Bells and Sugarplums

Russian Orange-Spiced Tea Mix

$1^1/_3$ cups Tang Orange Drink Powder
$^1/_2$ cup sugar

$^1/_3$ cup sweetened iced tea mix
1 teaspoon cinnamon
$^1/_2$ teaspoon ground cloves

Combine all ingredients in a tightly covered jar. To prepare 1 serving, dissolve 1 teaspoon mix in $^3/_4$ cup boiling water. For a quart, dissolve $^1/_3$ cup mixture in 1 quart boiling water.

Recipes to Remember

Dandelion Wine

1 gallon dandelion flowers
1 gallon water
4 oranges and 2 lemons

5 pounds sugar
Vintner's yeast

Remove any insects and the green parts of the flowers. Cover with boiling water and soak for 2 days. Add chopped oranges and lemons and return to a boil. Simmer for at least 15 minutes. Strain through a jelly bag or cheesecloth and add sugar, stirring to dissolve completely. When cooled to room temperature, add yeast. Pour into a fermenting jug with an air-lock or an open crock which you cover with cloth. Rack (siphon into a clean bottle) when the wine clears, and store up to 6 months before sampling. If you can't wait, it is okay to go ahead and drink it.

The Wild and Free Cookbook

Editors' Extra: Vintner's yeast is available at any local home brew shop.

Spiced Mocha Mix

1 cup sugar
1 cup nonfat dry milk powder
^{1}/$_2$ cup powdered non-dairy
  creamer
^{1}/$_2$ cup cocoa powder
3 tablespoons powdered instant
  coffee

^{1}/$_2$ teaspoon ground allspice
^{1}/$_4$ teaspoon ground cinnamon
Dash salt
Marshmallows (optional)

In large bowl, combine all ingredients. Store in airtight container. For single serving, place 3 tablespoons mix in mug or cup, and add ^{3}/$_4$ cup boiling water. Stir until mixture is dissolved. Top with marshmallows, if desired. Each 2^1/$_2$ cups mix makes 12–14 servings.

McNamee Family & Friends Cookbook

In 1971, the first Starbucks opened in Seattle's Pike Place Market. There are now more than 5,500 stores, 1,196 of which are international.

Jeannie's Famous Margaritas

2 cups tequila
1 cup triple sec
1 (12-ounce) can frozen
  lemonade
1 (12-ounce) can frozen lime-aid
2 (2-liter) bottles 7-UP

In a large container mix all ingredients except 1 bottle of 7-UP. Cover and put in freezer 24–48 hours. Pour in $^1/_2$–1 bottle of 7-UP, mix, and serve.

Favorite Recipes, Numerica Credit Union

Lemon Strawberry Punch

$1^1/_2$ cups strawberries
3 (6-ounce) cans frozen
  lemonade
3 (6-ounce) cans water
2 quarts chilled ginger ale

Blend strawberries, lemonade, and water in blender. Pour mixture in punch bowl. Add ginger ale and ice. Taste to see if some sugar is needed.

Costco Wholesale Employee Association Cookbook

Artichoke Dip

1 (14-ounce) can artichoke
  hearts (marinated okay)
$^3/_4$ cup grated mozzarella
  cheese
$^3/_4$ cup grated Cheddar cheese
$^1/_4$ cup grated Parmesan cheese
1 cup mayonnaise
1–2 cloves garlic to taste
Tortilla chips

Drain artichokes well. Place all ingredients in food processor. Blend until smooth. Place in baking dish. Bake at 375° for 20–30 minutes. Serve warm with tortilla chips.

Taste of the Methow

Peanut Butter Dip

Serve as a dip for celery sticks and slices of apple or pear.

$^1/_2$ cup creamy peanut butter $^1/_2$ teaspoon cinnamon
$^1/_2$ cup plain yogurt

Place all ingredients into a small mixing bowl. Stir until fluffy. This will keep for 1 week in a sealed container in the refrigerator. Yields 1 cup.

Food for Tots

Salmon Dip

16 ounces smoked salmon   2 (8-ounce) packages cream
2 tablespoons lemon juice   cheese, softened
1 bunch green onions, chopped   Pepper to taste
$^1/_2$ teaspoon liquid smoke   1–2 tablespoons mayonnaise
2–3 teaspoons horseradish   Red food coloring (optional)

Mix all ingredients in order given. Cover and refrigerate for 1–2 hours before serving. May be served with your favorite crackers or vegetables.

From Our Kitchen to Yours

Spicy Crab Dip with Corn Chips

1 (6- to 8-ounce) package frozen $^1/_3$ cup chili sauce
   Alaska King crab, thawed, or   1 teaspoon horseradish
   1 (7$^1/_2$-ounce) can crabmeat   2 tablespoons chopped green
1 (3-ounce) package cream   onions
   cheese, softened   Parsley for garnish
$^1/_2$ cup mayonnaise   King-size Fritos Corn Chips
1 tablespoon lemon juice

Drain and slice crab, reserving a chunk of leg meat for garnish. Blend cream cheese and mayonnaise until smooth. Add lemon juice, chili sauce, and horseradish. Stir in crab and green onions. Chill for 1 hour. Garnish with reserved crabmeat and parsley. Serve with Fritos.

Family Favorites Recipes

Curried Crabmeat Spread

1 pound (2 cups) crabmeat
¹/₄ cup plain yogurt or sour
  cream
¹/₄ teaspoon curry powder
1 tablespoon capers, drained

1 (8-ounce) package cream
  cheese, softened
Salt and red pepper to taste
¹/₄ cup chopped chives

Combine all ingredients, mixing well. Chill before serving to allow flavors to meld.

Note: Capers aren't always easy to find. You can make your own imitation capers by pickling the new seed pods of your nasturtium plants. It is just as good and a lot cheaper.

The Wild and Free Cookbook

Sandy's Smoked Salmon Spread

One day we were sharing fish stories with our Seattle neighbors and they served us this delicious spread. They like to use fresh salmon from the Puget Sound.

1 (8-ounce) can or package
  smoked salmon
¹/₃ cup sour cream
¹/₃ cup mayonnaise
1 teaspoon dried dill weed

¹/₃ cup chopped onion
2 tablespoons capers
Pepper to taste
Fresh parsley for garnish

In a bowl, combine all ingredients and mix until smooth. May add more sour cream or mayonnaise for the right consistency. Serve with rye rounds or other crackers.

Recipe by Lou Piniella, Manager, Seattle Mariners
Starters & Closers

Surprise Spread

1 (8-ounce) package cream
  cheese, softened
¹/₂ cup sour cream
¹/₄ cup mayonnaise
1 cup seafood cocktail sauce
3 cans small shrimp, rinsed and
  drained

1 green pepper, chopped
3 green onions, chopped
1 tomato, diced
2 cups shredded mozzarella
  cheese

Mix the first 3 ingredients together. Spread over a 12-inch cake plate or pizza pan. Cover with cocktail sauce. Scatter shrimp over cocktail sauce. (If desired, use only 2 cans shrimp and chop up a bit; it still covers well.) Add green pepper, onions, and tomato. Cover with cheese. Serve with thin crackers or chips and lots of napkins.

Nautical Niceaty's from Spokane Yacht Club

Savory Cheese Spread

The feta cheese gives a lot of "oomph"! Like a Boursin or Alouette cheese, this is best with bland crackers or melbas.

2 tablespoons finely chopped
  fresh herbs (thyme, summer
  savory, sage, chives, and/or
  dill weed)
¹/₂ pound feta cheese
¹/₂ pound cream cheese

1 tablespoon heavy cream
1 large clove garlic, pressed
Dash of cayenne pepper
Freshly ground black pepper to
  taste

Hand chop fresh herbs. Process feta cheese in food processor. Add cream cheese and cream; re-process. Combine with herbs, cayenne pepper, and black pepper. Chill. Serves 8–12.

The Overlake School Cookbook

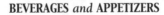

Blue Cheese Crisps

$^1/_2$ pound blue cheese
$^2/_3$ cup butter, room
 temperature

$^1/_4$ teaspoon cayenne
$1^1/_3$ cups flour
$^1/_2$ cup poppy seeds

Cream together blue cheese and butter until smooth. Mix cayenne with flour and add to butter-cheese mixture. Blend well. Divide mixture into two balls, wrap each in plastic and chill for 30 minutes.

 Roll each ball of dough into a 1-inch-thick cylinder, then roll each cylinder in poppy seeds, coating them well. Cut cylinders into $^1/_4$-inch slices. (They will slice better if slightly frozen first.) Place on a dry baking sheet and bake in preheated 350° oven until golden brown, about 15 minutes. Serve warm or at room temperature. Makes 60 crisps.

The Shoalwater's Finest Dinners

Apricot Almond Brie

Probably my favorite appetizer, and definitely the one I use most often. Serve with a glass of white wine and your guests will never know it took you less than ten minutes to put together.

1 (8- to 10-ounce) wedge Brie
 cheese
1 tablespoon Grand Marnier
 liqueur

$^1/_2$ cup apricot preserves
1 tablespoon toasted sliced
 almonds

Remove top rind from cheese. Place cheese on serving plate. In a small saucepan, combine liqueur with preserves and heat until hot, but do not boil. Spoon some of the sauce over cheese (save remainder for later). Sprinkle almonds over top. Serve with butter crackers.

Six Ingredients or Less

Chicken Bites in
Creamy Garlic-Almond Sauce

CREAMY GARLIC-ALMOND SAUCE:
1 tablespoon vegetable oil
3 tablespoons minced garlic
1 (1-inch) piece fresh ginger,
  peeled and minced
$^2/_3$ cup slivered almonds
2 -3 tablespoons water

In frying pan, combine oil, garlic, and ginger. Sauté on low heat, uncovered, until garlic is very tender, about 5–6 minutes, stirring often. Transfer to blender, add almonds and 2 tablespoons water, and pulse to purée, adding more water, if necessary.

CHICKEN BITES:
2 pounds skinned, boned chicken
  breasts, cut in 1-inch pieces
Salt and pepper to taste
2 tablespoons vegetable oil
$1^1/_2$ cups heavy cream
Chopped parsley and slivered
  almonds, for garnish

Season chicken pieces with salt and pepper. Heat oil in a frying pan on medium heat; add chicken and sauté, tossing until golden, about 5 minutes. Pour in Creamy Garlic-Almond Sauce and cream; simmer, stirring occasionally, until sauce thickens, 2–3 minutes. Transfer mixture to bowl and garnish with parsley and almonds. Serve with toothpicks and plenty of napkins.

Northwest Garlic Festival Cookbook

Japanese Chicken Rounds

When these chicken rounds are sliced, their colorful centers look like flowers.

MARINADE:

¹/2 cup mirin* or sweet white wine

¹/2 cup low-sodium soy sauce

¹/4 cup sugar

4 cloves garlic, finely chopped

2 tablespoons finely grated fresh ginger

1 tablespoon fresh lemon juice

Pinch of salt and pepper

Combine all ingredients in a small glass bowl. Whisk until well blended; set aside.

2 skinless, boneless chicken breasts (4 halves)

8 thin fresh string beans

1 medium carrot, peeled and cut into 5-inch strips a little thicker than matchsticks

2 or 3 green onions, cut into 5-inch strips

¹/2 medium red pepper, cut into thin strips

Preheat oven to 350°. Cut chicken breasts in half and trim fat. Remove tenderloin from underneath and use another time for stir-fry. Place each breast between plastic wrap and pound lightly on the underside until as thin as possible without tearing. Trim the ragged edges.

Place a couple pieces of each vegetable width-wise near the narrowest end of each chicken breast. Roll tightly into a log shape, trimming the ends of the vegetables, if necessary. Secure the chicken roll with wooden toothpicks and place in a baking dish, seam-side-down.

Pour Marinade over chicken and cover with foil; bake 35 minutes, or until juices run clear and chicken is springy to the touch. Remove from oven; strain Marinade and reserve. Let chicken stand until cool enough to handle. Carefully remove toothpicks. If you prefer to serve it cold, cover and chill in refrigerator 2 hours. Slice each roll into ¹/2-inch rounds with a serrated knife. Serve with Marinade on the side. Yields about 20 rounds.

*Mirin is a sweet cooking rice wine available in the Asian section of most supermarkets.

Good Times at Green Lake

Teriyaki Chicken Wings

A richly glazed appetizer that can also be served as a main dish.

16 chicken drumettes (the meaty
  leg portion of wings)
$^1/_4$ cup reduced-sodium soy
  sauce
$^3/_4$ cup firmly packed light
  brown sugar

1 tablespoon honey
4 thin slices fresh ginger
2 green onions, cut into 1-inch
  pieces

Clean wings; trim off excess fat and skin. Place in medium bowl. Combine remaining ingredients; stir to dissolve sugar. Pour over chicken. Cover; chill at least 3 hours, turning occasionally. When ready to bake, place chicken in foil-lined shallow baking pan. Bake at 350° for 15 minutes. Baste with marinade; bake 30–35 minutes or until tender, basting frequently. (Remove skin before eating.) Makes 8 hors d'oeuvre servings of 2 per person.

Per Serving: Calories 117; Prot. 10g; Carb. 10g; Fiber 0g; Fat 3g; Sat. Fat <1g; Chol. 27mg; Sod. 149mg.

Six Ingredients or Less: Cooking Light & Healthy

Asian Beef Skewers

Ginger flavored beef skewers are excellent as an appetizer as well as an entrée.

3 tablespoons hoisin sauce
3 tablespoons sherry
$^1/_4$ cup soy sauce
1 teaspoon barbeque sauce
2 green onions, chopped

2 cloves garlic, minced
1 tablespoon minced fresh
  ginger
1$^1/_2$ pounds flank steak

In a small bowl, mix together hoisin sauce, sherry, soy sauce, barbeque sauce, green onions, garlic, and ginger. Cut flank steak across grain on a diagonal, yielding thin, 2-inch-wide slices. Place slices in a 1-gallon, resealable plastic bag. Pour hoisin sauce mixture over slices, and mix well. Refrigerate 2 hours, or overnight.

  Preheat an outdoor grill for high heat. Thread steak onto skewers. Grill 3 minutes per side, or to desired doneness. Serves 3.

Allrecipes Tried & True Favorites

Butternut Pot Stickers with Raspberry Szechuan Sauce

1 onion, diced
4 tablespoons olive oil
1 tablespoon minced fresh sage
4 cups butternut squash,
   peeled and diced
1 cup chopped hazelnuts

1 package won ton wrappers
1^1/$_2$ cups canola oil
   (approximate)
^{1}/$_2$ cup Madeira
Salt and freshly ground pepper
   to taste

In a large skillet, sauté onion in olive oil until translucent. Add sage and squash and cook over medium heat until squash tests tender. Add hazelnuts and stir thoroughly. Place a spoonful of squash mixture in middle of won ton wrap, moisten edge of wrap with water and use a pot sticker press to seal, or hand pleat.

Heat canola oil in separate skillet and fry small batches of potstickers in ^{1}/$_2$ inch of oil. When pot stickers are half cooked, about 3 minutes, add Madeira to caramelize wrap. Cover briefly. Lift pot stickers from pan and serve upside-down with Raspberry Szechuan Sauce and garnish with fresh raspberries and bamboo leaves.

RASPBERRY SZECHUAN SAUCE:
^{1}/$_2$ cup soy sauce
^{2}/$_3$ cup raspberry vinegar
^{1}/$_2$ cup raspberry syrup
2 tablespoons toasted sesame oil
4 cloves garlic, pressed

2 teaspoons minced fresh ginger
1 whole scallion, minced
^{1}/$_2$ teaspoon dried red chili
   flakes
^{1}/$_2$ cup fresh raspberries

In a medium-size bowl, combine all ingredients and whisk gently. Yields about 2 cups of sauce. Pour a portion in small bowl and place in center of serving plate with potstickers. Serves 12.

Nutritional values per serving: Calories 348; Carb. 21g; Prot. 3.9g; Fiber 1.4g; Sugar 19.6g; Fat Cal. 265; Total Fat 29.4g; Sat. Fat 2.6g; Chol. 0.2g; Sod. 579.5mg.

LaConner Palates

In 1976, Dixy Lee Ray, former chairwoman of the U.S. Atomic Energy Commission, became the first woman governor of the state. In 1997 Gary Locke became the first Asian American governor in the continental United States.

Mediterranean Wrap-Ups

1 cup mixed nuts (almonds, cashews, and pecans are best)

1 (8-ounce) package pitted dates
1 pound bacon, cut in half

Slip the nuts into the pitted dates. Wrap each date with $^1/_2$ strip of bacon and secure with a toothpick. Broil until the bacon is cooked. Serve warm or cold.

Extraordinary Cuisine for Sea & Shore

Cheese Puffs with Smoked Salmon Filling

If you don't have time to make the Puffs, spread the Salmon Filling on crackers.

SALMON FILLING:

6–7 ounces smoked salmon, bones removed
1 (8-ounce) package cream cheese
1 tablespoon lemon juice

1 tablespoon grated onion
2 tablespoons mayonnaise
1 tablespoon horseradish
2 tablespoons chopped parsley

Place all ingredients in food processor and blend until smooth.

PUFFS:

1 cup water
$^1/_2$ cup butter or margarine, cut into small pieces

1 cup all-purpose flour, sifted
4 eggs
$^3/_4$ cup grated Cheddar cheese

Preheat oven to 400°. In a medium saucepan, bring water and butter to a boil over medium heat. Remove from heat. Add all the flour at once and beat vigorously until mixture is smooth, forming a ball. Return to heat and beat vigorously for 1–2 minutes. Remove from heat and add eggs, 1 at a time, beating well to incorporate until smooth and velvety. Add cheese. Spoon about $1^1/_2$ teaspoons of batter (or pipe with a pastry bag with no tip attached) onto greased cookie sheet (can use parchment). Makes approximately 50.

Bake 10 minutes. Open oven door slightly and keep ajar, using a wooden spoon, and bake an additional 15 minutes. (This allows steam to escape from oven.) Remove from oven and pierce each puff with a thin, sharp knife to let steam escape. Turn off oven; return puffs to oven for 30–45 minutes to dry out, leaving door ajar. Remove from oven; split and fill puffs with Salmon Filling. May be reheated briefly in a 350° oven to crisp before filling and serving.

Wandering & Feasting

Seafood Stuffed Filo

These appetizers can be made ahead of time and frozen uncooked or they can be made in the morning and baked just before guests arrive. Keep warm on a warming tray.

WHITE SAUCE:

1 tablespoon butter
1 tablespoon flour
$^1/_2$ cup milk
$^1/_2$ teaspoon salt

Melt butter in small saucepan over low heat; whisk in flour. Cook 1 minute. Whisk in milk. Cook, whisking constantly, until smooth and thickened, 3–4 minutes. Stir in salt.

FILLING:

3 green onions, minced
$1^1/_2$ tablespoons butter
1 cup flaked cooked crab meat
  or shrimp
1 egg yolk, lightly beaten
1 teaspoon lemon juice
$^1/_4$ teaspoon nutmeg
$^1/_4$ teaspoon white pepper

Sauté green onions in butter in 9-inch skillet over medium heat until soft, 3–5 minutes. Reduce heat to low; stir in White Sauce, crab meat or shrimp, egg yolk, lemon juice, nutmeg, and pepper. Cool.

WRAPPERS:

5 filo leaves (a Greek pastry
  that can be purchased frozen)
$^1/_2$ cup butter, melted

Place thawed filo leaves between slightly dampened paper toweling to prevent drying. Brush 1 leaf with melted butter; cut into 5 (2-inch-wide) strips. Place about 2 teaspoons of the Filling in top corner of 1 strip; fold corner over to opposite edge, making a triangle. Continue folding (as you would a flag), keeping triangular shape with each fold and brushing with butter as needed. Place on baking sheet. Repeat with remaining filo and Filling. Preheat oven to 400°. Bake until puffed and golden, about 15 minutes. Serve warm. Yields 3 dozen.

ALTERNATE FILLING:

1 (1-pound) carton ricotta
  cheese
$^1/_2$ cup Parmesan cheese
2 teaspoons basil
$^1/_2$ teaspoon oregano
1 egg, beaten

Combine Alternate Filling ingredients. (Replaces White Sauce and Filling above.) Proceed with wrapping.

Sharing Our Best

Tuna Puffs

PUFF SHELLS:
¹/₂ cup boiling water   ¹/₂ cup flour
¹/₄ cup butter or margarine   2 eggs
Dash of salt

Combine water, butter, and salt in saucepan; bring to boil. Add flour all at once; stir vigorously until mixture forms a ball and leaves sides of pan. Remove from heat. Add eggs, 1 at a time; beat thoroughly after each addition. Continue beating until stiff dough is formed. Drop by level teaspoonful onto well-greased cookie sheet. Bake in 450° oven 10 minutes. Reduce heat to 350°. Bake 10 more minutes. Cool.

2 cans tuna   2 tablespoons chopped sweet
1 cup finely chopped celery   pickle
¹/₂ cup mayonnaise   Salt to taste
2 tablespoons chopped onion

Drain and flake tuna. Combine all ingredients. Mix thoroughly.

   Cut tops from Puff Shells. Fill each shell with approximately 2 teaspoons of tuna mixture.

Nautical Niceaty's from Spokane Yacht Club

Zucchini Appetizer

This is yummy served hot or cold as finger food. Your guests will enjoy it!

4 eggs, well beaten
$^1/_2$ cup oil
1 cup biscuit mix
$^1/_2$ teaspoon salt
$^1/_4$ teaspoon pepper
$^1/_2$ teaspoon oregano

3 cups grated zucchini
1 cup finely chopped onion
2 tablespoons finely minced
 parsley
1 clove garlic, minced
$^1/_2$ cup grated Parmesan cheese

Beat eggs in large bowl. Add oil to eggs and beat well. Add remaining ingredients and stir together until well mixed. Spread batter into a greased 9x13-inch baking pan. Bake in 350° oven for 30–35 minutes or until golden brown.

Our Burnt Offerings

Banquet Mushrooms

Even people who don't like tofu will enjoy these mushrooms.

$^1/_2$ cup crumbled soft tofu,
 drained and patted dry
$^1/_4$ cup chopped walnuts
$^1/_2$ cup fine dried bread crumbs
2 tablespoons chopped green
 onions
1 medium clove garlic, minced
$^1/_2$ teaspoon minced fresh ginger
2 tablespoons prepared hoisin
 sauce

$^1/_2$ cup drained and coarsely
 chopped mandarin oranges
1 egg white
18 mushrooms (about 2 inches
 in diameter), washed and
 stemmed
1 tablespoon unsalted butter,
 melted

Preheat oven to 375°. In a small bowl combine tofu, walnuts, bread crumbs, green onions, garlic, ginger, hoisin sauce, mandarin oranges, and egg white. Brush mushroom caps with a little butter. Mound the filling into caps. Save stems for another recipe.

Place mushrooms on a baking sheet. Bake 12 minutes, or until tops are lightly browned. Remove and serve immediately. Yields 18 appetizers.

Good Times at Green Lake

Chanterelles with Hazelnuts and Madeira

Once you've eaten chanterelles, you'll have trouble substituting. But since the season is short and these very special mushrooms aren't available everywhere, you can substitute small button mushrooms. Chef Lucas says that, while it won't be the same, it will certainly be a treat.

4–6 tablespoons butter, clarified*
Salt and white pepper to taste
Dash of Tabasco
1 teaspoon Worcestershire sauce
1/2 teaspoon minced shallots
1 teaspoon minced garlic

2 tablespoons coarsely ground hazelnuts
1/8 teaspoon paprika
2 cups chanterelles, wiped and cut in half
Madeira
Chopped parsley

Place in a sauté pan butter, salt and white pepper, Tabasco, Worcestershire sauce, shallots, garlic, hazelnuts, paprika and chanterelles. Turn heat on high.

As the toasting aroma of nuts and garlic rises, deglaze with Madeira. Cook just long enough to reduce sauce slightly. Serve in casserole or chafing dish. Sprinkle with chopped parsley. Serves 2.

The Best of The Ark and More!

Editors' Extra: Clarified butter is unsalted butter that has been slowly melted, thereby evaporating most of the water and separating the milk solids (which sink to the bottom of the pan) from the golden liquid on the surface. The clear (clarified) butter is poured or skimmed off the milky residue and used in cooking.

Port Townsend hosts some of the nation's finest blues musicians at the June Blues Festival and Workshop.

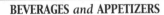

Onion Confetti

A friend gave us this recipe for a party and I love it. It makes a meal all by itself.

¹/₄ cup olive oil	6 tablespoons balsamic vinegar
¹/₂ cup sugar	2 tablespoons grenadine
1 teaspoon salt	(optional)
¹/₂ teaspoon black pepper	1 baguette
2 pounds onions, thinly sliced	Goat cheese, crumbled
1 cup dry red wine	

Preheat oven to 400°. In a large sauté pan, heat oil on medium-high. Add sugar, salt, black pepper, and onions. Cook covered for 30 minutes. Stir occasionally. Add wine, vinegar, and grenadine. Cook for an additional 30 minutes, or until thick. Slice baguette and brush with olive oil. Toast in oven for 6–8 minutes. Top toast with cooked onions and goat cheese. Makes about 22.

Recipe by Dan Wilson, Catcher, Seattle Mariners
Starters & Closers

Prawns Genovese

Impress your guests with an appetizer that will be remembered long after the evening is over. This easy-to-make and flavorful dish is a great beginning to a memorable meal.

3 tablespoons extra virgin olive oil	1¹/₂ tablespoons capers
8 large prawns, shelled and deveined	3 tablespoons diced tomatoes
	Juice of 1 lemon
1 tablespoon minced shallots	1 tablespoon chopped parsley
¹/₂ teaspoon minced garlic	1 tablespoon butter
¹/₄ cup dry white wine	Salt and pepper to taste

In a medium-size sauté pan, preheat olive oil over medium-high heat. Add prawns and lightly cook both sides. Add shallots and garlic. When garlic begins to brown, deglaze with wine. Add capers, tomatoes, lemon juice, and parsley. Cook until prawns lose their translucency. Take pan off heat and whisk in butter. Season to taste with salt and pepper. Serves 2.

Nutritional values per serving: Calories 394; Carb. 12.5g; Prot. 23.6g; Fiber 0g; Sugar 12.5g; Fat Calories 309; Total Fat 34.3g; Sat. Fat 9.3g; Chol. 187.5g; Sod. 3,790.mg.

LaConner Palates

Oysters Gino

GINO SAUCE:

1 thin slice bacon
1 teaspoon butter
1 teaspoon chopped garlic
$^1/_4$ teaspoon chopped parsley
2 shakes Tabasco
Salt and pepper to taste
Juice of $^1/_2$ lemon
1 cup crab meat

$^1/_3$ cup Madeira
3 ounces butter
4 tablespoons flour
$^1/_2$ cup fish stock
$1^1/_2$ cups half-and-half
$^1/_4$ cup Madeira
$^3/_4$ cup Parmesan cheese

Fry bacon in 1 teaspoon butter until brown. Add garlic, parsley, Tabasco, salt and pepper, lemon juice, and crab meat. Deglaze with $^1/_3$ cup Madeira. Set aside.

In a saucepan put 3 ounces butter on medium-high heat. Add flour and whisk for 1–2 minutes; add fish stock and half-and-half. Deglaze with $^1/_4$ cup Madeira. Whisk until sauce thickens and add Parmesan cheese. Fold into crab mixture and refrigerate. Yields 2 cups.

Oysters on half shell   Rock salt

Place oysters on half shell on rock salt in an ovenproof dish. Place 1–2 tablespoons Gino Sauce on each of the oysters. Bake in 425° oven for 12–15 minutes.

Note: Use Dungeness crab meat if possible. Fish bouillon may be substituted for fish stock.

The Best of The Ark and More!

Heavenly Caramel Corn

5 quarts popped corn
1 cup butter or margarine
2 cups brown sugar

$^1/_2$ cup light corn syrup
1 teaspoon salt
$^1/_2$ teaspoon baking soda

Spread freshly-popped corn in a large shallow sheet pan. Put it in a very slow oven (250°) to keep warm and crisp. Combine butter, brown sugar, corn syrup, and salt in a heavy saucepan. Boil and stir to firm-ball stage (248°), about 5 minutes. Remove from heat and stir in baking soda. Take popped corn from oven and pour hot caramel mixture over it in a fine stream. Stir to mix well. Return to oven for 45–50 minutes, stirring every 15 minutes. Cool. Store in airtight container.

Sleigh Bells and Sugarplums

BREAD *and* BREAKFAST

PHOTO © JEFF TETRICK.

Eastern Washington's Palouse Country between Spokane and Walla Walla is the most productive wheat-growing region in the world. The region is remarkably beautiful, especially in spring, when new growth mantles the rolling hills in brilliant green.

Butter-Crust Beer Bread

2 cups self-rising flour
3 tablespoons sugar

1 (12-ounce) can beer (not light)
1/2 stick unsalted butter, melted

Oil or butter standard loaf pan. In bowl, combine flour, sugar, and beer and mix with wooden spoon until well blended and sticky, about 1 minute. Pour dough in prepared pan and bake at 350° for 30 minutes. Remove bread from oven and pour melted butter over top. Bake 30 minutes more until lightly browned. Cool in pan, then remove and serve with whipped butter. Makes 1 loaf.

Favorite Recipes from Our Best Cooks

Dilly Casserole Bread

This is easy because you don't have to knead it, just stir!

1 package active dry yeast
2 tablespoons sugar
1/4 cup warm water
1 cup cottage cheese, heated to
  lukewarm
1 tablespoon instant (dry)
  minced onion flakes

1 tablespoon butter
2 teaspoons dill seed
1 teaspoon salt
1/4 teaspoon baking soda
1 egg
2 1/4–2 1/2 cups flour

Dissolve yeast and sugar in warm water. In mixing bowl, combine remaining ingredients (except flour) with the yeast mixture. Gradually add flour, beating well after each addition, until a stiff dough forms. Let rise, covered, for 50–60 minutes until doubled. Stir down with a spoon. Place in greased 8-inch-round casserole dish and let rise in warm place until doubled again, about 30–40 minutes. Bake at 350° for 40–50 minutes until golden brown; brush top with butter.

Western Washington Oncology Cook Book

Easy-Cheesy Bread

1 loaf French bread
1 cup shredded mozzarella
  cheese

1 cup shredded Cheddar cheese
1 cup real mayonnaise

Slice French bread in half long-way so you have 2 flat, long halves. Mix cheeses and mayonnaise. Spread mixture over both halves evenly. Warm in oven at 325° for 15–20 minutes. (If in hurry, broil for 5 minutes or until cheese is slightly browned.) Slice and serve.

Recipes from Our Friends

Fantastic Focaccia Bread

1 (10-ounce) package
  refrigerated pizza crust
2 garlic cloves, pressed
²/₃ cup grated Romano cheese,
  divided

2 cups shredded mozzarella
  cheese, divided
2 teaspoons oregano, divided
2 plum tomatoes

Preheat oven to 375°. Dip dough and pizza roller in flour and evenly roll dough into a 12-inch circle on a 13-inch baking stone. Press garlic with garlic press and spread evenly over crust. Grate half Romano cheese over crust with cheese grater. Sprinkle 1 cup mozzarella and 1 teaspoon oregano over Romano cheese. Slice tomatoes thinly with grater/slicer. Layer tomatoes in single layer over cheese. Sprinkle remaining Romano, mozzarella, and oregano over tomatoes. Bake for 30–35 minutes. Cut into squares and serve hot.

Costco Wholesale Employee Association Cookbook

 Cape Flattery on Washington's Olympic Peninsula is the northwestern most point in the contiguous United States.

Focaccia Bread

BREAD:

½ cup warm water
½ cup warm milk
2 tablespoons sugar
1 teaspoon salt
1 package active dry yeast

3 tablespoons shortening, melted
  (or butter flavored Crisco)
3 cups white all-purpose flour,
  divided
About ¾ cup olive oil

Combine water, milk, sugar, salt, yeast, and melted shortening that has cooled slightly. Mix enough to make sure yeast has dissolved. Add half of flour and mix well. Then add remaining flour and knead until you can form a large ball. Dough should be slightly sticky, which makes for a crisp crust. Place dough in lightly greased large bowl. Turn to grease all sides of dough. Cover with plastic wrap and a towel. Let rise at room temperature, until double in size, about 1–1½ hours. Remove and knead for 1–2 minutes. Divide into 2 portions. Flatten out with your hands to ½ inch thick, and oval in shape. Place in lightly oiled baking pan. Make deep impressions in the dough with fingertips. Drizzle oil over top.

TOPPING:

2 cloves fresh garlic, finely
  chopped
1 teaspoon rosemary
1 teaspoon dry basil

1 teaspoon dry parsley
1 teaspoon dry fennel seeds
1 teaspoon dry oregano

Sprinkle garlic evenly over dough. Crumble the rosemary as best you can. It is very coarse. Mix rosemary and remaining ingredients well and sprinkle generously over dough. Salt to taste. Let rise for about 30 minutes. Bake at 350° for 15–20 minutes, only until bottom is brown. Top does not need to be brown. Serve hot.

Cooking with Irene!

Before the coming of the Europeans, the Native American peoples inhabiting what is now the state of Washington included the Nez Percéé, Spokane, Yakima, Cayuse, Okanogan, Walla Walla, and Colville in the interior, and the Nooksak, Chinook, Nisqually, Clallam, Makah, Quinault, and Puyallup in the coastal area.

Country Gravy and Biscuits

MILK GRAVY:

$^1/_4$ pound sausage, bacon,
  ham, or hamburger
4 tablespoons drippings

4 tablespoons flour
2 cups milk
Salt and pepper

In a skillet, brown meat and drain grease, saving 4 tablespoons of drippings. Add flour to drippings and meat in skillet. Let this mixture bubble for 3 minutes, then add milk. Stir constantly until well thickened. Season and serve hot gravy over biscuits or mashed potatoes.

BISCUITS:

2 cups flour
3 teaspoons baking powder
1 teaspoon salt

6 tablespoons shortening
$^3/_4$ cup milk

Mix dry ingredients; cut in shortening; add milk; knead lightly about 10 times. Pat to $^1/_2$-inch thick, and cut into biscuits. Place in pan so that biscuits are not touching. Bake in preheated 400° oven until golden, about 15 minutes.

Variation: Buttermilk biscuits can be made by adding $^1/_4$ teaspoon each baking powder and baking soda and $^3/_4$ cup buttermilk in place of sweet milk.

Sleigh Bells and Sugarplums

Sausage Gravy

A real stick-to-the-ribs dish that is best when served over hot biscuits.

1 pound bulk pork sausage
6 tablespoons flour
1 quart milk
$^1/_4$ teaspoon salt
Dash Worcestershire sauce

Dash hot pepper sauce
$^1/_2$ teaspoon poultry seasoning
  (optional)
$^1/_2$ teaspoon ground nutmeg
  (optional)

Crumble sausage into large saucepan; cook until well browned over medium-low heat. Drain, discarding all but 2 tablespoons of drippings. Stir in flour; cook over medium heat about 6 minutes or until mixture bubbles and turns golden. Stir in milk; add seasoning and cook, stirring, until thickened.

Christmas in Washington Cook Book

Sweet Potato Rolls

These rolls are awesome! The pretty pumpkin-colored dough can be mixed a day ahead, refrigerated overnight, and made into rolls the next day. Remember when the dough is cold, it takes longer for the rolls to rise; allow for that time.

2 medium-size sweet potatoes (1¹/₂ cups pulp)	2 cups warm water
¹/₈ teaspoon nutmeg	4 tablespoons butter
¹/₂ cup plus 1 tablespoon packed dark brown sugar, divided	1¹/₂ cups water
2 packages yeast	4 teaspoons salt
	About 10 cups flour, divided
	2 eggs

Cook, peel, and mash sweet potatoes (can be done in microwave). Mash in nutmeg and ¹/₂ cup brown sugar until smooth. Stir yeast and 1 tablespoon brown sugar into warm (110°–115°) water. Let stand until yeast mixture foams. Meanwhile, in a saucepan, heat butter and 1¹/₂ cups water over low heat until warm. Butter does not have to completely melt.

In a large bowl, combine salt and 3 cups flour. Stir in yeast mixture, warm butter mixture, and sweet potato mixture until well blended. Add 1 whole egg and 1 egg yolk (refrigerate egg white to brush on rolls later), and stir until blended. Mix in 6 cups flour, 1 cup at a time, to make a soft dough. Flour board and knead bread until smooth and elastic, working in more flour to make a soft dough.

Shape each piece of dough into a ball and place in greased pans. For overnight rising, cover pans with plastic wrap and refrigerate overnight. When ready to bake, uncover and let rise in a warm place until doubled. After rising, brush rolls with beaten egg white. Bake at 400° for 25–30 minutes.

Bounteous Blessings

 Boeing, manufacturer of airplanes, missiles and space-related items, was long the primary employer in the Seattle area. In recent years, the Microsoft computer software company added a new dimension, pumping vast amounts of money into the economy and helping to create new high-tech ventures.

The Yogi's Banana Bread

Discovered in the '70s by a Yogi in Bellingham who taught it during a meditation.

1 cup brown sugar
1/2 cup butter, softened
2 eggs
3 or 4 very ripe bananas
2 cups flour
1 teaspoon baking powder
1/2 teaspoon salt

1/2 teaspoon baking soda
1 teaspoon cinnamon
1 teaspoon cloves
1 teaspoon nutmeg
1 cup frozen blueberries
1 cup chopped cashews

Mix brown sugar, butter, eggs, and bananas in food processor. Add flour, baking powder, salt, baking soda, cinnamon, cloves, and nutmeg; blend thoroughly. Add blueberries and cashews, and blend very lightly. Bake in well-greased loaf pan at 325° for about 1 hour. Test with a knife to see if it's done in the middle. Remove from pan and set on wire rack to cool. Slice and serve.

The Colophon Cafe Best Recipes

Liberty Lake Huckleberry Bread

3 cups flour
2 teaspoons baking powder
1 teaspoon baking soda
1/2 teaspoon salt
1 1/3 cups sugar
2/3 cup shortening
4 eggs

1/2 cup milk
1 1/2 teaspoons lemon juice
1 cup crushed pineapple
2 cups huckleberries
1 cup chopped nuts
1/2 cup coconut

Sift dry ingredients. Cream shortening and eggs. Add sifted mixture, milk, lemon juice and pineapple; beat well. Stir in huckleberries, nuts and coconut. Bake in 2 small greased loaf pans or 1 greased 9x13-inch pan for approximately 45 minutes at 350°.

Liberty Lake Community Cookbook

Banana Carrot Bread

1 cup mashed bananas (2 or 3)	1 teaspoon baking soda
1 cup sugar	$^1/_2$ teaspoon salt
$^3/_4$ cup salad oil	$^1/_2$ teaspoon cinnamon
2 eggs	1 cup finely grated carrots
$1^3/_4$ cups unsifted flour	$^1/_4$ cup chopped pecans

Combine bananas, sugar, oil, and eggs in mixer bowl; beat 2 minutes. Combine dry ingredients and stir to blend. Add banana mixture; stir until blended. Fold in carrots and pecans. Pour into greased and floured 9x5x2$^1/_4$-inch loaf pan. Bake at 350° for 55–60 minutes. Cool in pan 10 minutes. Remove to wire rack and allow to cool completely.

Our Best Home Cooking

Apple Bread

5 cups flour, divided	3 eggs, beaten
1 teaspoon baking soda	3 cups peeled, cored, and
1 teaspoon salt	shredded apples
1 teaspoon cinnamon	$^2/_3$ cup oil
$^1/_4$ teaspoon baking powder	1 teaspoon vanilla

Grease and flour three 7$^1/_2$x3$^1/_2$-inch or two 8x4-inch bread pans. Set aside. Mix 3 cups flour, baking soda, salt, cinnamon, and baking powder. Set aside. In large bowl combine eggs, apples, 2 cups flour, oil, and vanilla. Stir in flour mixture. Pour batter into pans. Bake 45–55 minutes at 325° until toothpick comes out clean. Cool in pans on rack 10 minutes. Remove from pans; finish cooling on racks. Wrap and store overnight before cutting.

Costco Wholesale Employee Association Cookbook

Washington State Apple Muffins

2 cups sugar
$^1/_2$ cup vegetable oil
2 eggs
2 teaspoons vanilla
2 cups flour

2 teaspoons baking soda
2 teaspoons cinnamon
1 teaspoon salt (optional)
4 cups chopped apples

In large bowl, beat sugar, vegetable oil, eggs, and vanilla. Slowly stir in dry ingredients just until flour is moistened. Fold in chopped apples. Fill greased muffin tins $^2/_3$ full. Bake at 400° for approximately 20 minutes. Makes 8 muffins.

Recipe by The Guest House B&B, Seattle
Another Taste of Washington State

Apple Crisp Muffins

These low-fat and nutritious muffins are always a hit with the toddler crowd!

$1^1/_4$ cups flour
$^3/_4$ cup quick-cooking oats
$^1/_2$ cup brown sugar
1 tablespoon baking powder
1 teaspoon cinnamon
$^1/_2$ teaspoon salt
1 cup milk

$^3/_4$ cup applesauce
1 egg
2 tablespoons vegetable oil
1 teaspoon vanilla
$1^1/_2$ cups peeled diced apples (2
    medium apples)

Set oven to 375°. Lightly grease a muffin pan. In medium bowl, combine flour, oats, brown sugar, baking powder, cinnamon, and salt. In separate bowl, whisk together milk, applesauce, egg, oil, and vanilla. Stir milk mixture into flour mixture until just moistened. Stir in diced apples.

Fill medium muffin cups $^3/_4$ full, mini-muffin cups to the top.

TOPPING:
$^1/_3$ cup quick-cooking oats
$^1/_4$ cup flour

2 tablespoons brown sugar
2 tablespoons butter, melted

Combine Topping ingredients until crumbly and sprinkle over muffins. Bake 16–18 minutes for medium muffins, 10–12 minutes for mini-muffins or until tops spring back when lightly touched. Yields 12 medium muffins or 36 mini-muffins.

Food for Tots

Chunky Monkey Muffins

1 cup walnuts

Preheat oven to 350°. Toast walnuts in oven, then coarsely chop and set aside. Prepare muffin papers for 16 muffins. Set pans aside.

CREAM CHEESE FILLING:

4 ounces cream cheese, softened

2 tablespoons powdered sugar

Pinch salt

¹/₂ cup semisweet chocolate chips

Combine and cream well soft cream cheese, powdered sugar, and salt. Blend in chocolate chips. Set aside.

MUFFIN BATTER:

2 cups all-purpose flour

1 cup sugar

¹/₂ teaspoon salt

1 teaspoon baking powder

1 teaspoon baking soda

2 tablespoons salad oil

1 large egg

¹/₂ cup orange juice

2 large bananas, peeled

1 teaspoon vanilla

In a bowl, sift dry ingredients. Add chopped nuts. Set aside. In mixer bowl, blend oil, egg, orange juice, bananas, and vanilla. Slowly add dry ingredients and blend. Divide batter evenly between prepared muffin cups, reserving a small amount. Top each muffin with a teaspoon of Cream Cheese Filling and press down slightly. Put a small amount of reserved batter on top of each muffin to cover cream cheese. Bake at 350° for 20–25 minutes.

Recipe by Kangaroo House B&B, Orcas Island
Another Taste of Washington State

Washington was nicknamed "The Evergreen State" by C.T. Conover, pioneer Seattle realtor and historian, for its abundant evergreen forests. Unlike the other state symbols, the nickname has never been officially adopted by law.

David's Bran Muffins

These are very healthful bran muffins that taste good and moist.

1 cup oat bran
$^{1}/_{2}$ cup whole wheat flour
$^{1}/_{2}$ cup unbleached all-purpose
   flour
1 tablespoon baking powder
$^{1}/_{2}$ teaspoon baking soda
$^{1}/_{2}$ teaspoon salt
$^{1}/_{2}$ cup skim milk or Soy Moo
$^{1}/_{2}$ cup brown sugar or honey

2 tablespoons olive oil
1–1$^{1}/_{2}$ teaspoons vanilla
3 egg whites, unbeaten
1 ripe banana, mashed
$^{3}/_{4}$ cup unsweetened applesauce
$^{1}/_{2}$ cup raisins and/or chopped
   walnuts (optional)
1 cup quick oatmeal, uncooked

Preheat oven to 375°. Mix together bran, both flours, baking powder, baking soda, and salt. In a separate bowl, combine milk, honey, oil, vanilla, eggs, banana, and applesauce. Add raisins and/or chopped walnuts. Combine wet and dry ingredients, stirring only until dry ingredients are moistened. Do not over mix. Spray muffin tins with Pam olive oil or line with muffin paper. Fill each one to top. Sprinkle quick oatmeal on top of each muffin. Bake for 15–17 minutes.

    After removing from tins and cooling, muffins can be frozen in an airtight plastic bag. Remove, one at a time, to pack in a lunch or for a great snack. Yields 12 muffins.

Note: Raisins can be substituted with date pieces.

Family Favorites Recipes

Piña Colada Muffins

This is a very moist muffin—that's why everyone likes them.

¹/₂ cup sugar
1 egg
¹/₃ cup vegetable oil
1 cup sour cream
1 teaspoon vanilla
1¹/₂ cups flour

1 teaspoon baking powder
¹/₂ teaspoon salt
¹/₂ teaspoon baking soda
1 small can crushed pineapple, drained
¹/₂ cup coconut

Measure sugar, egg, oil, and sour cream; beat well. Add vanilla and mix well. Add remaining ingredients except pineapple and coconut. Mix well. Stir in pineapple and coconut. Spray muffin tin or line with paper baking cups; fill ²/₃ full. Bake at 375° approximately 20 minutes. Do not over bake.

Bounteous Blessings

Berry Muffins

3 cups flour
¹/₂ cup sugar
1 tablespoon baking powder
1 teaspoon salt
¹/₂ cup brown sugar

¹/₂ cup butter, melted
3 large eggs
1 cup milk
1¹/₂ cups berries

Sift flour, sugar, baking powder, and salt into a bowl. Add brown sugar and stir to blend. Combine melted butter, eggs, and milk; stir into dry mixture until just blended. Fold in berries very lightly and carefully. Spoon into well-greased muffin tins. Bake at 400° for 20 minutes.

Tastes of Country

Streusel Raspberry Muffins

A nice change for those frozen raspberries. This muffin is like cake; the raspberries give such a summery taste.

PECAN STREUSEL TOPPING:

$^1/_4$ cup flour

$^1/_4$ cup packed brown sugar

$^1/_4$ cup chopped pecans

2 tablespoons butter, melted

Combine flour, sugar, and pecans; stir in melted butter. Set aside.

MUFFINS:

$1^1/_2$ cups flour

$^1/_2$ cup sugar

2 teaspoons baking powder

$^1/_2$ cup milk

$^1/_2$ cup butter, melted

1 egg, beaten

1 cup fresh or frozen
raspberries

Combine flour, sugar, and baking powder. In a small bowl, combine milk, butter, and egg until blended. Stir into flour mixture until moistened. Spoon half of batter into greased muffin cups. Divide raspberries among 12 cups then top with remaining batter. Sprinkle Pecan Streusel Topping over tops. Bake at 375° for 25–30 minutes.

Bounteous Blessings

Lemon Cream Scones

2 cups unbleached flour
2 tablespoons sugar
1 teaspoon cream of tartar
$^{1}/_{2}$ teaspoon baking soda
$^{1}/_{2}$ teaspoon salt
Grated zest of 2 lemons
4 tablespoons unsalted butter,
  cut into pieces

2 eggs
$^{1}/_{2}$ cup heavy cream
Cinnamon-sugar mixture,
  optional ($^{1}/_{2}$ teaspoon
  cinnamon mixed with
  2 tablespoons sugar)

Preheat oven to 400°. Combine flour, sugar, cream of tartar, baking soda, salt, and zest; blend. This can be blended in the work bowl of a food processor. With pastry blender, 2 knives or steel blade of a food processor, cut or process butter in until mixture resembles coarse meal. Whisk together eggs and heavy cream. Add to dry mixture and stir until sticky dough is formed. If using a food processor, pour mixture in feed tube and pulse until dough starts to form a rough ball (don't over process or scones will be tough).

Turn dough out onto lightly floured work surface and knead gently just until dough holds together, about 6 times. Pat out dough into an 8- to 10-inch round, and with a knife, cut into 8 wedges (a biscuit cutter can also be used). Remember that, as with biscuits, you stamp or punch and not slice. Place scones about 1 inch apart on a greased or parchment-lined baking sheet. Sprinkle with cinnamon-sugar mixture, if desired. Bake until crusty and golden brown, about 15–20 minutes. Serve hot with butter and jam.

Recipe by The Whalebone House, Ocean Park, Long Beach Peninsula
Another Taste of Washington State

Every spring since 1974, the Walla Walla Balloon Stampede has drawn hot-air balloons to the skies over Walla Walla, Washington. This spectacular show is one of the area's longest running events and has always been free to the public.

Wonderful Buttermilk Scones

In years past, I opened my home and studios to a group of Seattle's Lakeside High School students and teachers. While camping out here, they did art projects. Lakeside Library's glowing stained glass window is the product of one of these visits.

3 cups flour	$^3/_4$ cup butter
$^1/_4$ cup sugar	1 cup currants
$2^1/_2$ teaspoons baking powder	Grated peel of 1 orange
$^1/_2$ teaspoon baking soda	1 cup buttermilk
$^1/_2$ teaspoon salt	

Preheat oven to 425°. Combine the first 5 ingredients in a mixing bowl; cut in butter until mixture is in pea-sized grains. Add currants and orange peel. Make a well in the center and pour in buttermilk. Stir with a fork until dough leaves the sides of the bowl. Knead dough briefly on a floured board.

Divide dough into 3 balls. Flatten each with the palm of your hand until $^1/_2$–$^3/_4$ inch thick. Shape into a circle and cut into quarters. Place 12 quarter-pieces on ungreased cookie sheet. Bake for approximately 12 minutes or until golden. The scones freeze well. Makes 12 scones.

Skagit Valley Fare

Country Cinnamon Rolls

1¹/₂ cups milk
1¹/₂ cups water
1 cup shortening
²/₃ cup sugar
2 teaspoons salt
4 packages yeast

9 cups flour, divided
4 eggs, beaten
Butter, cinnamon, and brown
   sugar, to taste
Applesauce, raisins, or nuts
   (optional)

Heat milk, water, shortening, sugar, and salt to 120°–130°; mix undissolved yeast with 3 cups flour. Add liquid mixture to the flour-yeast mixture. Beat 2 minutes at medium speed. Add eggs and 1 cup flour. Beat 2 minutes on high speed. Stir in remaining flour. Turn out onto floured board. Let rest 10 minutes. Knead 12–15 times, until smooth. Place in an oiled bowl in a warm place and let rise until doubled, about 1 hour. Melt butter, brown sugar, and cinnamon in 3 (9x13-inch) pans. Punch dough down and form into rolls; place in prepared pans. Top rolls with additional melted butter, brown sugar, cinnamon and applesauce, raisins, or nuts (if desired); let rise. Bake in a 350° oven for 20 minutes or until golden brown.

A Taste of Heaven

Overnight Brunch Rolls

Easy, exciting, tender rolls—your guests and family will think you've been up all night making and baking.

1 (15-ounce) package frozen
   dinner rolls
1 small package butterscotch,
   lemon or other desired flavor
   pudding mix (not instant)

¹/₂ cup brown sugar
¹/₂ cup butter, melted
¹/₂ teaspoon cinnamon
   (optional)
¹/₂ cup chopped nuts

The night before serving, arrange frozen dinner rolls in greased Bundt pan. Sprinkle dry pudding over top; then brown sugar. If using cinnamon, mix with melted butter. Pour melted butter (or butter and cinnamon mixture) over top and sprinkle with nuts. Cover with towel; set on counter overnight. Pop in oven next morning at 350° for 25–30 minutes. Cool 5 minutes in pan; then flip over onto serving plate.

Sleigh Bells and Sugarplums

Christmas Tea Ring

My family says it wouldn't be Christmas without the Christmas Tea Ring.

2 packages dry yeast	5–5$^1/_2$ cups flour, sifted
$^1/_4$ cup warm water	Melted butter
$^1/_2$ cup sugar	$^1/_2$ cup firmly packed brown
$^1/_4$ cup shortening	sugar
1 teaspoon salt	2 teaspoons cinnamon
1 cup milk, hot, scalded	Chopped nuts and Maraschino
2 eggs, unbeaten	cherry halves for garnish

Soften yeast in warm water; set aside. Combine sugar, shortening, salt, and milk in large mixing bowl. Stir in eggs and softened yeast; add flour gradually to form stiff dough. Knead on floured surface until smooth and satiny, 5–8 minutes. Place in greased bowl and cover. Let rise in warm place until doubled, about 1$^1/_2$ hours. While waiting for dough to rise, make Pineapple Date Filling.

After dough has risen, divide in half and roll out 1 portion on floured surface to 20x12-inch rectangle. Brush with melted butter. Spread with half the Filling to within 1 inch of one long side and to edge of other side. Combine brown sugar and cinnamon; sprinkle half over Filling. Roll as for jellyroll, starting with 20-inch edge. Shape into a ring on greased cookie sheet. With scissors, make cuts 1 inch apart through top of ring to 1 inch from bottom. Alternate cut slices, bringing one to center and the next to the outside of the ring. Cover. Repeat with remaining dough. Let rise in warm place until light, 45–60 minutes. Bake at 375° for 20–25 minutes. While warm, frost with Vanilla Glaze. Garnish with nuts and cherries.

PINEAPPLE DATE FILLING:

1 (20-ounce) can crushed	1 tablespoon cornstarch
pineapple, well drained	$^3/_4$ cup chopped dates
$^3/_4$ cup sugar	$^1/_2$ cup chopped walnuts

Combine in saucepan, pineapple, sugar, and cornstarch; cook over medium heat until thick. Add dates and nuts; cool.

VANILLA GLAZE:

1 cup powdered sugar, sifted	$^1/_2$ teaspoon vanilla
2 tablespoons cream	

Beat Glaze ingredients until spreading consistency.

Christmas in Washington Cook Book

Sunrise Coffee Cake

NUT TOPPING:

2 teaspoons cinnamon	$^1/_2$ cup chopped nuts

Mix Topping ingredients together; set aside.

COFFEE CAKE:

$^1/_2$ cup margarine	$^1/_2$ teaspoon baking soda
1 cup sugar	$^1/_2$ teaspoon salt
1 teaspoon vanilla	$^3/_4$ cup sour cream
2 eggs	$^1/_2$ cup orange juice
2 cups sifted flour	1 tablespoon grated orange rind
1 teaspoon baking powder	

Cream margarine, sugar, and vanilla. Beat in eggs, 1 at a time. Sift flour, baking powder, baking soda, and salt. Stir alternately with sour cream and orange juice. Fold in orange rind. Spoon half of batter into greased 9-inch-square pan. Top with half of Nut Topping. Repeat layer. Bake at 375° for 40 minutes or until done.

Nautical Niceaty's from Spokane Yacht Club

Overnight Coffee Cake

TOPPING:

$^3/_4$ cup brown sugar	$^3/_4$ cup finely chopped nuts
$^3/_4$ teaspoon cinnamon	

Mix Topping ingredients together. Set side.

COFFEE CAKE:

1 cup butter, softened	$1^1/_2$ teaspoons baking powder
$1^1/_2$ cups sugar	$1^1/_2$ teaspoons baking soda
$^3/_4$ cup brown sugar	1 teaspoon cinnamon
3 eggs	$^3/_4$ teaspoon salt
3 cups flour	$1^1/_2$ cups buttermilk

Cream butter and sugars. Add eggs, 1 at a time, beating well. Sift flour, baking powder, baking soda, 1 teaspoon cinnamon, and salt. Add alternately with buttermilk, mixing gently. Pour into a greased 9x13-inch pan. Sprinkle with Topping. Cover and refrigerate overnight. Bake at 350° for 45 minutes.

Your Favorite Recipes

Coffee Cake with
Cinnamon Walnut Topping

CINNAMON WALNUT TOPPING:

1¼ cups brown sugar   1¼ cups chopped walnuts

1 tablespoon cinnamon

Combine Topping ingredients. Set aside

COFFEE CAKE:

1 box yellow cake mix, with   4 whole eggs
   pudding in the mix   ¼ cup oil

1 stick margarine or butter,   1½ cups sour cream
   melted

Mix cake mix, margarine, eggs, oil, and sour cream together. Batter will be thick; don't overmix. Grease 9x13-inch pan or 2 square glass pans. Pour in batter, then top with Cinnamon Walnut Topping. Swirl topping into batter with tip of knife. Bake at 350° for 40–45 minutes. This freezes well and is good served warm or cold.

Recipe by Otters Pond Bed & Breakfast of Orcas Island
Another Taste of Washington State

Plum Kuchen

$^1/_3$ cup butter	Flour to make a stiff batter
$^1/_3$ cup sugar	(about $3^3/_4$ cups)
$^1/_2$ teaspoon salt	24 fresh plums, halved and pitted
1 cup scalded milk	2 teaspoons cinnamon
1 cake yeast	$1^1/_2$ cups sugar
$^1/_4$ cup lukewarm water	1 egg yolk, well beaten
2 eggs, well beaten	5 tablespoons cream

Add butter, $^1/_3$ cup sugar, and salt to the scalded milk and let it cool to lukewarm. Soften yeast in lukewarm water and stir in lukewarm milk mixture. Add well beaten eggs, then the flour and stir until well blended and smooth. Cover and let rise in a warm place until double in bulk. Punch down, beat thoroughly, and then spread the dough $^1/_2$ inch thick in a large well-buttered baking pan. Let rise again until doubled. Lay plum halves, skin down, on top. Mix cinnamon with $1^1/_2$ cups sugar, egg yolk, and cream; drizzle this over the plums. Bake in 350° oven for 35–50 minutes. This can also be made in cake pans or pie tins, and thickness made as desired.

Unser Tagelich Brot (The Staff of Life III)

Peach French Toast

Plan ahead, start the night before.

1 cup packed brown sugar
¹/₂ cup butter or margarine
2 tablespoons water
1 (29-ounce) can or 6 fresh
  sliced peaches (drained
  blueberries can also be used)

12 slices of day-old French bread
5 eggs
1¹/₂ cups milk
1 tablespoon vanilla extract
Cinnamon to taste

In a saucepan, bring brown sugar, butter, and water to a boil. Reduce heat; simmer for 10 minutes, stirring frequently. Pour into greased 9x13x2-inch baking dish; top with peaches. Arrange bread over peaches. In a bowl, whisk the eggs, milk, and vanilla; slowly pour over bread. Cover and refrigerate overnight. Remove from refrigerator 30 minutes before baking. Sprinkle with cinnamon. Cover and bake at 350° for 20 minutes. Uncover and bake 25–30 minutes longer or until golden brown. Serve with a spoon. Makes 6–8 servings.

Bounteous Blessings

French Toast Decadence

6 eggs
¹/₂ cup orange juice
¹/₃ cup orange liqueur
¹/₂ cup half-and-half
1 teaspoon vanilla

¹/₄ teaspoon salt
Grated peel of 1 orange
1 loaf cinnamon bread, sliced
4 tablespoons butter, divided

The night before serving, beat the eggs in a large mixing bowl. Add orange juice, liqueur, half-and-half, vanilla, salt, and orange peel. Mix well. Dip the sliced bread in egg mixture and place bread in a baking dish. Cover dish with plastic wrap and refrigerate overnight.

To prepare the French toast, melt 1 tablespoon butter in a skillet. Brown the soaked bread on both sides. Continue with all pieces.

MAPLE RUM SYRUP:
1 cup maple syrup
1 cup honey

2 tablespoons dark rum

In a small saucepan heat syrup, honey, and rum over low heat. Pour into a small pitcher and serve with French toast. Makes 6 servings.

Simply Whidbey

Banana Pecan Pancakes

This batter is wonderfully versatile. In this recipe, the bananas and pecans give a distinctively appealing texture and flavor.

2 bananas	1/2 teaspoon salt
2 eggs	1 cup cornmeal
3 cups buttermilk	1/2 cup bran
3 tablespoons butter, melted	1 tablespoon honey
2 cups unbleached flour	1/2 cup pecans, sautéed in
1 teaspoon baking soda	butter until golden

In a medium mixing bowl, mash bananas with fork until lumps are mostly worked out. Add eggs, buttermilk, and melted butter; mix thoroughly. In separate bowl, sift flour with baking soda and salt. Stir in cornmeal and bran; add dry ingredients to banana mixture, stirring until moistened. Add honey and pecans (that have been sautéed in butter until golden). Prepare as any other pancake.

Christmas in Washington Cook Book

Morning Mix-Up

2 cups frozen hash browns	6 eggs
1 cup chopped ham	Salt and pepper
1/2 cup chopped onion	1 cup shredded Cheddar
2 tablespoons oil	Minced fresh chives

Mix hash browns, ham, onion, and oil in large saucepan. Then cook for 10 minutes. Beat eggs, salt and pepper. Add to mixture. Stir occasionally. Remove from heat and gently stir in cheese. Sprinkle with chives.

Costco Wholesale Employee Association Cookbook

The best kite flying in Washington can be found in Long Beach during the week-long Washington State International Kite Festival held each August. Among the country's largest kite events, the festival has drawn contestants from as far away as Indonesia and Europe.

Breakfast Pinwheels

6 eggs
¹/₂ cup cream
Salt and white pepper to taste
Parmesan cheese to taste
2 cups broccoli flowerets
1 cup slivered mushrooms
Garlic to taste
Salt and pepper to taste

1 cup sour cream
1 cup shredded white cheese
2 tablespoons butter
2 tablespoons flour
Milk, as needed
Shredded sharp Cheddar cheese
   to taste

Mix eggs, cream, salt and white pepper. Pour into well-greased 9x13-inch baking dish. Bake at 350° for 20–30 minutes. Carefully slip out onto waxed paper covered with Parmesan cheese. Precook broccoli, mushrooms, garlic, salt and pepper until tender. Layer sour cream, white cheese, and broccoli-mushroom mixture onto eggs. Roll into a log and slice into medallions. Mix butter, flour, milk, and Cheddar cheese together in saucepan on medium heat, stirring until smooth. Pour cheese sauce onto serving plate; place medallions in center. Garnish and serve.

Recipe by Inn at Barnum Point, Camano Island
Another Taste of Washington State

Northwest Oven Omelets

For an elegant presentation, bake these in individual soufflé dishes.

10 eggs	3 tablespoons small capers,
¹/₂ cup milk	rinsed and drained
4 ounces smoked salmon, flaked	¹/₄ teaspoon white pepper
1 cup (4 ounces) grated	¹/₄ teaspoon salt
medium Cheddar cheese	Dill sprigs for garnish
4 ounces light cream cheese,	
cut into small pieces	

Preheat oven to 375°. Oil 6 individual soufflé dishes (10 ounces each), or an 8x8-inch baking dish. In a large bowl, whisk eggs and milk. Add salmon, Cheddar cheese, cream cheese, capers, white pepper, and salt; mix well.

Divide egg mixture between the soufflé dishes. Lay sprigs of dill on top in a decorative fashion. Bake 30 minutes or until center of each omelet is firm and sides have pulled away. Serve immediately. Yields 6 servings.

Good Times at Green Lake

Skagit Bay Crab and Havarti Omelet

5–6 mushrooms, thinly sliced	¹/₈ pound fresh Dungeness crab
2+ tablespoons butter	¹/₂ of a plum tomato, chopped
4 eggs	1–2 green onions, chopped
1¹/₂ tablespoons cream	Fresh nasturtium for garnish
Havarti cheese, thinly sliced	

Sauté mushrooms in 2 tablespoons butter over low heat. Melt additional butter in 10-inch omelet pan. Mix eggs and cream well, and pour into pan. Cook over low heat for 20–30 minutes. After eggs are set, place thin slices of Havarti cheese to cover omelet and let melt. Add crab, sautéed mushrooms, and most of tomato and green onions (reserve enough for garnish). Fold omelet in half and slide onto serving dish. Serve with garnish of tomatoes, green onions, and fresh nasturtium on top. Makes 1 omelet.

Recipe by Skagit Bay Hideaway, LaConner
Another Taste of Washington State

24 Hour Wine & Cheese Omelet

This is an excellent dish for brunch.

1 large loaf day-old French
  bread, broken in small pieces
6 tablespoons butter, melted
³/4 pound Swiss cheese,
  shredded
¹/2 pound Monterey Jack cheese,
  shredded
9 thin slices Genoa salami,
  coarsely chopped
16 eggs

3¹/4 cups milk
¹/2 cup white wine
4 large green onions, minced
1 tablespoon Düsseldorf
  German mustard
¹/4 teaspoon pepper
¹/8 teaspoon cayenne pepper
1¹/2 cups sour cream
²/3–1 cup freshly grated
  Parmesan cheese

Butter 2 (9x13-inch) dishes. Spread bread over bottom of each dish and drizzle with melted butter. Sprinkle bread with Swiss and Monterey Jack cheeses and salami. Beat together the eggs, milk, wine, green onions, mustard, and peppers until foamy. Pour over the cheeses. Cover dishes with foil, crimping edges. Chill overnight or up to 24 hours.

Remove dishes from refrigerator ¹/2 hour before baking. Bake 1 hour at 325°. Uncover, spread with sour cream, and sprinkle with Parmesan. Bake, uncovered, 10 minutes.

Extraordinary Cuisine for Sea & Shore

Ports on Puget Sound and the Pacific Ocean handle almost all commercial fishing landings; less than 1% comes from fresh water. In value, salmon accounts for about ¹/3 of the catch, followed by oysters, crab, shrimp and other shellfish. Other fish caught include halibut, flounder, tuna, cod, rockfish, pollock, and sablefish.

Baked Egg Omelet

This is great to make ahead for overnight guests, but can be made just prior to serving. It is unbeatable!

Butter	4 cups milk
8 slices bread	2 teaspoons salt
1 pound Cheddar cheese, grated	Dash cayenne pepper
1 cup diced, cooked sausage, bacon or ham	Sautéed sliced mushrooms (optional)
10 eggs	Chopped green onions (optional)

Butter bread and cut into 1-inch cubes. Place bread evenly in well-greased 9x13-inch pan. Sprinkle with cheese. Top with meat that has been patted with paper towels to remove grease. Beat together eggs, milk, salt, and pepper; add sautéed mushroom slices and chopped green onions if desired; pour over bread mixture. Cover and refrigerate overnight. Bake covered at 350° for 1 hour or until egg mixture is set. Remove cover for last 15 minutes of baking.

Bounteous Blessings

Breakfast Sausage Soufflé

This makes a wonderful breakfast for company and has become something of a tradition for Christmas breakfast.

8 slices bread, cubed	4 eggs
1¹/₂ pounds sausage, browned	3 cups milk, divided
Sliced mushrooms	³/₄ teaspoon dry mustard
1 cup chopped onion	1 can cream of mushroom soup, condensed
2 cups shredded sharp Cheddar cheese	

Cube bread and spread on bottom of a greased 9x13-inch pan. Brown sausage, adding mushrooms and onions just before done. Drain. Layer sausage mixture and cheese over bread. Beat together eggs, 2¹/₂ cups milk, and dry mustard. Pour over bread, sausage and cheese; stir lightly until mixed. Refrigerate overnight. Just before baking, combine mushroom soup and ¹/₂ cup milk. Pour over casserole. Bake at 300° for 1¹/₂ hours.

Harvest Feast

Tortilla Torta

6 (10-inch) flour tortillas
6 eggs
2 tablespoons flour
$^1/_2$ cup buttermilk
2 cups (about 8 ounces) grated
  pepper jack cheese

3 green onions, sliced (optional)
4 ounces roasted red peppers,
  drained and chopped
$^1/_2$ teaspoon salt
$^1/_4$ teaspoon pepper
1 tablespoon butter, melted

Preheat oven to 375°. Spray 9x3-inch springform pan lightly with vegetable oil. Line with 5 tortillas, overlapping them and gently pressing them against sides of pan. (Be careful not to tear them.) You may have to pleat them in some places. Extend the tortillas about 2 inches above rim. Set aside.

Whisk eggs in a large bowl. Add flour, buttermilk, cheese, green onions, red peppers, salt and pepper; stir well. Pour filling into tortilla shell. Gently bend edges of tortillas over filling. With scissors or knife, trim remaining tortilla so it will fit on top. Brush edges with water. Brush tops of tortillas in the pan with water. Put tortilla on top and gently press. Brush melted butter on top.

Bake about 1 hour, checking it after 15 minutes for browning. Cover top with foil after it has browned. To check for doneness, make a small slit in the top and press gently. If the egg is runny, continue baking. Remove torta from oven and let stand 20 minutes. Release the springform. Place torta on a serving platter. Serve with Salsa Fresca and sour cream. Yields 6 servings.

SALSA FRESCA:
4 plum tomatoes, seeded and
  coarsely chopped (about
  2 cups)
1 shallot, peeled and chopped
1 fresh jalapeño chile pepper,
  finely chopped*

2 cloves garlic, chopped
1 teaspoon olive oil
3 tablespoons roughly chopped
  cilantro
Freshly squeezed lemon or lime
  juice to taste

Combine the ingredients in a small bowl. Add coarse salt and freshly ground pepper to taste. Let stand at room temperature for 1 hour. Serve with the Tortilla Torta. Yields about 2 cups.

*Use a serrano chile if you like hot foods. You can also add more garlic.

Good Times at Green Lake

Creamy Christmas Eggs

Very filling and men like this elegant dish, especially when served with cinnamon rolls.

STEP ONE:

2 tablespoons butter
2 tablespoons flour

1 cup sour cream

In a saucepan, melt butter; stir in flour and cook over medium heat until bubbly. (Be sure the flour cooks to avoid raw taste.) Remove from heat, then blend in sour cream; return to heat and cook until bubbly and smooth. Set aside.

STEP TWO:

2 dozen eggs
$^1/_4$ teaspoon salt
$^1/_8$ teaspoon pepper

2 tablespoons butter
Chopped parsley

Beat eggs, salt, and pepper. Melt butter in a wide frying pan over medium-low heat; pour in eggs and cook slowly, gently lifting cooked portion from bottom. Cook just until softly set; remove from heat and gently blend in sour cream mixture. Turn into a serving dish, garnish with parsley, and keep warm on an electric warming tray.

GARNISHES:

1–1$^1/_2$ pounds bacon, crisply
   fried and crumbled
3 cups shredded mild Cheddar
   or Swiss cheese
10–12 green onions, sliced

2–3 (2$^1/_2$-ounce) cans sliced
   ripe olives
1 pound small cooked shrimp
1 pint sour cream

Serve the eggs with the above Garnishes. Yields 10 servings.

Sharing Our Best

Cheese Blintzes

These blintzes are very delicate. What a surprise for Sunday brunch. You'll just have to try them.

1 cup nonfat cottage cheese	$^1/_2$ teaspoon vanilla
1 cup nonfat ricotta cheese	2 cups sliced strawberries
$^1/_3$ cup nonfat cream cheese	16 low-fat crepes
$^2/_3$ cup sugar, divided	

Place cottage cheese, ricotta cheese, cream cheese, $^1/_3$ cup sugar, and vanilla in food processor or blender. Process until smooth. Pour mixture in bowl, cover, and chill. Mix strawberries with remaining $^1/_3$ cup sugar. Toss gently. Spoon 2 tablespoons cheese mixture in center of each crepe. Fold sides and ends over. Place seam down on a platter. Serve with strawberry mixture over crepes. Serves 8.

From My Heart For Yours

Apples with Granola and Cider Cream

Cinnamon-sugar mixture, to taste	$^1/_2$ cup dried cranberries
4 large apples (reds, goldens, Braeburn or Fuji)	4 cups granola
	8 tablespoons melted butter, plus extra for buttering dish

Generously butter 9x9-inch glass pan or 8 large ramekins. Sprinkle bottom of pans with cinnamon-sugar, reserving some for later use. Peel, halve, and core apples. Maintain shape of apple half and place in dish. Sprinkle tops of apples with more cinnamon-sugar and dried cranberries. Pour $^1/_2$ cup granola on each apple half. Pour melted butter onto granola. Cover with foil and bake at 350° for 45–60 minutes. Serve apples topped with Cider Cream and a dash of cinnamon. Makes 8 servings.

CIDER CREAM:

1 cup apple cider	1 cup whipping cream

Boil cider until reduced to $^1/_4$ cup. Cool. Beat cream until stiff. Blend in cider syrup.

Recipe by Autumn Pond Bed & Breakfast, Leavenworth
Another Taste of Washington State

Sprouts' Granola

This recipe was a favorite at Sprouts' Fresh Cafe. Granola makes a great gift—for yourself and for your friends!

6 cups old-fashioned rolled oats
  (not quick variety)
$^1/_2$ cup brown sugar
1 cup slivered or sliced almonds
$^1/_4$ cup raw sunflower seeds
$^1/_4$ cup pumpkin seeds
1 tablespoon cinnamon

$^1/_2$ cup apple juice
$^2/_3$ cup honey
2 tablespoons vanilla extract
2 tablespoons butter, melted or
  olive oil
1 cup dried fruits

Preheat oven to 400°. Combine all dry ingredients in a large bowl. In a small bowl, whisk together apple juice, honey, vanilla, and melted butter. Drizzle over dry ingredients and mix well. Spread onto a baking sheet and bake for about 30–40 minutes turning and mixing granola every few minutes until just golden brown. Caution—watch closely toward end of baking time, it starts to brown quickly.

   When granola is completely cool, add 1 cup of dried fruits such as craisins, bananas, dates, mangos, raisins, coconut flakes, etc. Store in a sealed, airtight container. Makes about 2 quarts.

Good Food for (Mostly) Good People Cookbook

SOUPS, CHILIES *and* STEWS

Long famous as the earliest-opening downhill skiing resort in Washington, the Mt. Baker Ski Area reported 1,140 inches of snowfall for the 1998-99 snowfall season, setting a record for the most snowfall ever measured in the United States in a single season.

Puget Sound Oyster Bisque

The distinctive taste of oysters is a favorite of many Whidbey Island residents. This bisque makes the perfect starter to any entrée. It is equally suitable as a meal in itself when accompanied by a warm loaf of freshly baked bread.

$1/4$ cup flour
$1/4$ cup water
2 teaspoons salt
4 teaspoons Worcestershire
3 (10-ounce) jars shucked
   oysters

6 cups half-and-half
3 tablespoons margarine
Snipped parsley for garnish

In a large saucepan, whisk together flour, $1/4$ cup water, salt, and Worcestershire. Add oysters and their liquid. Depending on the size of the oysters, you may want to cut them into bite-size pieces. Cook over medium heat for 10 minutes, stirring constantly. The centers will be firm and the edge of oysters will curl a bit when cooked.

Add half-and-half and margarine and heat to boiling. Let the bisque stand at least 15 minutes to blend flavors. Garnish with snipped parsley, if so desired. Makes 6 servings.

Simply Whidbey

Fiddlehead Cream Soup

2 cups fiddleheads
4 tablespoons butter
1 tablespoon walnut oil
2 cups chicken stock or water

1 cup heavy cream
2 tablespoons white wine
   (optional)

Sauté fiddleheads in butter and nut oil for 10 minutes over medium-low heat and add chicken stock. Bring to a boil, cover and reduce heat, and simmer 20 minutes more. Add cream and simmer 10 more minutes, adding wine, if desired, at this time.

The Wild and Free Cookbook

Editors' Extra: Fiddleheads are the fronds of ostrich ferns. In the spring they are available fresh in many food stores.

Lavone's Italian Fish Soup

This is my version of traditional Italian fish soup. It is a meal in itself when served with fresh-baked sourdough French bread.

$^1/_2$ pound fresh sweet or hot Italian sausage

3 tablespoons olive oil

1 medium onion, diced

$^3/_4$ cup chopped celery including leaves

1 small red sweet pepper, chopped

1 small yellow sweet pepper, chopped

3 (14$^1/_2$-ounce) cans Italian-style chopped tomatoes with basil

4 medium potatoes, diced

1 teaspoon salt

Fresh-ground pepper to taste

4 cups fish stock or clam nectar

1 pound firm white fish, such as cod or halibut, cut into chunks

$^1/_2$ pound fresh scallops

$^1/_2$ pound fresh cooked and peeled medium-size shrimp

$^1/_2$ cup dry white wine

$^1/_4$ cup chopped fresh parsley, divided

1 tablespoon lemon juice or to taste

1 teaspoon lemon zest

3 dashes Tabasco sauce

In large soup pot, sauté Italian sausage in olive oil until lightly browned. Add onion, celery, and peppers and continue to sauté until vegetables are limp. Add tomatoes, potatoes, salt, pepper, and fish stock to sautéed vegetables and bring to a simmer.

Cook for about 10 minutes and then add fish and scallops. Simmer for 5–7 minutes. Add shrimp, wine, half of the parsley, lemon juice, lemon zest, and Tabasco. Bring back to a simmer and serve immediately. Serve in large soup plates with remaining chopped parsley sprinkled over the top. Serves 6–8.

Skagit Valley Fare

Moushella

This soup is referred to as a German version of won ton soup.

NOODLE DOUGH:

3 eggs   1 teaspoon salt
3 cups flour

Mix noodle ingredients, kneading with hands, to make very firm dough. You may need to add flour or a little water. Cut dough into quarters; roll until very thin. Cut into 4x4-inch squares; set aside until Meatballs are made.

MEATBALLS:

1¹/₂ pounds hamburger   ¹/₈ teaspoon thyme
¹/₂ pound pork sausage,   Dash cloves
   unseasoned   Dash mace
1¹/₂ teaspoons salt   Dash savory
³/₄ teaspoon pepper   2 cloves garlic, crushed
¹/₄ teaspoon allspice

Combine all meatball ingredients; form into small balls. Wrap in noodle squares, making triangles. Seal edges of dough with water, or a bit of egg white.

SOUP:

2 large cans beef broth   1 clove garlic, crushed
2 large onions, diced   4 quarts water, approximately

In large kettle, combine ingredients; bring to boil. Drop in noodle meat triangles, 1 at a time. They will rise to the top. Boil gently for about 20 minutes.

Christmas in Washington Cook Book

The first Americans interested in the Pacific Northwest were merchants who came from Boston as early as the 1780s, among them Robert Gray, who explored the Columbia River in 1792. The Lewis and Clark expedition (1804-06) stimulated public interest, and in 1811 John Jacob Astor established a fur-trading post, Astoria, near the mouth of the Columbia and a fort at the mouth of the Okanogan River.

Hamburger Soup

2 tablespoons butter
1 medium onion, chopped
1 pound ground beef
2$^{1}/_{2}$ quarts hot water
2 beef bouillon cubes
2 cups diced potatoes
1 cup chopped celery with leaves

1 cup diced carrots
1 (1-pound) can tomatoes
1 (7-ounce) can whole-kernel
corn
2 teaspoons salt
$^{1}/_{2}$ teaspoon pepper
$^{1}/_{4}$ cup rice or barley

Melt butter in soup kettle; add onion. Cook until soft, but not brown. Add ground beef; cook until crumbly. Add hot water and bouillon cubes. Bring to a boil, stirring to dissolve bouillon cubes. Add remaining ingredients; return mixture to a boil. Reduce heat and simmer for 1$^{1}/_{2}$ hours. Taste before serving and adjust seasonings. Yields 12 cups.

Heavenly Fare

Ox-Tail Vegetable Soup

Knuckle soup bone or ox-tail
chuck roast of beef
1 (29-ounce) can tomatoes,
put through blender
$^{1}/_{4}$ cup chopped fresh carrots,
small pieces
$^{1}/_{4}$ cup chopped celery, small
pieces
$^{1}/_{4}$ cup chopped onion, small
pieces
$^{1}/_{4}$ cup corn (fresh, if possible)

$^{1}/_{4}$ cup fresh green beans
$^{1}/_{4}$ cup finely cut cabbage
1 teaspoon sugar
$^{1}/_{3}$ cup barley
1 tablespoon chopped fresh
parsley
Salt to taste
1 cup V-8 or tomato juice
1 potato, chopped in small
pieces
$^{1}/_{2}$ cup rice

Cover meat with water and blended tomatoes, bring to a boil, skim, then add all vegetables and ingredients except potato and rice. May vary amount of vegetables as desired. Cook at least 2 hours. Then add potato and rice and cook an additional $^{1}/_{2}$ hour. May serve meat separately or shred throughout soup. Add more juice or water if more liquid is needed.

McNamee Family & Friends Cookbook

Tortilla Soup

2 (16-ounce) cans tomatoes
  with liquid
2 (8-ounce) cans tomato sauce
2 cloves garlic, minced
4 cups water
2 tablespoons sugar
1 tablespoon chili powder
1 teaspoon salt

$1/2$ teaspoon black pepper
$1/2$ teaspoon dried oregano
1 ($4^1/2$-ounce) can chopped
  green chiles
$1/2$ cup tomato salsa
2 cups cubed, cooked chicken
  breast meat
Tortilla chips

CONDIMENTS:
Sour cream
Avocado
Shredded Cheddar cheese

Chopped green onions
Chopped black olives
Chopped tomatoes

Combine all ingredients except chips and Condiments. Cover and simmer over low heat for 1 hour. When ready to serve, put a handful of chips in a bowl and add soup. Top with desired Condiments. Serves 8.

Gold'n Delicious

Pig Out Taco Soup

1 pound ground beef
1 medium onion, chopped
1 package taco seasoning
1 large can tomatoes, undrained
1 (16-ounce) can kidney beans,
  undrained
1 (16-ounce) can corn,
  undrained

1 (4-ounce) can chopped chile
  peppers, undrained
1 (4-ounce) can sliced black
  olives
Condiments: Sour cream, salsa,
  chips, shredded cheese,
  guacamole, etc.

Brown ground beef. Add onion; sauté. Add taco seasoning, tomatoes, beans, corn, peppers, and olives. (Do not drain any veggies.) Simmer at least $1/2$ hour. Serve with condiments.

Pig Out

Mexican Corn & Bean Sopa

One of the most popular soups ever to come from the Colophon, the Mexican Corn & Bean Sopa has been featured in many publications since we created it. It's vegetarian and low in fat.

1 medium onion, finely diced	3 teaspoons chili powder
3 cloves garlic, minced	1 teaspoon sugar
1 (15-ounce) can diced tomatoes, or equal amount of fresh tomatoes and juice	1/2 teaspoon black pepper
	1 teaspoon cumin
	Hot water
2 (15-ounce) cans red kidney beans, drained	1 (1-pound) bag frozen corn
	Sour cream for garnish
1 (24-ounce) can vegetable juice	Tortilla chips for garnish

Sauté onion and garlic in a little olive oil in a large pot. Add tomatoes, beans, and vegetable juice to pot and heat to a slow boil. Mix chili powder, sugar, black pepper, and cumin in a small bowl, then add hot water to make a paste-like consistency; add to pot. Add corn to pot, heat to slow boil, reduce heat, and simmer for about 20 minutes. Garnish with sour cream and tortilla chips. Serves 4–6.

The Colophone Cafe Best Soups

Gazpacho Soup

This is a wonderful cold soup for warm summer days.

4 medium ripe tomatoes, peeled and chopped	2 cups tomato juice
	1/4 cup wine vinegar
2 cloves garlic, mashed	Dash of Tabasco sauce
1 medium cucumber, chopped	1 cup ice water
1 large green pepper, chopped	Salt and pepper
1 large red pepper, chopped	Croutons for garnish
1 cup onion, minced	Chopped chives for garnish
1/4 cup olive oil	

Mix all ingredients in a large bowl and refrigerate 3 hours or longer. You may want to add more vinegar. Pour into chilled bowls and serve with croutons and chopped chives. Serves 6.

Heavenly Fare

Cheri's Creamy Potato Soup

1 small onion, chopped fine
4 tablespoons margarine
2 cups water
3 cubes chicken bouillon
6 potatoes, peeled and cubed
1 (8-ounce) package cream
  cheese, softened

$^1/_3$ cup flour
4 cups milk
$^1/_2$ pound bacon, fried crisp and
  crumbled
1 can cream of potato soup
Salt and pepper to taste

Sauté onion in margarine until tender. In large kettle, put water, bouillon, and potatoes with onion. Cover and cook until potatoes are tender. Blend cream cheese and flour until smooth. Stir into potato mixture. Add milk, bacon, and can of soup. Bring to a boil, and boil for 1 minute. Season with salt and pepper.

Very good soup base for clam chowder! Just omit can of soup and add 1 can clams, juice and all.

Tastes of Country

Baked Potato Soup

4 large baking potatoes
$^2/_3$ cup butter or margarine
$^2/_3$ cup flour
6 cups milk
$^3/_4$ teaspoon salt
$^1/_2$ teaspoon pepper
1$^1/_2$ cups shredded Cheddar
  cheese, divided

12 slices bacon, cooked and
  crumbled, divided
4 green onions, chopped,
  divided
8 ounces sour cream

Bake potatoes, scoop out pulp, and let cool. Melt butter, add flour, and cook for 1 minute on low. Gradually add milk, then cook over medium heat until thick and bubbly.

Stir in potato, salt, pepper, 1 cup cheese, $^1/_2$ cup bacon, and 2 tablespoons green onions. Cook until heated (do not boil). Stir in sour cream and cook until heated (do not boil). Serve with remaining cheese, bacon, and green onions, or anything else you put on baked potatoes.

Pig Out

The Original African Peanut Soup

This often-copied, never-duplicated recipe was created by Ray Dunn in the fall of 1985. The gingerroot, chiles, and garlic give it a distinctive, spicy taste which some people call "addictive."

1 ounce fresh gingerroot, scrubbed and chunked
2 cloves garlic
1 teaspoon crushed chile peppers
$7^1/4$ cups canned or fresh diced tomatoes, divided
$1^3/4$ cups dry roasted unsalted peanuts

1 medium onion, chopped
$1^1/2$ cups chicken stock
3 cups water
$^1/2$ pound cooked and cubed turkey or chicken
$^1/4$ cup butter, melted
$^1/4$ cup flour

Blend gingerroot, garlic, and chile peppers in food processor. Add $3^1/4$ cups diced tomatoes and chop (leave chunky). Place in large soup pot; add peanuts, onion, remaining diced tomatoes, chicken stock, 3 cups water, and cubed turkey or chicken. Make a paste of butter and flour; add as needed to thicken mixture in pot, and heat to 160°. Reduce heat to 145°. Thin with water to desired consistency. Garnish with peanuts. Serves 6–8.

Note: For a vegetarian version, leave out the turkey and use a vegetable-based stock instead of chicken stock.

The Colophon Cafe Best Soups

Lentil Soup

1 pound hamburger
1 (46-ounce) can tomato juice
4 cups hot water
1 cup lentils (not cooked)
1 cup diced carrots
1 cup chopped celery

$^1/_2$ cup minced onion
1 bay leaf
1 teaspoon green pepper flakes
1 teaspoon salt
$^1/_2$ teaspoon pepper
$^1/_2$ teaspoon Accent

Sauté hamburger, drain excess fat. Add juice and water. Bring to boil. Add all other ingredients and bring to a boil. Simmer $1^1/_2$–2 hours, uncovered.

Family Favorites Recipes

Gourmet Lentil Soup

5 slices bacon, diced
1 cup chopped onion
1 cup diced carrots
1 cup diced raw potatoes
$1^1/_2$ cups dry lentils
$^1/_2$ cup tomato paste
2 whole cloves

2 bay leaves
$^1/_2$ clove garlic
6 cups cold water
4 cups beef broth
2 tablespoons red wine vinegar
2 cups smokey sausage links,
   sliced

Sauté bacon, onion, and carrots. Add potatoes, lentils, tomato paste, cloves, bay leaves, garlic, water, and beef broth. Simmer $1^1/_2$ hours. Add vinegar and sausage and cook $^1/_2$ hour more. Serves 10–12.

Recipes from Our Friends

 Llama trekking is a popular way to explore the wilderness areas of Washington including the Olympic Peninsula, the Cascade Range and the Okanogan National Forest. The sure-footed Llama lightens the load by carrying up to 125 pounds of gear.

Pea Soup

The secret to this soup is a good stock. Make it with the bone that's left from the Easter ham, or whenever you cook a whole or half ham. I have used smoked pork hocks, but the best stock is really from a ham bone. I learned to make this soup from my mom when I was quite young.

STOCK:

1 ham bone (shank)	1 bay leaf
1 large onion	$^1/_2$ tablespoon crushed, black
2 medium carrots	peppercorns

Remove the rest of the usable ham from the bone and reserve. Cut onion into quarters. Chop carrots in large pieces. Put bone, onion, and carrot into stockpot and cover with cold water. Add bay leaf and peppercorns; simmer for 3 hours. Strain Stock. Return strained Stock to soup pot; bring to boil.

1 package split peas (green or yellow)	$^1/_2$–1 cup diced ham, from ham bone
1 onion, diced	Freshly ground black pepper to
1–2 carrots, diced	taste

Add peas, onion, carrots, and ham to stock. Simmer 1$^1/_2$ hours, or until peas are cooked. Serve with a good bread and freshly ground black pepper.

Liberty Lake Community Cookbook

Palouse Split Pea Soup

Make enough of this hearty soup to reheat the next day.

2 tablespoons vegetable oil
$1/2$ chopped cup onion
$1/2$ cup chopped baked ham
1 pound dry split peas (rinsed
  and drained)
A ham hock (optional)
5 cups water
6 cups chicken stock or broth
1 cup chopped celery
1 cup peeled and chopped
  carrots
1 medium potato, peeled,
  diced

1 bay leaf
A little sugar
1 tablespoon lemon juice
2 tablespoons minced parsley
$1/8$ teaspoon nutmeg, preferably
  freshly ground
$1/8$ teaspoon marjoram
1 teaspoon salt, or to taste
  (amount of salt depends on
  salt content of chicken stock)
Freshly ground pepper to taste
Dry sherry to taste (optional)

Place oil in large stockpot over medium heat. Sauté onion in oil until tender, and add chopped ham, peas, optional ham hock, water, broth, celery, carrots, potato, bay leaf, sugar, and lemon juice. Bring to boil, reduce heat, and simmer, partially covered, for 2 hours over low heat. Remove bay leaf.

Remove from stockpot and place solids in food processor, with steel blade inserted, and purée (or press through coarse sieve to get purée). Combine purée with remaining liquid in stockpot and mix together. Add parsley, nutmeg, and marjoram, and season with salt and freshly ground pepper to taste. Serve in soup bowls. Add about $1/2$ teaspoon sherry to each bowl, if desired. Serves 8–10.

Wandering & Feasting

In Palouse Falls State Park, the Palouse River plunges over a wide semicircle of volcanic rock into an enormous pool almost 200 feet below, creating one of the most incredible waterfalls in Washington state.

Clam Chowder

Like spaghetti, the flavor of chowder improves with age.

8–10 pounds live clams (or
  4 cups cooked, ground clams)
1 cup water
$^1/_2$ pound bacon, finely chopped
1 medium onion, finely chopped
2 cloves garlic, minced
1 stalk celery, peeled and finely
  chopped*
10 medium-sized potatoes,
  peeled and diced, divided*

Reserved clam nectar (1–2 pints)
1 (12-ounce) can corn, or 2 cups
  grilled, fresh corn
2 bay leaves
2 carrots, diced
1 pint milk
$^1/_4$ cup butter, melted
Salt and pepper to taste

Steam clams in a pot with 1 cup water (or a $^1/_2$ can of beer) for 7–10 minutes, until clams are open. Reserving the nectar, separate meat from shells; grind or finely chop clam meat. Rinse meat in a fine mesh colander to expel the softer bits.

Brown bacon over medium heat, discarding all but 2 tablespoons of grease. Add onions, garlic, and celery to the bacon and sauté until translucent; then add chopped clams. Remove from heat and set aside.

Combine the reserved nectar (adding water to equal 2 pints of liquid if you are short on the nectar) and half of the diced potatoes in a large pot. Cook on medium heat until the potatoes are completely broken down, stirring frequently to prevent them from sticking and burning. Add corn, bay leaves, carrots, remaining potatoes, and bacon and clam mixture to the pot. Simmer for 1 hour. Stir in milk and butter; season to taste with salt and pepper. Remove bay leaves before serving. Serve with a fresh sourdough loaf or crusty French bread. Serves 10–12 as a main entrée.

*Keep covered in water until ready to use.

Washington Farmers' Markets Cookbook and Guide

One Gallon of Clam Chowder

4 tablespoons butter, divided
1 medium onion, diced
2 cloves garlic, minced
1 quart clam juice
1¹/₂ pounds potatoes, cubed
　¹/₂-inch-square
1 medium carrot, small dice
¹/₄ cup dried potatoes

1 teaspoon chopped parsley
1 teaspoon thyme
1 teaspoon tarragon
1 quart water
2 tablespoons flour
1 pint half-and-half
1 pound chopped clams (fresh,
　frozen, or canned)

In large soup pot, melt 2 tablespoons butter and sauté onion and garlic until tender. Add clam juice, potatoes, carrot, dried potatoes, parsley, thyme, and tarragon, with enough water to cover all the ingredients. Bring to a boil and cook until potatoes are done (test with a fork). Melt remaining butter in a small pan and mix in flour to make a roux. Stir into soup, mixing well to avoid lumps. Heat to high simmer for about 10 minutes to thicken. Add half-and-half and clams and bring back up to a low simmer. Do not boil!

　You may add whatever seafood you have conjured, bought, or caught at this time. If you add halibut or other meatier fresh seafood, put it in 6–7 minutes before you serve the soup. Shrimp or scallops only need about 3–4 minutes to cook before serving. If you add crab, do it on the way to the table or as a garnish on top. Serves 8.

20,000 Gallons of Chowder

Bouillabaisse

This recipe makes a lot of soup. Prepare for a big party; you won't regret the leftovers. You will never taste a better bouillabaisse.

5 onions	2 tablespoons whole coriander
$^{1}/_{2}$ bunch celery (6–7 good-- sized ribs)	3 bay leaves
3 bell peppers	3 tablespoons sage
8 ounces butter	$^{1}/_{2}$ teaspoon cayenne
3 tablespoons cumin	1 cup fish bouillon
$^{1}/_{4}$ cup oregano	4 cups diced tomatoes
$^{1}/_{4}$ cup sweet basil	4 cups tomato purée
5 tablespoons garlic	1 quart sauterne
5 tablespoons whole fennel	2 gallons fish stock
3 tablespoons celery seed	Seafood of choice*
	Aïoli sauce

Peel and cut off the ends of onions. Cut bottom off celery. Clean seeds and membrane from bell peppers. Run vegetables through food processor to chop fine. (Don't purée.) Sauté vegetables with butter in the stockpot you'll be using, 10–15 minutes. Be sure to stir vegetables occasionally to keep them from sticking to bottom of pot.

Measure all spices into bowl. Add spices to vegetables. Add bouillon and blend well. Add tomatoes and tomato purée. Add sauterne and allow it to marry with mixture. Add fish stock and bring to rumbling boil over high heat. Reduce temperature and simmer to a low rumbling boil for 30 minutes. (You may want to give the soup another 10–15 minutes to reduce.)

Cut the fish you choose into chunks (larger chunks for whitefish so it doesn't disintegrate.) Just before you're ready to serve, add fish and cook for 2–3 minutes. Serve with a generous dollop of aïoli sauce in each bowl. *This* is Bouillabaisse.

***Suggestions for seafood per serving:** 2 sections of crab body, 1 or 2 crab legs, 2 prawns, 4–5 ounces scallops, 1 or 2 chunks salmon or whitefish. You can use pieces of chicken breast in addition to the seafood.

The Best of The Ark and More!

Editors' Extra: If you can't find prepared aïoli sauce: combine 3 tablespoons milk; 4 large cloves garlic, minced; 2 tablespoons red raspberry vinegar; 2 coddled egg yolks; $^{1}/_{2}$ teaspoon salt; and $^{1}/_{4}$ teaspoon white pepper in blender. Blend until thick. Slowly add $^{1}/_{2}$ cup olive oil while machine is running. Quickly add 2 tablespoons lemon juice and 1–2 tablespoons heavy cream.

Northwest Cioppino

2 onions, finely chopped
4 cloves garlic, minced
12 sprigs parsley, finely chopped
$^1/_2$ cup olive oil
6 cups peeled, seeded and
  coarsely chopped Roma
  tomatoes
3 cups tomato sauce
2 cups red wine
2 cups water
4 tablespoons red wine vinegar
$1^1/_2$ cups fish stock (or clam
  nectar)

$1^1/_2$ teaspoons each: basil,
  rosemary, marjoram, and
  oregano
Salt and pepper to taste
24 steamer clams
$^1/_2$ cup clarified butter*
24 large scallops (about $^3/_4$
  pound)
24 medium shrimp (about 1
  pound)
$1^1/_2$ pounds fresh fish

Sauté onion, garlic, and parsley in olive oil over medium heat until onion is transparent. Add tomatoes, tomato sauce, wine, water, vinegar, stock, herbs, salt and pepper. Bring to a boil, reduce heat, and simmer for 40 minutes. The cioppino base freezes wonderfully at this point.

In a separate large saucepan, sauté the clams in the clarified butter until they open. Turn down the heat and add the rest of the seafood all at once. Sauté lightly until about halfway cooked.

Add cioppino base and bring soup to a boil to heat through and finish cooking the seafood. Dish into 8 bowls, making sure everyone has some of everything! Accompany with garlic bread croutons (top slices of buttered French bread with minced garlic and Parmesan cheese, then lightly brown them under the broiler). Makes 8 servings.

*See Editors' Extra on page 27 for more information on clarified butter.

Note: The stock for this cioppino makes a wonderful sauce for spaghetti when thickened with a bit of tomato paste.

The Shoalwater's Finest Dinners

When gold was discovered in Alaska in 1896, Seattle promoted itself as the best place to take off for the Yukon gold rush. Prospectors could get to Seattle on the Great Northern Railroad and then take the Inside Passage to Alaska.

Chunky Meat Stew

A meat lover's favorite dish.

5 slices bacon
$^1/_2$ pound Italian sausage, sliced
$1^1/_2$ pounds beef stew meat, diced
1 cup chopped onion
1 green pepper, chopped
1 garlic clove, minced
2 pickled jalapeño peppers, rinsed, seeded and chopped

$1^1/_2$ tablespoons chili powder
$^1/_2$ teaspoon crushed red pepper
$^1/_2$ teaspoon salt
$^1/_4$ teaspoon oregano
$2^1/_2$ cups water
1 (12-ounce) can tomato paste
1 ($15^1/_2$-ounce) can pinto beans

Cook bacon until crisp. Drain and crumble. Brown sausage. Reserve 2 tablespoons drippings. Brown beef, onion, green pepper, and garlic. Add bacon, sausage, jalapeños, chili powder, red pepper, salt, and oregano. Stir in water and tomato paste. Bring to a boil. Simmer $1^1/_2$ hours. Stir in beans. Simmer for 30 minutes. Serves 8.

Recipe by John McLaren, Coach, Seattle Mariners
Mariners Mix'n and Fix'n Grand Slam Style

Italian Chili

This is a nice chili, not too spicy, and the cinnamon gives it a nice flavor. We enjoy this when we are camping.

$1^1/_2$ pounds sweet Italian sausage
1 large onion, diced
4 cloves garlic, minced
2 tablespoons olive oil
2 (15-ounce) cans chili beans, undrained
2 (15-ounce) cans Italian tomato sauce

1 (28-ounce) can crushed tomatoes
1 cup of beer or beef broth
2 tablespoons chili powder
1 teaspoon cinnamon
Shredded cheese, sour cream, and onions for garnish

Sauté the first 4 ingredients. Crumble sausage; cook until sausage is no longer pink. Add the remaining ingredients except garnishes; simmer uncovered, 1 hour or more. Serve with shredded cheese, sour cream, and onions.

Taste of Balboa

Ray's Turkey Chili

An amazing chili made without beef or beans!

3 tablespoons vegetable or
  olive oil
1 red onion, chopped
1 yellow onion, chopped
2 leeks, chopped
6 garlic cloves, chopped
2 tablespoons flour
4–6 tablespoons chili powder
1 tablespoon oregano
1 tablespoon salt
2 tablespoons cumin powder
1–2 teaspoons cayenne pepper

Bottle of cold beer
3 pounds cooked, chopped
  turkey breast
2 (14½-ounce) cans stewed
  tomatoes (with juice)
1 (14-ounce) can tomato sauce
1 tablespoon peanut butter
6–8 tablespoons beer (or water),
  divided
Chopped onion for garnish
Shredded Cheddar cheese for
  garnish

Heat oil in a large soup pot and add onions, leeks, and garlic, stirring until cooked. Mix together, flour, chili powder, oregano, salt, cumin, and cayenne pepper. Add just enough beer (1–2 tablespoons) to form a thin paste. Stir paste into cooked vegetables. Add and stir well chopped turkey, tomatoes with juice, tomato sauce, and peanut butter. Stir often and simmer on low heat 2–5 hours. Add beer or water to thin, but not too much. Serves 8–10. Garnish with chopped onion and Cheddar cheese. Serve with tortilla chips or corn bread.

The Colophon Cafe Best Recipes

SALADS

The 605-foot-high, steel-and-glass Space Needle in Seattle was built for the 1962 World's Fair and still attracts over 1.3 million visitors a year.

Northwest Seafood Salad

SESAME DRESSING:

$^1/_3$ cup white vinegar

$^1/_4$ cup vegetable oil

3 tablespoons soy sauce

2 tablespoons dry mustard

2 tablespoons sesame oil

2 tablespoons sherry

1 tablespoon sugar

$^1/_3$ cup water

Combine all ingredients in a jar. Shake well to mix; set aside.

SALAD:

2 dozen large shrimp, shelled
  and deveined

$1^1/_2$ pounds scallops

$^1/_2$ pound snow peas

2 cucumbers, peeled and sliced

4 celery stalks, sliced

1 lemon, quartered for garnish

Cook shrimp in boiling water for 2 minutes or until they are pink. Drain well and transfer to a small bowl. Cool slightly. When they are cool, spoon 3 tablespoons dressing over shrimp and refrigerate until serving.

Cook scallops in boiling water until white and opaque. Drain well and chill. Place snow peas in a colander and pour boiling water over them. Drain well. Transfer snow peas to a salad bowl and add cucumbers and celery. Toss slightly and chill.

To assemble, add scallops and shrimp to the salad bowl. Pour Sesame Dressing over all and toss to coat. Garnish each serving of this colorful main dish salad with a lemon quarter. Let it be the focus of a summer party. Makes 4 servings.

Simply Whidbey

Turkey Waldorf Salad

A great way to serve Washington's abundant apples and tasty turkey for a luncheon.

3 Red Delicious apples, cored,
cut into ¹/₂-inch chunks
3 Granny Smith apples, cored,
cut into ¹/₂-inch chunks
2 tablespoons lemon juice
4 stalks celery, diced
³/₄ cup chopped pitted dates

3 cups cubed roast turkey
¹/₂ cup whipping cream
¹/₂ cup mayonnaise
³/₄ cup coarsely chopped
walnuts
Salt and freshly ground pepper
to taste

Toss apple chunks with lemon juice in mixing bowl. Mix in celery, dates, and turkey. In separate small bowl, whip the whipping cream gently fold in mayonnaise. Blend into salad ingredients until well combined. Fold in walnuts and season to taste. Cover; refrigerate until serving.

Christmas in Washington Cook Book

Smoked Turkey, Pecan and Blue Cheese Salad

This surprising meld of flavors will have your guests asking for extra servings—and the recipe, of course!

¹/₂ cup vegetable oil
¹/₄ cup white wine vinegar
¹/₄ cup honey
¹/₂ cup chopped onion
4 teaspoons Tabasco sauce
Salt and pepper to taste
6 cups assorted salad greens,
bite-size pieces

2 cups curly endive, bite-size
pieces
8 ounces smoked turkey, diced
²/₃ cup crumbled blue cheese
²/₃ cup toasted and chopped
pecans
1 avocado, peeled, pitted, and
diced

In a blender, purée oil, vinegar, honey, onion, and Tabasco. Season dressing to taste with salt and pepper. Rinse and dry greens in salad spinner. Greens have to be as dry as possible for dressing to adhere. In a large bowl, combine greens and endive and toss with enough dressing to coat. Add remaining ingredients and drizzle with more dressing. Toss gently. May be made up to 4 hours ahead. Serves 4.

Nutritional values per serving: Calories 880; Carbo. 42.1g; Prot. 22.2g; Fiber 10.3g; Sugar 31.8g; Fat Calories 666; Total Fat 74g; Sat. Fat 14.6g; Chol. 34.6g; Sod. 807.6mg.

LaConner Palates

Chicken Yakitori Salad

1 large head garlic, roasted
1/3 cup soy sauce
1/2 cup Japanese sake (or dry
  sherry)
2 tablespoons sugar
1/4 cup peanut oil
4 cups Romaine lettuce, torn
  bite size

1 pound chicken breasts,
  skinned, boned, cut into
  1-inch strips, and cooked
6–8 green onions, cut in 2-inch
  lengths
Fresh snow peas and red onion
  rings for garnish

Place garlic, soy sauce, sake, and sugar in blender; purée. With motor running, slowly drizzle in oil and process until dressing thickens.

In a large bowl, gently toss lettuce, chicken, and onions. Pour enough dressing over to lightly coat, toss. Transfer mixture to serving bowl, garnish with snow peas and onion rings and drizzle lightly with additional dressing.

Note: To roast garlic, slice about 1/4 inch off top of garlic head, place head in heavy foil and drizzle with 2 tablespoons peanut oil. Pull foil up and fold to seal. Place packet in small ovenproof dish. Bake in preheated 250° oven for 40–50 minutes, or until garlic is soft when pressed.

Northwest Garlic Festival Cookbook

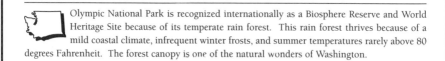

Olympic National Park is recognized internationally as a Biosphere Reserve and World Heritage Site because of its temperate rain forest. This rain forest thrives because of a mild coastal climate, infrequent winter frosts, and summer temperatures rarely above 80 degrees Fahrenheit. The forest canopy is one of the natural wonders of Washington.

Vegetable Bacon Salad

DRESSING:
1 cup sour cream   1 teaspoon garlic powder
1 cup mayonnaise

SALAD:
1 head cauliflower, cut into   1 pound bacon, fried crisp,
  bite-size pieces   broken into bite-size pieces
1 bunch broccoli, cut into   1 can Durkee Fried Onions
  bite-size pieces
5–10 ounces frozen peas,
  thawed

Mix Dressing and toss with vegetables and bacon.   Refrigerate
overnight (or all day). Before serving, top with canned onions.

Crime Stoppers: A Community Cookbook

Chattaroy Gardens
Marinated Vegetables

1 can tomato soup   1 head cauliflower
1/2 cup oil   2 cups sliced carrots
1 cup sugar   2 green peppers
3/4 cup vinegar   1 medium white onion
1 teaspoon prepared mustard   1 can cut green beans, drained
1 tablespoon Worcestershire
  sauce

Mix tomato soup, oil, sugar, vinegar, prepared mustard, and
Worcestershire sauce. Cut cauliflower into flowerets. Boil lightly.
Boil sliced carrots lightly. Cut green peppers into rings or bite size.
Slice and separate onion into rings. Drain green beans. Mix veg-
etables together. Mix marinade well and pour over vegetables. Let
set for 2 days.

Our Best Home Cooking

Three Bean Salad

$^1/_2$ cup sliced red onion
3 cloves garlic, crushed
1 tablespoon olive oil
1 red pepper, cubed
1 teaspoon ground cumin
Pinch of fresh ground pepper
$^1/_4$ cup balsamic vinegar

$^1/_4$ cup water
2 tablespoons honey
$^1/_2$ cup chopped cilantro
1 cup cooked garbanzo beans
1 cup cooked kidney beans
1 cup cooked black beans

Sauté onion and garlic in olive oil over medium-high heat until onions turn light brown (approximately 7 minutes). Add red pepper, cumin, and fresh ground pepper to sauté and reduce heat to medium. Mix balsamic vinegar, water, honey, and cilantro in a bowl with a small whisk or fork until combined or smooth. Combine sauté with liquid mixture into a bowl. Add all beans, toss and serve. Yields 8 servings.

Nutritional profile per serving: Calories 184; Prot. 3.4g; Carb. 31.8g; Fat 8.8g; Sat. Fat 0.3g; Chol. 0.0mg; Fiber 3.1g; Sod. 96.5mg.

The Ingredients: Fresh Pacific Northwest Cuisine

Summer Corn and Cabbage Salad

3 medium-size fresh ears of corn, or 1 (10-ounce) package frozen whole-kernel corn
$1^1/_2$ cups shredded green cabbage
1 medium sweet red pepper, chopped
1 stalk celery, thinly sliced

1 medium onion, thinly sliced to taste
$^1/_4$ cup olive or vegetable oil
$^1/_4$ cup lemon juice
1–2 tablespoons honey
1 teaspoon dry mustard
$^1/_2$ teaspoon salt
$^1/_4$ teaspoon black pepper

Cook ears of corn; cut corn from cob. (If using packaged corn, cook according to directions, and then drain.) Combine corn along with remaining vegetables in a salad bowl. Mix olive oil, lemon juice, honey, dry mustard, salt, and pepper. Mix well. Pour over salad mixture. Toss to coat. Cover and refrigerate 2–24 hours. Adjust salt and pepper to taste. Spoon salad onto leaf lettuce.

Taste of the Methow

Black Bean and Corn Salad

You will enjoy the lively flavors of the Southwest in this colorful, robust salad.

2 (15-ounce) cans black beans, drained and rinsed
1½ cups corn kernels, fresh or thawed
1 large red bell pepper, diced
1 cup chopped celery
¾ cup minced red onion
2 fresh jalapeño peppers, seeded and minced
½ cup chopped fresh cilantro
2 teaspoons cumin seed

In a large bowl, combine all ingredients and set aside.

LIME DRESSING:
¼ cup lime juice
½ tablespoon lime zest
2 tablespoons brown sugar
1 tablespoon Dijon mustard
½ teaspoon red pepper flakes
½ teaspoon salt
Freshly ground pepper to taste
¼ cup vegetable oil
Cilantro sprigs for garnish

In a small bowl, combine all dressing ingredients, except oil and garnish. Add oil gradually, beating with a whisk until blended. Pour dressing over salad and toss to combine. Cover and refrigerate for at least 1 hour. Salad can be served cold or at room temperature. Garnish with cilantro sprigs before serving. Makes 6–8 servings.

San Juan Classics II Cookbook

Crunchy Pea Salad

$^1/_2$ cup Miracle Whip or
  mayonnaise
$^1/_4$ cup Zesty Italian dressing
1 (10-ounce) package frozen
  peas, thawed and drained
1 cup chopped celery

1 cup roasted peanuts
6 pieces bacon, fried crispy and
  crumbled
1 (8-ounce) can ($^1/_4$ cup) water
  chestnuts, diced
Parmesan cheese

Mix lightly all ingredients except Parmesan cheese; chill. Before serving, sprinkle top with Parmesan cheese. Serve with tomato wedges, if desired.

Taste of Balboa

Spinach Salad with Bacon and Apples

2 large bunches spinach
6 strips bacon
$^1/_3$ cup sliced almonds
$^1/_3$ cup olive or salad oil
3 tablespoons tarragon vinegar
  or white wine vinegar

$^1/_8$ teaspoon salt
1 teaspoon sugar
$^1/_2$ teaspoon dry mustard
Dash pepper
1 large red-skinned apple
3 tablespoons sliced green onion

Remove and discard tough spinach stems; wash leaves, drain well, and chill for at least 2 hours.

In frying pan over medium heat, cook bacon until crisp; drain (reserving 1 tablespoon drippings), crumble, and set aside. Place almonds in remaining bacon drippings and sauté until lightly browned (3 or 4 minutes); lift from pan and set aside. Combine oil, vinegar, salt, sugar, mustard, and pepper; blend well. Core and dice apple. Break spinach into bite-sized pieces and place in a large bowl; add onion, apple, and almonds. Pour dressing over salad, top with reserved bacon, and toss gently. Makes 6–8 servings.

Extraordinary Cuisine for Sea & Shore

Jamie's Cranberry Spinach Salad

Everyone I have made this for raves about it. It's different and so easy to make.

1 tablespoon butter
3/4 cup blanched and slivered
  almonds
1 pound spinach, rinsed and torn
  into bite-size pieces
1 cup dried cranberries
2 tablespoons toasted sesame
  seeds

1 tablespoon poppy seeds
1/2 cup sugar
2 teaspoons minced onion
1/4 teaspoon paprika
1/4 cup white wine vinegar
1/4 cup cider vinegar
1/2 cup vegetable oil

In a medium saucepan, melt butter over medium heat. Cook and stir almonds in butter until lightly toasted. Remove from heat, and let cool. In a large bowl, toss spinach with toasted almonds and cranberries.

In a medium bowl, whisk together sesame seeds, poppy seeds, sugar, onion, paprika, white wine vinegar, cider vinegar, and vegetable oil. Toss with spinach just before serving. Makes 12 servings.

Allrecipes Tried & True Favorites

Craisin-Spinach Salad

3 bunches spinach, washed
  and torn into bite-size pieces
2 Gala apples, washed and
  chopped

3/4 cup craisins
1/2 cup almonds

Combine ingredients in a large bowl. Add Dressing and toss well.

DRESSING:
1/2 cup sugar
2 teaspoons salt
2 tablespoons chopped onion
1 1/2 cups oil

2 teaspoons dry mustard
2/3 cup apple cider vinegar
2 tablespoons poppy seeds

Combine well. Extra Dressing keeps well for a couple of weeks in refrigerator.

Taste of Balboa

The Best Avocado Caesar Salad

No eggs needed in this one. We like it with heavy garlic, so use less if you don't want to taste it all day. Also, many people put the dressing in the bowl first and then add the lettuce. That's fine if you want most of the dressing to stay in the bowl. We prefer to drizzle over the top, then toss.

DRESSING:
$^1/_3$ cup olive oil	1 teaspoon Worcestershire sauce
6 garlic cloves, pressed or minced	Freshly ground pepper to taste
3 teaspoons lemon juice	

Mix all Dressing ingredients in cruet with lid and shake until blended. May be done hours ahead and held in refrigerator.

SALAD:
2 large heads of green leaf or romaine lettuce	2 or 3 peeled, sliced ripe avocados
1 cup shredded Parmesan cheese	Croutons (optional)

Wash lettuce thoroughly, dry, and tear into bite-size bits. Place in a large bowl. Drizzle Dressing over lettuce. Toss with Parmesan. Garnish top of salad with avocado slices and croutons, if you wish. Serve with French bread.

The Colophon Cafe Best Vegetarian Recipes

Jane's Chinese Cabbage Salad

1 head (5 cups) cabbage	$^1/_2$ cup oil
2 tablespoons sunflower seeds	3 tablespoons vinegar
4 green onions	$^1/_2$ teaspoon salt
$^1/_4$ cup almonds	1 package ramen noodles
2 tablespoons sugar	

Shred cabbage; add sunflower seeds, onions, and almonds. Make dressing of sugar, oil, vinegar, and salt. Just before serving, break noodles in the package and sprinkle over cabbage mixture. Pour on dressing.

Heavenly Fare

Kentucky Fried Chicken Cole Slaw

DRESSING:

$^1/_3$ cup sugar

$^1/_2$ teaspoon salt

$^1/_8$ teaspoon pepper

$^1/_2$ cup mayonnaise

$^1/_4$ cup milk

$^1/_4$ cup buttermilk

$2^1/_2$ tablespoons lemon juice

$1^1/_2$ tablespoons white vinegar

Mix all ingredients.

SALAD:

$^1/_4$ cup finely chopped carrots   8 cups diced cabbage

Marinate vegetables in Dressing at least 2 hours prior to serving.

Recipes to Remember

Ginger Mustard Coleslaw

A crisp-textured coleslaw loaded with spicy mouth-watering flavor.

DRESSING:

3 tablespoons apple cider
  vinegar

3 tablespoons lemon juice

2 tablespoons Dijon mustard

4 cloves garlic, crushed

1 jalapeño chile pepper, minced

2 teaspoons peeled and grated
  fresh ginger

$^2/_3$ cup olive oil

3 tablespoons minced cilantro
  leaves

Kosher salt

Freshly ground pepper

Whisk together vinegar, lemon juice, mustard, garlic, chile pepper, and ginger. Slowly whisk in oil; add cilantro. Season with salt and pepper to taste. Set aside.

SALAD:

$^1/_2$ head red cabbage, shredded

$^1/_2$ head bok choy, shredded

1 red pepper, sliced into
  matchsticks

4 carrots, grated

$^1/_2$ cup chopped green onions

1 small red onion, diced

Toss together cabbage, bok choy, red pepper, carrots, and onions in a large bowl; set aside. Pour dressing over cabbage mixture and toss until all vegetables are well coated. Let rest at least 10 minutes before serving, or cover and chill until ready to use. Serves 6.

Washington Farmers' Markets Cookbook and Guide

Picnic Coleslaw

6 cups shredded cabbage
2 cups shredded carrots
8 bacon strips, cooked and
  crumbled
12 green onions with tops, thinly
  sliced

¹/₂ cup cider vinegar
¹/₃ cup vegetable oil
¹/₃ cup sugar
1 teaspoon salt

Combine cabbage, carrots, bacon, and onions. In jar with tight fitting lid, mix vinegar, oil, sugar, and salt. Shake well. Just before serving, pour dressing over cabbage mixture and toss. Makes 12–16 servings.

Recipes from Our Friends

Putter's Potato Salad

Savor the Greek flavors of this nontraditional potato salad.

DRESSING:
3 tablespoons white wine vinegar
1 tablespoon fresh lemon juice
2 cloves garlic, chopped
1 teaspoon sugar

¹/₂ teaspoon salt
¹/₄ teaspoon freshly ground
  pepper
¹/₂ cup extra-virgin olive oil

Combine vinegar, lemon juice, garlic, sugar, salt and pepper in a small bowl. Gradually whisk in the olive oil.

6 small to medium white
  potatoes (about 2 pounds),
  peeled
¹/₂ red onion, thinly sliced
³/₄ cup Greek olives, pitted
  and cut in half
1¹/₂ tablespoons chopped fresh
  dill, or 1 teaspoon dried

1¹/₂ teaspoons chopped fresh
  marjoram, or ¹/₂ teaspoon
  dried
³/₄ cup (about 3 ounces) grated
  kasseri cheese, or good-quality
  Parmesan

Boil or steam potatoes in salted water until just tender. Drain potatoes and cool just enough to handle; cut into slices about ¹/₄ inch thick. Put in a large bowl. Pour Dressing over the potatoes and stir carefully, until well coated. Add onion, olives, dill, marjoram, and cheese; stir carefully. Put in a covered container and chill in the refrigerator. Good served at room temperature. Yields 6 servings.

Good Times at Green Lake

Dianne's Potato Salad

7–8 medium-size potatoes
7–8 eggs, hard-cooked
5–6 green onions, sliced
Salt
Paprika
5–6 medium-size sweet pickles, chopped
4 medium-size dill pickles, chopped
1 1/2 cups Miracle Whip
1 tablespoon prepared mustard
2/3 cup sweet relish

Cook potatoes with peel on until almost done. (They should be a little crunchy for this salad.) Remove peel when potatoes are just cool enough to handle. Slice potatoes and eggs into large salad bowl, layering with green onions. Sprinkle with salt and paprika, to taste. Add chopped sweet and dill pickles.

Combine Miracle Whip, mustard, and sweet relish. Spoon over salad and mix until thoroughly moistened.

Sharing Our Best

Hot Potato Salad

6 medium potatoes, cooked in jackets
6 slices bacon
1/4 cup finely minced onion
2 tablespoons finely chopped green pepper
2 tablespoons sugar
2 teaspoons salt
1/4 teaspoon pepper
1/3 cup vinegar
1/4 cup water
2 tablespoons minced parsley

Peel and dice potatoes. Set temperature control at 325°. Fry bacon until crisp and remove from fry pan. Drain all but 1 tablespoon bacon grease. Reduce heat to simmer. Combine potatoes with onions, green pepper, sugar, salt, pepper, vinegar, and water. Place in fry pan, cover, and heat thoroughly. Sprinkle crumbled bacon and parsley over potatoes.

Unser Tagelich Brot (The Staff of Life III)

Taco Macaroni Salad

1 (7-ounce) package macaroni
1 (12-ounce) package ground sausage
1 (15-ounce) can kidney beans, drained
1 (8-ounce) can whole-kernel corn, drained
2 tomatoes, diced

1 green pepper, diced
$^1/_4$ cup diced onion
$^1/_2$ cup sliced ripe olives
1 cup grated cheese
$^1/_2$ cup taco sauce
$^1/_4$ cup salad oil
1 teaspoon seasoning salt
1 tablespoon sweet basil leaves

Cook macaroni and drain. Fry sausage and drain. Combine sausage, beans, corn, tomatoes, peppers, onion, olives, and cheese. In another bowl, blend together taco sauce, oil, salt, and basil. Combine with sausage mixture; add cooked macaroni. Toss all together and chill. Serves 6–8.

Washington Cook Book

Oriental Pasta Salad

5 ounces uncooked rotini noodles
4 ounces fresh Chinese pea pods
$^1/_2$ cup thinly sliced carrots
2 tablespoons sugar

$^1/_4$ cup olive oil
1 (3-ounce) package Top Ramen Chicken Sesame Oriental Noodles

Cook rotini noodles according to directions on package. Meanwhile, steam pea pods until just crisp-tender. Cut in half, crosswise. Drain cooked noodles; rinse. Place noodles in mixing bowl. Add pea pods, carrots, sugar, olive oil, and seasoning packet from Ramen Noodles (do not use the sesame oil). Toss thoroughly to blend. Cover; chill 2 hours to blend flavors. When ready to serve, break up $^1/_2$ of the uncooked ramen noodles and add to salad; toss to combine. Makes 8 servings.

Per Serving: Calories 172; Prot. 4g; Carb. 23g; Fiber 1g; Fat 7g; Sat. Fat 1g; Chol. 0mg; Sod. 42mg.

Six Ingredients or Less: Cooking Light & Healthy

Chinese Noodle Salad

1 (10-ounce) package frozen peas, heated to boiling and cooled
1 head lettuce, chopped
4 stalks celery, sliced

2 cups cooked and chopped chicken or shrimp
1 (5-ounce) can crunchy Chinese noodles

DRESSING:
1 cup mayonnaise
1/3 cup soy sauce

Garlic powder to taste

When ready to serve, mix all salad ingredients in a bowl. Stir in dressing and serve immediately.

Western Washington Oncology Cook Book

Vermicelli with Salami and Cheese

8 ounces vermicelli or spaghetti, or your favorite pasta
1 (6-ounce) jar marinated artichoke hearts (reserve marinade)
1 small zucchini, diced
1 medium carrot, diced

1 (3-ounce) package sliced salami, cut in julienne strips
2 cups shredded mozzarella cheese
1/3 cup grated Parmesan
Lettuce leaves
Tomato wedges for garnish

DRESSING:
Reserved marinade from artichoke hearts
1/3 cup salad oil
1/3 cup white wine vinegar
1 1/2 teaspoons dry mustard
1 teaspoon oregano leaves

1 teaspoon dry basil
1/4 teaspoon dry rosemary
1/4 teaspoon pepper
2 cloves garlic, pressed (remove membrane)

Cook pasta; rinse. In a large bowl, combine Dressing ingredients. Add pasta to Dressing, stirring to combine. Add vegetables, meat, and cheeses. Serve in a bowl lined with lettuce leaves. Garnish with tomato wedges. This may be served at room temperature or chilled, if made ahead. Serves 6.

Liberty Lake Community Cookbook

LaConner Slough Salad

This is a definite pleaser for pasta lovers. In combination with sun-dried tomatoes, Greek olives and feta cheese, this salad is mouthwatering. Fourth of July celebrations aren't complete without this crowd-pleaser.

16 ounces rotini pasta, uncooked

10 ounces Greek olives, pitted and chopped; reserve brine

$8^{1}/_{2}$ ounces sun-dried tomatoes in oil, drained and chopped; reserve oil

1 large red onion, chopped

8 ounces feta cheese, crumbled

3 cups large shrimp, fresh cooked and chilled

DRESSING:

3 tablespoons red wine vinegar

$1^{1}/_{4}$–$1^{1}/_{2}$ cups mayonnaise

2 tablespoons chopped fresh basil leaves

2 tablespoons chopped fresh oregano

2 tablespoons chopped fresh parsley

2 cloves garlic, minced

Salt and pepper to taste

Cook pasta according to package directions and cool. In a large bowl, combine olives, tomatoes, and onion. Add pasta and mix together. In a separate bowl, whisk together Dressing ingredients. Mix into salad. Before serving, add feta cheese and shrimp and toss. May substitute chicken for shrimp, if desired. Serves 10–12.

Note: This salad is best if made the day before serving.

Nutritional values per serving: Calories 306; Carb. 20.2g; Prot. 16.7g; Fiber 0.9g; Sugar 19.4g; Fat Calories 175; Total Fat 19.4g; Sat. Fat 4.8g; Chol. 135.1g; Sod. 1305.5mg.

LaConner Palates

Washington ranks second in the country for premium wine production with more than 29,000 acres planted in vinifera grapes, 11,000 of which are located in the Yakima Valley.

Tomato and Bread Salad

This is one of those salads that makes you want to pack a picnic basket with some cheese and a bottle of red wine, and take off for a day on the beach.

1¹/2 pounds Roma tomatoes, seeded and coarsely chopped (about 2¹/2 cups)

1/2 English cucumber, seeded and chopped

1/2 cup chopped green bell pepper

1 (15-ounce) can garbanzo beans, drained and rinsed

1/2 red onion, chopped

1/2 cup chopped fresh parsley

1/4 cup chopped fresh basil

1 cup sliced green olives (optional)

3 tablespoons red wine vinegar

1¹/2 tablespoons extra-virgin olive oil

1 clove garlic, minced

1/4 teaspoon salt

1/4 teaspoon coarsely ground pepper

4 cups coarse-grained bread cubes (¹/2 inch)

In a large bowl, combine first 8 ingredients (tomatoes through olives). Sprinkle next 5 ingredients (vinegar through pepper) over tomato mixture and toss to blend. Cover and set aside to marinate. Mixture can be refrigerated at this time.

Preheat oven to 300°. Arrange bread cubes in a single layer on baking sheet. Bake in oven, stirring frequently, until toasted, about 15 minutes. Set aside to cool.

Thirty minutes before serving, combine bread cubes with marinated tomato mixture. Serve at room temperature. Makes 4–6 servings.

San Juan Classics II Cookbook

Dorothy's Seafood Aspic

3³/₄ cups tomato juice, divided
2 (3-ounce) packages lemon
  Jell-O
2 tablespoons Worcestershire
  sauce

2 cans shrimp or crab (or mixed)
2 cups chopped celery
1 cup chopped green pepper
2 green onions, cut fine

Heat 2 cups of the tomato juice and dissolve Jell-O. Add rest of tomato juice and refrigerate until slightly thickened. Add rest of ingredients and pour into mold.

Unser Tagelich Brot (The Staff of Life III)

Beet Salad

1 (3-ounce) package raspberry
  Jell-O
1 (3-ounce) package strawberry
  Jell-O
1 (3-ounce) package cherry
  Jell-O

¹/₂ cup sweet pickle juice
1 can crushed pineapple and
  juice
1 can shredded beets and juice

Dissolve all Jell-O in 4 cups boiling water. Cool, then add pickle juice, pineapple and juice, beets and juice. Pour into 9x13-inch pan. Refrigerate until ready to serve.

DRESSING:
¹/₂ cup mayonnaise
¹/₂ cup chopped stuffed green
  olives

1 green onion, chopped (top and
  all)
¹/₂ cup diced pimiento

Combine; spread over salad. Make salad the night before, but put dressing on just before serving.

Nautical Niceaty's from Spokane Yacht Club

 In 1975, petrified wood was adopted as the state gem. The best place to see petrified wood is the Gingko Petrified Forest State Park in Vantage.

Cranberry Salad

1 package fresh cranberries
1 cup sugar
1 small can crushed pineapple, drained
1 large orange, cut up

2 (3-ounce) packages lemon Jell-O
2 cups hot water
1 cup pineapple juice

Grind fresh cranberries (medium blade). Add sugar, crushed pineapple, and orange. Let stand 1 hour.

Make lemon Jell-O with hot water and pineapple juice. When slightly thickened, add the fruit and stir together. Pour into 1-quart mold and refrigerate.

TOPPING:
1 (3-ounce) package cream cheese
1 tablespoon lemon juice

3 tablespoons currant jelly (or red jelly)
$^3/_4$ cup heavy cream, whipped

Mix and chill; serve with cranberry salad.

Our Burnt Offerings

Linde Salad

1 (3-ounce) package lime gelatin
1 cup boiling water
$^1/_2$ cup diced pineapple, undrained

$^1/_2$ cup sugar
1 cup 1% cottage cheese
1 cup light whipped cream topping

Dissolve lime gelatin in boiling water. In quart pan, mix pineapple, juice, and sugar. Gently boil for 5 minutes, stirring occasionally. Add mixture to gelatin. Place in refrigerator and chill until gelatin is soft set. Add cottage cheese and whipped cream. Fold in gently. Pour mixture into mold and chill until firm. Yields 8 servings.

Nutritional profile per serving: Calories 132; Prot. 4.8g; Carb. 24.8g; Fat 2.0g; Sat. Fat 1.0g; Chol. 6.4mg; Fiber 0.1g; Sod. 132.1mg.

The Ingredients: Fresh Pacific Northwest Cuisine

Lime Cottage Cheese Salad

1¹/₂ cups hot water
2 packages lime Jell-O
1 (9-ounce) can crushed
   pineapple
1 pint cottage cheese

1 cup salad dressing
1 cup canned milk, chilled,
   whipped
1 cup chopped nuts

Add hot water to Jell-O. Stir until dissolved. Add crushed pineapple. Cool until slightly thickened; add cottage cheese, salad dressing, and whipped canned milk. Add nuts; stir until thoroughly mixed. Chill thoroughly and serve.

The Historic Mid-1900's Cookbook

Cottage Cheese Salad

1 package lemon Jell-O
1 cup boiling water
1 cup crushed pineapple
15 marshmallows

1 cup cottage cheese
1 cup whipping cream, whipped
1 cup chopped nuts

Mix Jell-O with boiling water. Drain pineapple and add water to make 1 cup juice, then add to Jell-O mixture. Cut marshmallows in small pieces and add to hot mixture. Cool. Add cottage cheese, whipped cream, and nuts. Allow to set. Can be poured into molds or into suitable dish or pan and cut into squares when firm.

Tastes of Country

VEGETABLES

Home to the native Roosevelt Elk, the Hoh Rainforest in Olympic National Park receives over 150 inches of rain per year and is the only temperate rain forest in the United States. Some trees in the forest are more than 1,000 years old.

Addictive Sweet Potato Burritos

Once you've had one, you'll want another. Serve these with sour cream, chopped green onions, and salsa.

3 teaspoons vegetable oil
1 onion, chopped
4 cloves garlic, minced
6 cups canned kidney beans, drained
2 cups water
3 tablespoons chili powder
2 teaspoons ground cumin
4 teaspoons prepared mustard

1 pinch cayenne pepper, or to taste
3 tablespoons soy sauce
4 cups cooked and mashed sweet potatoes
12 (10-inch) flour tortillas, warmed
8 ounces Cheddar cheese, shredded

Preheat oven to 350°. Heat oil in a medium skillet, and sauté onion and garlic in until soft. Stir in beans, and mash. Gradually stir in water, and heat until warm. Remove from heat, and stir in chili powder, cumin, mustard, cayenne pepper, and soy sauce.

Divide bean mixture and mashed sweet potatoes evenly between warm flour tortillas. Top with cheese. Fold up tortillas burrito-style. Bake for 12 minutes in preheated oven, and serve. Makes 12 burritos.

Allrecipes Tried & True Favorites

Coconut Baked Sweet Potatoes

10 medium-size sweet potatoes	³/4 cup brown sugar
¹/3 cup butter	¹/2 cup flaked coconut

One day before serving, cook the sweet potatoes in boiling water until almost tender (approximately 20 minutes). Drain, cool, peel and cut them in half lengthwise. Arrange the potatoes in a greased 9x13-inch baking dish.

In a small saucepan over medium heat melt the butter, brown sugar and ¹/4 cup water. Pour this over the cooked potatoes. Cover the potatoes and allow them to stand overnight. On the day of serving, pour Glaze over the potatoes. Bake in a 350° oven to heat thoroughly. Sprinkle coconut over the potatoes before serving. Serves 12.

GLAZE:

¹/4 cup butter	¹/4 cup heavy cream
¹/2 cup brown sugar	

Preheat oven to 350°. Combine butter, brown sugar, and cream in a small saucepan. Melt over medium heat until smooth.

Simply Whidbey

Hash Brown Bake

1 (32-ounce) package frozen hash browns	1 pint sour cream
	1 pound shredded Cheddar cheese
1–2 cups chopped onions (to taste)	¹/2 cup margarine, melted
2 cans cream of chicken soup	4 cups crushed corn flakes

Mix first 5 ingredients. Spread into casserole dish. For topping, mix melted margarine and corn flakes. Spread over top of casserole. Bake until brown on top, about 1 hour at 350°.

Pig Out

Potatoes Romanoff

1¹/₂ cups shredded Cheddar
cheese, divided
1 bunch green onions, chopped
fine
1 pint sour cream

1¹/₂ teaspoons salt
¹/₂ teaspoon pepper
6 large potatoes, baked, cooled,
and shredded
Paprika

Mix well 1 cup cheese, onions, sour cream, and seasonings. Add potatoes. Place in greased casserole and top with remaining cheese. Sprinkle with paprika. Can be covered and refrigerated overnight. Bake, uncovered, at 350° for 30–40 minutes.

Nautical Niceaty's from Spokane Yacht Club

Disgustingly Rich Potatoes

6 large Idaho potatoes
³/₄ cup butter or margarine,
softened
2 teaspoons salt
1 teaspoon pepper

1 cup heavy cream
4 tablespoons butter or
margarine
1 cup grated Cheddar or
Gruyère cheese

Bake potatoes until soft. Split and scoop pulp into mixing bowl. (Leave as is—do not mash or chop.) Add softened butter, salt, pepper, and cream, mixing lightly. Transfer to flat baking dish. Dot with butter and sprinkle with cheese. Bake at 375° for at least 20 minutes.

Note: Half-and-half can be substituted for heavy cream and isn't quite so deadly.

Recipes from Our Friends

Towering 500 feet above Seattle as part of the Space Needle, SkyCity™, a revolving restaurant, makes one complete revolution every 48 minutes. Ironically, the first Space Needle Manager, Hoge Sullivan, had acrophobia, a fear of heights.

Potato Torte

1 egg
2 egg yolks
4 cups whipping cream
1 teaspoon salt
1/2 teaspoon freshly ground
   black pepper
4 large baking potatoes, peeled
   and thinly sliced
1 medium onion, minced
1 (10-ounce) package frozen,
   chopped spinach, thawed and
   drained

1 tablespoon Dijon mustard
1/2 pound shredded Gruyère
   cheese
1 pound baked ham, very thinly
   sliced
1 large jar sweet, roasted
   peppers, sliced, or 3 sweet
   red peppers, roasted and
   peeled

Combine egg, yolks, cream, salt, and pepper in large bowl. Add potatoes to cream mixture, stirring until well coated. Drain off cream mixture and reserve. Combine onion, spinach, and mustard in small bowl. Butter a 9x13-inch casserole.

Layer 1/4 of potatoes and 1/4 of shredded cheese in bottom of pan, drizzle with cream mixture; top with ham. Repeat potato-cheese layer; top with spinach mixture. Repeat potato-cheese layer, top with peppers. Add final potato-cheese layer and remaining cream mixture. Bake torte, uncovered, in 325° oven for 2 hours. Top should be well browned. Makes 12 servings.

Liberty Lake Community Cookbook

Oven-Fried Potatoes

12 medium potatoes, peeled and
   cubed
1/4 cup grated Parmesan cheese
2 teaspoons salt

1 teaspoon garlic powder
1 teaspoon paprika
1/2 teaspoon pepper
1/3 cup vegetable oil

Place potatoes in 2 large resealable plastic bags. Combine Parmesan cheese and seasonings; add to potatoes and shake to coat. Pour oil into 2 (15x10x1-inch) pans; pour potatoes into pans. Bake uncovered at 375° for 40–50 minutes or until tender.

Taste of Balboa

Roasting Walla Walla Sweets & Potatoes

3 large Walla Walla sweet
  onions
3–4 medium russet potatoes

2 tablespoons vegetable oil
$1/8$ teaspoon black pepper

Halve each onion lengthwise through the top and root, then skin, peeling away any slippery membrane. Dig into center of each half with a metal spoon, and scoop out flesh, leaving a $1/2$-inch-thick shell. Chop enough of the inner flesh to measure 2 cups and set aside. Scrub potatoes and cut enough of the potatoes into $1/4$- to $1/2$-inch dices to make 4 cups. Heat oil in large skillet, adding chopped onion, potatoes, salt and pepper. Sauté over medium-high heat, stirring occasionally, about 5 minutes until onion begins to soften.

Arrange 6 scooped-out halves in large greased baking dish. Spoon about $1/2$ cup of potato mixture into the onion shells, then arrange remaining potato mixture all around them in a layer no deeper than 1 inch. Bake in 375° oven for 1 hour, until potatoes are thoroughly cooked and deeply browned. Serves 6.

Washington Cook Book

Only onions grown in the Walla Walla Valley of southeast Washington and northeast Oregon can be called Walla Walla Sweet Onions, as protected by a Federal marketing order designating Walla Walla Sweet Onions as a unique variety and establishing a specific growing area for the crop.

Parmesan Steamed Onions

Best when made with Walla Walla sweet onions.

1/4 cup margarine
5 medium onions, sliced 1/4 inch
   thick
1/4 teaspoon salt
1/4 teaspoon pepper

1/4 teaspoon sugar
1/4 cup cooking sherry or white
   wine vinegar
1 tablespoon Parmesan cheese

Place margarine into wok or fry pan; heat to 225° until margarine melts. Separate onions into rings. Add onions, salt, pepper, and sugar; stir. Cover and simmer for 20 minutes. Stir every 5 minutes. Add cooking sherry or wine vinegar and cheese. Increase heat to 300°. Stir gently and cook for 3 minutes. Reduce heat to warm for serving. Yields 4–6 servings.

Sharing Our Best

Herb Roasted Vegetables

Vary this recipe by substituting whatever vegetables you have on hand!

1 red bell pepper, quartered,
   seeded, and cut into triangles
1 yellow bell pepper, quartered,
   seeded, and cut into triangles
2 medium-sized sweet onions,
   peeled and cut into 1-inch
   wedges

5 medium red potatoes, cut into
   1-inch pieces
2 small zucchini and yellow
   squash, halved lengthwise and
   cut into 1-inch slices
1/2 cup grated Parmesan cheese
   (optional)

MARINADE:
2 tablespoons each: chopped
   fresh rosemary, thyme and
   parsley, or 1 tablespoon each
   dried

4–6 cloves garlic, minced
2 tablespoons olive oil
1 tablespoon balsamic vinegar

Place vegetables in a 9x13-inch roasting pan. Combine Marinade ingredients and toss with vegetables. Let stand for up to 2 hours and then bake, uncovered, at 400° for 30 minutes, stirring 3–4 times. Toss with Parmesan, if desired, and serve immediately. Serves 6–8.

Gold'n Delicious

Vegetable Casserole with Cream Cheese

This combination of vegetables makes an attractive and delicious dish.

1 (16-ounce) package cauliflower, broccoli and carrots (or vegetables of your choice)
4 tablespoons butter
4 tablespoons flour
2 cups milk

1 (8-ounce) package cream cheese
Salt
Pepper
Parmesan cheese

Cook vegetables until almost done. In saucepan add butter, flour, milk, cream cheese, salt and pepper to taste. Heat and stir until creamy and smooth. Pour over vegetables in casserole dish and sprinkle with Parmesan cheese. Bake at 350° for 30 minutes

Tastes of Country

Eggplant Parmesan

This is my specialty to cook. I make it all of the time. Sometimes I refrigerate the finished dish overnight and make a sandwich. It's delicious.

5 eggs
5 tablespoons water
2 or 3 large eggplants
Vegetable oil

Salt to taste
1 large jar spaghetti sauce
1 cup fresh Parmesan cheese

Beat eggs with water. Peel eggplant and slice about 1/4 inch thick. Dip each eggplant slice in egg wash. Then fry in frying pan with vegetable oil until it is golden brown. May salt lightly. Place eggplant on paper towels to drain grease. When done with each slice, make casserole.

In a 9x13-inch casserole dish, pour a small amount of spaghetti sauce on bottom. Layer eggplant. Pour a little more sauce and lightly dust with cheese. Repeat layers until dish is full. Cover top with sauce and cheese. Bake in oven at 350° for 30 minutes. Serves 4–6.

Recipe by Rick Rizzs, Announcer, Seattle Mariners
Mariners Mix'n and Fix'n Grand Slam Style

Stuffed Eggplant Foggiano

This delicious recipe brings memories of my childhood. I can still see my mother, Antionette, an Italian immigrant, pushing a chair to the table for me to kneel on to assist in the preparation of a tasty main meal for our large family.

2 medium-size eggplants	2 tablespoons finely chopped
$^1/_4$ cup lean ground pork or	fresh or dried parsley
sausage	3 cloves crushed garlic
$^1/_2$ pound lean ground beef	Salt to taste
$^1/_2$ teaspoon black pepper	$^1/_2$ cup dried bread crumbs
2 well beaten eggs	$^1/_2$ cup grated Parmesan
1 teaspoon finely chopped fresh	1 (16-ounce) can peeled,
or dried basil	crushed tomatoes

Blanch whole eggplant 2–3 minutes. Cool and cut in half, lengthwise. Scoop out centers, leaving about $^3/_4$-inch edge. Cut scooped portion into $^1/_2$-inch cubes. Combine with remaining ingredients. Mix well and spoon into eggplant shells.

$^1/_2$ cup grated Parmesan	1 (16-ounce) can peeled,
$^1/_2$ cup dried bread crumbs	crushed tomatoes
1 cup water	4 small potatoes

Place filled eggplant shells in deep casserole; sprinkle cheese and bread crumbs over tops. Combine water and tomatoes; pour around filled shells. Cover and bake at 350° for 2 hours or until eggplant is tender. Add raw, whole peeled potatoes to tomatoes around casserole. Return to oven and bake for additional 20 minutes. Serves 4.

Cooking with Irene!

Broccoli Cheddar Pot Pie

A rich and creamy pot pie with a Parmesan Biscuit Topping. Great winter day food.

$^1/_2$ cup butter
1 large onion, chopped
2 carrots, peeled and diced
3 celery stalks, sliced
2 large potatoes, cut in small
 cubes
$^1/_4$ cup sherry
2 tablespoons minced garlic
3 cups milk

2 cups shredded Cheddar cheese,
 divided
50 ounces canned cream of
 potato soup
3 cups chopped broccoli (if
 frozen, thaw first)
$^1/_4$ teaspoon white pepper
$^1/_3$ tablespoon garlic powder

Preheat oven to 350°. Microwave butter, onion, carrots, celery, potatoes, sherry, and garlic on HIGH until potatoes are soft; place into
large bowl. Microwave milk and 1 cup shredded cheese (can substitute 1 cup processed cheese spread) for 3 minutes, or until they can
be blended together. Pour mixture over vegetables.

 Mix potato soup, remaining Cheddar cheese, broccoli, pepper,
and garlic powder; add to vegetable mixture and mix thoroughly.
Scoop $1^1/_2$ cups of mixture into oven-proof soup bowls. Top with
Parmesan Biscuit Topping.

PARMESAN BISCUIT TOPPING:
2 cups flour
1 tablespoon baking powder
1 teaspoon sugar
$^1/_2$ teaspoon salt
$^1/_2$ teaspoon pepper
$^1/_2$ teaspoon paprika

$^1/_2$ cup shredded Parmesan
2 tablespoons chopped green
 onions
$^1/_3$ cup unsalted butter cut into
 $^1/_2$-inch pieces
$^3/_4$ cup milk

Mix everything, except butter and milk, on slow speed of mixer just
until blended. Add butter pieces and mix until coarse. Blend in milk.

 Turn out onto a floured board and knead until dough is no longer
too sticky to work with. Roll out dough to $^1/_4$ inch thick. Cut dough
with paring knife, tracing around top of an upside-down soup bowl.
Place biscuit rounds on the filled bowls. Brush tops with egg whites.
Bake for 20–25 minutes until pot pies are bubbly and golden brown.
Makes 6 large pot pies.

The Colophon Cafe Best Vegetarian Recipes

Sesame Asparagus

Tired of the butter, cheese, or hollandaise sauce usually served with asparagus? Try this for a change. It's tasty, and the combination of sesame seeds and bread crumbs will add valuable protein to your menu.

1 pound asparagus	1/2 cup bread crumbs
3 tablespoons oil or butter	Salt and pepper to taste
2 tablespoons sesame seeds	

Cut off the bottom part of the asparagus stalks as necessary to remove any tough fiber. Slice them in 2-inch lengths and sauté in oil or butter until almost tender. Toast the sesame seeds by stirring them in a frying pan over fairly high heat. Then add a little oil or butter and the bread crumbs, and stir together until well blended. Pour this mixture over the hot asparagus, season with salt and pepper, and stir gently until the asparagus is well coated with the seeds and bread crumbs. Serve immediately. Serves 4.

Note: This does wonders for broccoli and cauliflower, too!

The 99¢ a Meal Cookbook

Stuffed Acorn Squash

1 acorn squash	1/4 cup raisins
Brown rice	Curry powder
1 small onion	1 tablespoon cornstarch
1 cup sliced carrot	1/2 cup water
1 cup sliced celery	Shredded coconut
1 cup diced green pepper	

Slice acorn squash in half and cook in microwave (about 6–8 minutes on HIGH, covered). Cook a serving of brown rice, enough for 2. Stir-fry chopped onion, carrot, celery, and pepper. Add approximately 1/4 cup raisins and curry powder to taste. Stir in cornstarch mixed with water. Mix rice and stir-fry together; fill hollows in squash. Serve excess filling on side.

Harvest Feast

Fried Zucchini Blossoms

I consider this a gourmet treat.

12 large freshly picked zucchini
  blossoms
$^1/_2$ cup all-purpose flour
$^1/_2$ teaspoon baking powder
$^1/_4$ teaspoon granulated garlic

$^1/_4$ teaspoon salt
1 egg
$^1/_2$ cup milk
1 tablespoon vegetable oil
Additional oil for frying

Rinse blossoms in cold water (gently, as they are very fragile). In medium bowl combine flour, baking powder, garlic, and salt. In another bowl beat egg, milk, and oil. Add to dry ingredients and stir until smooth. Heat 2 inches oil in skillet. Dip blossoms separately into batter and fry in oil, a few at a time until crisp. Drain on paper towels. Keep warm until served. Makes 4 servings.

Cooking with Irene!

Zucchini Pickles

This is a really good way to preserve your surplus zucchini crop for later use. If you like bread-and-butter pickles, you'll love these.

2 pounds zucchini, sliced
  $^1/_8$ inch thick
2 medium onions, sliced
$^1/_4$ cup salt
$^1/_2$ cup honey

1 pint white vinegar
1 teaspoon celery seed
1 teaspoon mustard seed
1 teaspoon turmeric
$^1/_2$ teaspoon dry mustard

Place the sliced zucchini and onions in a pot, cover them with water, and add the salt. Stir, then let stand for 1 hour. Drain. Mix the remaining ingredients and bring them to a boil. Pour over the zucchini and onions, and let stand 1 hour. Bring to a boil and cook 3 minutes. Fill hot sterile jars and seal. Makes about 3 pints.

The 99¢ a Meal Cookbook

Mock Baked Beans

3 cups small white beans
  (Great Northern)
Water, to cover beans
4 tablespoons garlic salt

$^1/_2$ cup chopped onions
$^3/_4$ cup water
$^1/_2$ cup catsup
$^1/_4$ cup molasses

Soak beans overnight. Rinse well and drain. Cover with water and add garlic salt. Bring to boil and boil approximately 45 minutes until tender. In large frying pan cook onions with $^3/_4$ cup water until tender. Approximately 10 minutes, or until water has cooked off. Add beans, catsup, and molasses to frying pan with onions and cook just until everything is heated through. No baking necessary. Can be served hot or cold. Makes 6 servings.

From My Heart For Yours

Calico Beans

A good dish to take to a picnic or a potluck dinner. Serve with raw or lightly steamed vegetable sticks and a dip for a complete meal.

$^1/_4$ pound bacon (4–5 slices)
$^1/_2$ cup chopped onion
1 large (31-ounce) can pork and
  beans, drained
1 (15-ounce) can black beans,
  drained
1 (15-ounce) can white beans,
  drained

$^1/_2$ cup crushed pineapple,
  drained
$^1/_4$ cup chopped green pepper
$^1/_2$ cup ketchup
$^1/_4$ cup brown sugar
1 tablespoon cider vinegar
1 teaspoon mustard

Set oven to 325°. Fry bacon, drain off grease, and chop or tear into bite-size pieces. Cook onion in a small amount of bacon grease until golden in color. Pour all 3 cans of beans into a 9x13-inch casserole dish. Add bacon, onion, pineapple, and green pepper. In small bowl mix together ketchup, brown sugar, vinegar, and mustard. Stir ketchup mixture into bean mixture. Bake for 40–50 minutes or until juices bubble.

Food for Tots

Mexican Black Beans with Rice

You don't have to be a vegetarian to love this easy dish. It's also delicious rolled in a tortilla.

2 (16-ounce) cans black beans
1 (15-ounce) can Mexican-style
   stewed tomatoes
1 (4¹/₂-ounce) can chopped
   green chiles

¹/₄ cup barbecue sauce
¹/₂ teaspoon ground cumin
1 tablespoon lime juice
1 cup frozen corn kernels
1 cup rice, cooked

Drain and rinse beans. Combine beans, tomatoes, chiles, barbecue sauce, cumin, and lime juice in medium saucepan. Bring to a boil and simmer, uncovered, for 5 minutes. Add corn and simmer an additional 5 minutes. Spoon beans over rice. Serves 6.

Gold'n Delicious

*Kalama, Washington, claims to have the tallest, one-piece totem in the world—
a colorful 140-foot-tall totem pole located in the Marine Park. Washington contains more than 20 Native American reservations, including one of the largest in
the country, belonging to the Yakama peoples.*

Linguine with Lemon Clam Sauce

A simply delicious and healthy clam dish laced with lemon. For a meal in a hurry, this is the entrée to choose. You will take your seat at the table less than thirty minutes from walking in the door and reaching for the pasta pot.

1 (16-ounce) package linguine
5 tablespoons extra-virgin olive oil, divided
3 tablespoons basil pesto sauce
4 cloves garlic, minced
1^1/$_2$ teaspoons dried oregano
^{1}/$_2$ teaspoon red pepper flakes
2 cups minced fresh clams, including nectar or 2 (6^1/$_2$-ounce) cans chopped clams

^{1}/$_2$ cup freshly squeezed lemon juice
^{1}/$_2$ cup chopped fresh Italian parsley
Salt and freshly ground pepper, to taste
^{1}/$_3$ cup freshly grated Parmesan cheese

In a large pot, cook pasta al dente, according to package directions. Drain and return to pot, add 2 tablespoons oil and the pesto; toss to coat. Cover to keep warm.

While pasta is cooking, over medium heat in a large frying pan, heat remaining 3 tablespoons oil. Sauté garlic, oregano, and red pepper flakes about 1 minute. Add clams, lemon juice, and parsley and simmer until clams are cooked, about 5 minutes. (If using canned clams, simmer about 3 minutes.) Be careful not to overcook the clams.

Just before serving, salt and pepper to taste. Turn pasta onto individual heated plates and top with clam sauce and sprinkle with cheese. Serve with additional Parmesan. Makes 6 servings.

San Juan Classics II Cookbook

Smoked Salmon Fettuccine

This eye-pleasing pasta dish uses smoked or cooked salmon in a tomato-cream sauce seasoned with basil and garlic.

1 (16-ounce) package fettuccine	2 cups heavy cream
5 tablespoons extra-virgin olive oil, divided	2 cups smoked salmon
3 tablespoons pesto sauce	$1^1/2$ teaspoons dry basil or $^1/4$ cup chopped fresh basil
3 cloves garlic, minced	$^1/3$ cup chopped fresh parsley
1 cup sliced mushrooms	Salt and freshly ground pepper to taste
4 Roma tomatoes, seeded and chopped	Parmesan cheese for garnish
$^1/2$ cup dry white wine	

In a large pot, cook pasta al dente, according to package directions. Drain and return to pot. Add 3 tablespoons oil and pesto sauce; toss to coat. Cover to keep warm.

Over medium heat in a large frying pan, heat remaining 2 tablespoons oil and sauté garlic about 1 minute; add mushrooms and cook about 5 minutes or until golden brown. Stir in tomatoes and wine and cook 2–3 minutes. Add cream and gently simmer to reduce, about 10 minutes. Do not boil.

Add salmon, basil, and parsley to sauce and heat through to blend flavors, about 5 minutes. Just before serving, salt and pepper to taste. Turn pasta onto individual heated plates and top with salmon sauce, garnish with cheese. Serve with additional Parmesan. Makes 6 servings.

San Juan Classics II Cookbook

Salmon caught in the Columbia River was canned as early as 1866, and fisheries expanded their output steadily until the early 1900s.

Shrimp Fettuccine

3 ounces fettuccine
4 cups water
2 cups (loose packed) frozen
  broccoli, carrots and
  cauliflower
1 (8-ounce) package frozen
  shrimp
1 tablespoon margarine

1 tablespoon cornstarch
1 chicken bouillon cube
$^1/_4$ teaspoon garlic powder
$^1/_8$ teaspoon lemon pepper
$^3/_4$ cup skim milk
2 tablespoons white wine
2 tablespoons Parmesan cheese

In large saucepan, cook pasta in hot water for 8 minutes. Add frozen vegetables; return to boiling. Reduce heat; simmer 3 minutes. Add shrimp; cook until pink. Drain and leave in saucepan.

While pasta, vegetables, and shrimp are cooking, melt margarine in another pan; stir in cornstarch and seasonings. Add milk; cook and stir over medium heat until thick and bubbly. Cook 2 minutes more. Stir in wine (can substitute milk). Pour over pasta; toss and serve with Parmesan cheese. Serves 3.

Our Best Home Cooking

Fresh Seafood Fettuccine

Seafood lovers will enjoy this gourmet fare of lobster, scallops, and prawns swimming in creamy sauce splashed with fresh herbs.

1 pound fresh fettuccine
$^1/_4$ pound scallops
$^1/_4$ pound prawns
1 small lobster tail, peeled and
  cut into 1-inch pieces
2 tablespoons butter or
  margarine

2 cloves garlic, minced
1 teaspoon chopped fresh basil
1 teaspoon snipped fresh
  rosemary
3 cups cream sauce (for a lighter
  sauce, use 1 cup cream and 2
  cups chicken stock)

Boil water in large pot and cook fettuccine until al dente. Sauté scallops, prawns, and lobster in butter or olive oil till almost done, then add garlic. Toss cooked fettuccine with seafood, fresh herbs, and cream in a large serving bowl. Serves 6.

Washington Farmers' Markets Cookbook and Guide

Microwave Chicken Alfredo

8 ounces fettuccine noodles,
    uncooked
6 boneless chicken breast fillets
$^1/_2$ teaspoon garlic powder
4 tablespoons margarine
$^1/_4$ cup finely chopped onion
2 cups sliced fresh mushrooms
3 tablespoons flour

$1^1/_2$ cups chicken broth
$1^1/_2$ cups half-and-half
$^1/_4$ teaspoon nutmeg
$^1/_4$ cup Parmesan cheese
$^1/_4$ teaspoon salt
$^1/_4$ teaspoon pepper
$^1/_2$ cup mozzarella cheese

Boil noodles for 10 minutes; drain. Sprinkle chicken breasts with garlic and cook 10–12 minutes on HIGH in microwave. Slice into cubes after cooled. In baking dish, cook margarine, onions, and mushrooms for 3–4 minutes on HIGH. Add flour and cook 1 more minute. Add remaining ingredients (except mozzarella cheese) and cook on HIGH 10–12 minutes, or until sauce is boiling and thick. Stir in noodles and chicken. Cover with cheese. Serves 4.

Liberty Lake Community Cookbook

Seafood Lasagna

Fresh seafood is layered with pasta and sauces in this scrumptious lasagna. Serve with a green salad, Italian bread, and fresh fruit for dessert.

2 tablespoons olive oil
1 cup chopped onion
2 cloves garlic, minced
1 (14$^1\!/_2$-ounce) can chopped tomatoes, with juice
$^1\!/_4$ cup tomato paste
2 bay leaves, divided
$^1\!/_8$ teaspoon dried thyme
1 tablespoon minced parsley
1 teaspoon salt, divided
Freshly ground pepper to taste
Lasagna (8 ounces, or about 8 large 2-inch-wide strips)
2$^1\!/_2$ cups milk
$^1\!/_8$ teaspoon mace
6 peppercorns

Slice of onion
3 tablespoons butter or margarine
4 tablespoons all-purpose flour
$^1\!/_2$ pound Dungeness crab meat, drained
$^1\!/_2$ pound small cooked shrimp, drained
8 large scallops, sliced in about $^3\!/_4$-inch rounds, drained (or 16 small scallops)
2 cups sliced mushrooms
$^1\!/_3$ cup freshly grated Parmesan cheese
1$^1\!/_2$ cups grated mozzarella cheese

Make tomato sauce by heating olive oil in a large saucepan over medium heat; add 1 cup chopped onion, and cook until soft. Add garlic, cook lightly; add tomatoes with juice, tomato paste, 1 bay leaf, thyme, parsley, $^1\!/_2$ teaspoon salt and pepper to taste. Partly cover and simmer gently for 20 minutes.

Cook lasagna noodles in boiling salted water according to directions on package. Place under cool running water. Drain and lay pieces on clean towel to dry.

Make white sauce (béchamel) by heating milk over low heat for about 10 minutes with 1 bay leaf, mace, peppercorns, and onion slice. In another saucepan, melt butter over low heat; add flour and cook, stirring constantly for about 3 minutes. Take butter mixture off heat; add heated milk through a sieve to catch peppercorns, onion, and bay leaf. Return to medium heat and stir constantly until slightly thickened. Add reserved $^1\!/_2$ teaspoon salt or to taste. Cover sauce with buttered waxed paper to prevent a skin from forming, and set aside.

Preheat oven to 375°. Lightly butter 8x8- or 9x9-inch-square baking dish. (Before mixing seafood with tomato sauce, be certain that

(continued)

(continued)

all seafood is dry. If not, dry completely with paper towel.) Mix crab, shrimp, uncooked scallops and mushrooms with tomato sauce.

Spread about 1 tablespoon white sauce on bottom of pan. Layer $^1/_2$ lasagna in bottom, cutting off ends that do not fit. Spoon $^1/_2$ of the tomato sauce on pasta, cover with about $^1/_2$ of white sauce and sprinkle with all the grated Parmesan cheese (or sprinkle first layer with $^1/_2$ of the Parmesan cheese and reserve the rest to sprinkle over mozzarella cheese on top layer). Repeat layers. Sprinkle top with grated mozzarella cheese. Bake, uncovered, in 375° oven for 30–35 minutes. Remove from oven, cover with loosely vented foil, and let stand for 10–12 minutes. Serves 4–6.

Wandering & Feasting

Everyone's Favorite Lasagna

An excellent lasagna recipe that doesn't take all day to make. If desired, make two smaller dishes and serve one for dinner and freeze one for later. The lasagna can be prepared and then frozen or baked and frozen and reheated at another time.

2 pounds lean ground beef
1 tablespoon light brown sugar
1 (32-ounce) jar chunky
   spaghetti sauce with
   mushrooms

10–12 lasagna noodles, cooked
2$^1/_2$ cups (10 ounces) shredded
   Cheddar cheese
3 cups (12 ounces) shredded
   mozzarella cheese

Brown ground beef in large skillet; drain fat. Stir in brown sugar and spaghetti sauce. Bring to a boil; reduce heat and simmer 20 minutes.

Meanwhile, cook noodles according to directions on package. Spread about $^1/_2$ cup of the meat sauce in sprayed 9x13-inch baking dish. Layer, starting with noodles, then sauce, Cheddar cheese and mozzarella cheese, making 2 layers of everything. Bake for 30 minutes at 350° or until hot. Makes 10–12 servings.

Six Ingredients or Less

Vegetable Lasagna

A low-fat pasta recipe with all the goodness of fresh farm produce for robust flavor.

2 teaspoons oil
3 cups chopped unpeeled
  eggplant
³/4 cup chopped onion
1 teaspoon minced garlic
1 (28-ounce) can crushed
  tomatoes
¹/2 teaspoon sugar
¹/4 teaspoon basil
1 pound carrots, peeled and
  shredded

1 (10-ounce) package thawed
  frozen spinach
15 ounces ricotta cheese
1 cup shredded part-skim
  mozzarella cheese
1 egg, well beaten
Dash each of salt and nutmeg
1 package lasagna noodles,
  cooked
Parmesan cheese

Heat oil in skillet over low heat. Stir in eggplant, onion, and garlic; sauté for 5 minutes. Stir in crushed tomatoes, sugar, and basil. Add a dash of salt to taste. Cover and simmer for 20 minutes or till eggplant is tender.

Meanwhile, boil 2 quarts water and cook carrots 3–5 minutes. Drain well and add spinach, ricotta cheese, mozzarella cheese, beaten egg, dash of salt and nutmeg. Add eggplant mixture and stir to combine—this is your sauce.

In a greased 9x13-inch baking dish, make layers of cooked noodles, then sauce, then repeat, ending with a last layer of sauce. Sprinkle Parmesan cheese on top. Bake at 350° for 30 minutes or till heated through. Serves 8–10.

Washington Farmers' Markets Cookbook and Guide

The Ed Hendler Memorial Bridge between Kennewick and Pasco, when originally constructed, was the longest-span, concrete cable-stay suspension bridge in the world.

Spaghetti Pie

10 ounces spaghetti
1 1/2 pounds hamburger, browned
  with 1 teaspoon onion flakes
1 (32-ounce) jar spaghetti sauce
1 teaspoon oregano
1/8 teaspoon garlic powder
24 ounces ricotta cheese
1/2 cup Parmesan cheese
2 teaspoons salt
1/2 teaspoon pepper
2 eggs beaten
1 pound mozzarella cheese,
  grated

Cook and cool spaghetti. Combine browned hamburger, spaghetti, spaghetti sauce, oregano and garlic powder. Mix ricotta cheese, Parmesan cheese, salt and pepper into beaten eggs. Grease 2 (9x13-inch) pans and layer with 1/2 spaghetti mixture, then cheese mixture, then grated mozzarella cheese. Make 2nd layer of each. Bake at 375°, covered for 20 minutes, then uncovered for 25 minutes. Let stand 15 minutes before serving. Makes 2 pans.

Sleigh Bells and Sugarplums

Frigoly

1 onion, chopped
1 green pepper, chopped
2 tablespoons butter or oil
1 1/2 pounds ground beef
1 package noodles or macaroni,
  boiled in salted water
1 can corn
1 can tomatoes
1 small can ripe, sliced olives
1 (8-ounce) package cream
  cheese

Fry onion and pepper in butter or oil. Add meat and fry lightly. Add noodles, corn, and tomatoes. Boil 10 minutes, then add olives and cheese. Put in baking dish and bake 30 minutes at 350°. Serves 8.

Liberty Lake Community Cookbook

Chicken, Walnuts and Gorgonzola with Pasta

Toasted walnuts add a crunchy contrast to the rich creamy Gorgonzola sauce.

1¼ cups walnut halves, divided
2 boned and skinned chicken breasts (4 breast halves)
5 tablespoons vegetable oil, divided
1 (16-ounce) package fettuccine pasta

3 tablespoons butter
4 ounces Gorgonzola cheese (1 cup crumbled)
1 cup milk
1 cup light or heavy cream
Salt and freshly ground pepper to taste

Preheat oven to 325°. Place walnut halves in shallow baking dish and toast until lightly browned, about 7 minutes. Remove from oven and allow to cool. With a sharp knife, coarsely chop and set aside.

Cut chicken into bite-size pieces. In a large frying pan, over medium-high, heat 3 tablespoons oil and sauté chicken until done. Remove from pan and set aside.

In a large pot cook pasta al dente, according to package directions. Drain, return to pot and add remaining 2 tablespoons oil; toss to coat. Cover to keep warm.

While pasta is cooking, combine butter, Gorgonzola, milk, and cream in a small saucepan over low heat. Stir until cheese and butter melt and sauce has a creamy consistency, about 6 minutes. Increase heat to medium, stir, and cook until sauce is reduced by ¼; do not boil. Add chicken and 1 cup of walnuts to sauce; heat through. Pour sauce over reserved pasta and gently toss. Salt and pepper to taste. Turn pasta mixture into heated individual pasta bowls. Sprinkle with remaining ¼ cup walnuts. Makes 4 servings.

San Juan Classics II Cookbook

Famous Washingtonians include: Bob Barker, Dyan Cannon, Carol Channing, Kurt Cobain, Bing Crosby, Bill Gates, Jimi Hendrix, Robert Joffrey (choreographer), Hank Ketchum (cartoonist), Kenny Loggins, and Adam West (original Batman).

Thai Chicken Pasta

³/4 pound dry pasta
¹/4 teaspoon hot chile flakes
³/4 cup chicken broth
¹/4 cup rice vinegar
2 tablespoons soy sauce
1 tablespoon ginger or garlic
¹/2 pound cooked chicken
2 tablespoons lime juice
2 tablespoons roasted nuts
¹/3 cup mixed fresh cilantro

Cook pasta. Mix all ingredients except cilantro. Put chicken and sauce on noodles. Mix; add cilantro.

Costco Wholesale Employee Association Cookbook

Garlic Mushroom Stuffed Rigatoni

10 ounces rigatoni pasta,
  uncooked
3 tablespoons virgin olive oil
10 large garlic cloves, finely
  chopped
1 cup each chopped portabello
  and chanterelle mushrooms
¹/2 cup chopped fresh basil
1 (15-ounce) can chicken broth
2 tablespoons butter
Salt and pepper to taste
¹/4 cup Italian bread crumbs
1 cup heavy cream
2 ounces freshly grated Romano
  cheese

In a large pot, cook pasta according to package directions, al dente. Drain and set aside. In a small bowl, mix oil, garlic, mushrooms, basil, broth, butter, salt, pepper, and bread crumbs; mix well. Transfer mixture to a pastry bag with a pastry tip. Stuff each pasta evenly with mixture and place pasta in a large baking dish. Pour cream evenly over pasta. Cover and bake in a 350° oven for 15–18 minutes. Spread cheese over top and bake, uncovered, an additional 5 minutes. Serves 4.

Northwest Garlic Festival Cookbook

Macaroni and Cheese

Everyone loves my macaroni and cheese. It is creamy and easy to make. A terrific potluck casserole. Very rich and yummy!

1 (7-ounce) package elbow macaroni
6 tablespoons butter, divided
3 tablespoons flour
2$^1/_2$ cups milk (can use part canned milk)
1 (8-ounce) package cream cheese

3 cups grated Cheddar cheese, divided
$^1/_2$ teaspoon salt
$^1/_2$ teaspoon pepper
1 cup dry bread crumbs

Cook macaroni until tender, as directed on package. Melt 4 tablespoons butter in saucepan. Stir in flour until smooth. Gradually add milk. Bring to a boil, stirring constantly. Add cream cheese, 2 cups Cheddar cheese, salt and pepper. Stir over low heat until cheeses are melted and mixture is smooth. Drain and rinse macaroni and mix cheese mixture into macaroni. Transfer to a greased casserole dish or 9x13-inch pan. Sprinkle remaining 1 cup Cheddar cheese on top. Melt remaining 2 tablespoons butter and add bread crumbs. Spread on top of cheese. Bake uncovered at 400° for 20–25 minutes or until golden brown.

Bounteous Blessings

Marlanara

Don't be alarmed if this looks like enough to feed you and your neighbors. That's the point—we always freeze at least a quart or two to keep on hand for those "cooking emergencies." You may invent your own uses for this delicious sauce besides pouring it over pasta.

1 tablespoon olive oil
2 medium onions, cut in half and thinly sliced
²/₃ cup chopped, fresh basil leaves (stemmed and loosely packed) or 2 teaspoons dried
2 teaspoons ground oregano
2 teaspoons dried thyme
1 teaspoon fennel seed
2 teaspoons dried marjoram
¹/₂ teaspoon freshly ground black pepper
Pinch of dried, crushed red pepper flakes
5–6 large garlic cloves, finely chopped or minced
1¹/₂ cups dry red wine
4 (28-ounce) cans diced tomatoes in juice
1 (8-ounce) can tomato paste

In a heavy, 6-quart pot, sauté onions with olive oil on medium heat until onions are soft. Add all other spices (basil through garlic). Sauté another couple of minutes until spices are well blended. Add red wine, tomatoes, and tomato paste. Turn heat up to medium-high and bring to a boil. When it starts to boil, turn down the heat to low and let simmer as long as possible, stirring occasionally. One or two hours is great if you have the time. The longer it simmers the more flavorful the sauce will be.

Cool sauce and blend with a hand blender or transfer to large blender using small pulses in smaller batches to make a smooth puréed sauce. If you like a chunky version, leave it as it is except dice onions and chop basil leaves into smaller pieces for the sauté. I like a smooth version and the blending distributes the flavors and the sweetness from the onions. Makes about 4 quarts.

Note: If you are freezing the sauce, make sure to leave some room at the top for expansion.

Good Food for (Mostly) Good People Cookbook

Browned Butter with Myzithra

This quick and easy recipe has a nice blend of flavors and is similar to a pasta served at the Spaghetti Factory.

8 ounces spaghetti	2 medium garlic cloves, minced
1/3 cup butter	1/2 cup grated Myzithra cheese*

Cook pasta according to package directions; drain. In a small skillet, melt butter over medium-low heat. Add garlic and cook until butter turns light brown. (Watch carefully at this point. If it turns too dark, it will have to be discarded.) Add butter to pasta and toss to coat. Place on individual serving dishes and sprinkle with about 2 tablespoons cheese. Makes 4 side-dish servings or 2 main dishes.

*Myzithra Cheese, also known as Mitzithra cheese, is available both fresh and aged. Fresh Myzithra is soft, similar to cottage cheese. Aged Myzithra is shaped like an ostrich egg and is firm and pungent, rather like Italian Ricotta Salata. The aged variety is known as Xinomyzithra and makes an excellent grating cheese. Myzithra can be found in the fresh cheese department of most supermarkets.

Six Ingredients or Less: Pasta & Casseroles

Sundried Tomato Pesto

Great as a pizza topping, on crackers with cream cheese, tossed into salads, or baked into bread dough. Try it in soups and stews, or even stir into pasta.

2 cups sun-dried tomatoes, packed in oil; drain and reserve oil	1/2 cup fresh oregano
	3–5 cloves garlic
	1/2 cup pine nuts or walnuts (optional)
3/4 cup oil, preferably olive oil	3/4 cup shredded Parmesan cheese
1/2 cup fresh rosemary	
1/2 cup fresh parsley	

Process all the above ingredients except for cheese in food processor until smooth. Add cheese, mix well, and refrigerate up to 2 days. Can also be frozen.

Washington Farmers' Markets Cookbook and Guide

Basil Pesto

How do you say "yummy" in Italian?

1 cup chopped fresh basil leaves
3 cloves garlic, peeled
1/2 cup freshly grated Parmesan
  or Romano cheese
Pinch of salt
1/4 cup finely chopped walnuts
  or pine nuts

1/2 cup chopped parsley
1 teaspoon dried marjoram, or a
  sprig of fresh marjoram
6 tablespoons olive oil

In Genoa you would use a mortar and pestle to make this sauce. A blender is a good substitute, however. Put in everything but the olive oil and blend, then add the oil a few drops at a time. Pour this sauce over about a pound of hot pasta (spaghetti, noodles, or macaroni) and toss. Serves 4–6.

The 99¢ a Meal Cookbook

Pesto Quiche

Traditional egg pie with an Italian touch.

1 (9-inch) unbaked pie shell
2 cups shredded mozzarella,
  divided
3/4 cups ready-made pesto

1/2 cup sun-dried tomatoes
4 eggs
1 1/2 cups milk

In unbaked pie shell, layer 1 cup mozzarella, pesto, sun-dried tomatoes and then remaining cheese. Blend together eggs and milk. Pour batter over top of tomato/cheese mixture. Bake at 400° for 10 minutes, or until crust is lightly browned. Reduce temperature to 300° and bake until quiche is set and knife comes out clean.

The Colophon Cafe Best Recipes

 If the more than half a million Seattle residents drank and bathed only in water captured from Mount Rainier's snow and ice fields, the water supply would last 200 years.

Super Scented Play Dough

This simple-to-make play dough is soft, smooth, scented, and nontoxic. Kids can stir the dry ingredients and help knead the cooled dough.

1¼ cups flour
¼ cup salt
1 packet unsweetened flavored
   soft drink mix (such as Koolaid)

1 cup boiling water
1½ tablespoons vegetable oil

In a mixing bowl, combine flour, salt, and drink mix. In a separate container, combine oil and water. Make a well in the flour mixture and pour in oil and water mixture. Mix thoroughly with a large spoon.

On a large cutting board, knead dough until it is cool. Don't use the countertop as the drink mix can stain before it is mixed into the other ingredients.

Play! You probably have lots of tools in the kitchen to use with the play dough such as a rolling pin and cookie cutters, a garlic press to make grass or hair, chopsticks to poke holes, etc. Yields 1¾ cups of fun.

Note: Store in a sealed container in the cupboard for several months. Its lifetime depends upon the amount of use and time it is left out of the container. In spite of the vibrant colors, this play dough does not stain hands or most surfaces once it is thoroughly mixed.

Food for Tots

MEATS

The Columbia River (pictured here in eastern Washington) flows for more than 1,200 miles, from the base of the Canadian Rockies in southeastern British Columbia to the Pacific Ocean at Astoria, Oregon, and Ilwaco, Washington.

Walla Walla Steak Sandwich with Horseradish Sauce

2 pounds flank steak

MARINADE:
3/4 cup beer	1/2 teaspoon black pepper
1/4 cup olive oil	2 cloves garlic, minced
1 teaspoon salt	1/4 teaspoon crushed red pepper

Trim steak of fat and score both sides. Place in a covered container or ziplock bag. Combine Marinade ingredients and add to steak. Refrigerate for 4–24 hours, turning occasionally.

ONIONS:
3 tablespoons butter	6 cups Walla Walla sweet onions,
3/4 teaspoon paprika	sliced into 1/4-inch rings

Melt butter in large skillet over medium-low heat. Add paprika and onions and sauté until onions are tender, 20–25 minutes. Keep warm until ready to serve.

HORSERADISH SAUCE:
1 cup sour cream	1/4 teaspoon salt
2 tablespoons horseradish	1/8 teaspoon paprika
1 tablespoon parsley	

Combine sauce ingredients in a small saucepan and cook over low heat until thoroughly heated, about 7 minutes. Keep warm until ready to serve.

Remove steak from Marinade and grill or broil about 5 minutes per side or until steak reaches desired degree of doneness. Slice steak thinly on the diagonal and keep warm until ready to serve.

ROLLS:
1/4 cup butter, softened	6 French rolls, split
1 tablespoon Italian herb seasoning	

Combine butter and Italian seasoning and spread on rolls. Toast rolls briefly under broiler. To serve, place steak on rolls, then top with Onions and Horseradish Sauce. Serves 6.

Note: If you can't find Walla Walla sweets, substitute Vidalia or Maui onions. Be sure to sauté them slowly over low heat to bring out their natural sweetness.

Gold'n Delicious

Mustard Flank Steak

1¹/₂ pounds flank steak
2 tablespoons each butter and oil
1 onion, thinly sliced
1 cup regular-strength beef
  broth
2 teaspoons cornstarch

2 teaspoons Dijon mustard
2 tablespoons white vinegar
¹/₂ teaspoon salt
¹/₄ teaspoon each pepper and
  paprika

Slice flank steak thinly on diagonal. Sauté in oil and butter. Remove steak and keep warm. Using the same pan, sauté onion over medium heat, adding more butter if needed. Cook onion until it is limp and translucent. Turn into dish with meat and keep warm. Gradually stir beef broth into cornstarch until smooth. Add mustard, vinegar, salt, pepper, and paprika. Pour both mixtures into frying pan and cook, stirring to release brown particles, until sauce boils and is thickened. Return meat and onions to pan of sauce and stir to mix. Reheat quickly, then serve. Serves 4.

Crime Stoppers: A Community Cookbook

Killer Flank Steak

This is a deliciously different soy-based marinade.

1 (2-pound) flank steak,
  trimmed of fat
¹/₄ cup soy sauce
¹/₄ cup olive oil

¹/₂ tablespoon dried Italian
  seasoning
1 tablespoon lemon juice
2 cloves garlic, minced

Place steak in a covered container or ziplock bag. Combine remaining ingredients and pour over steak. Marinate at least 20 minutes at room temperature or up to 24 hours in the refrigerator, turning occasionally.

Grill over medium coals for 6 minutes. Turn and grill for an additional 6–8 minutes or until cooked to desired doneness. Slice thinly on the diagonal. Serves 4.

Gold'n Delicious

Beef Tenderloin with Mustard Caper Sauce

This wonderful sauce can be made one to two hours ahead and kept warm in a well-insulated thermos. Leftover sauce can be gently reheated. In addition to beef tenderloin, the sauce can be served with pork chops, pork tenderloin, beef and pork kabobs, beef fondue, and prime rib.

1 (3-pound) beef tenderloin (purchase the butt section)
2 tablespoons butter, divided
3 green onions, divided

2 cups heavy cream (no substitute)*
3 tablespoons Dijon mustard
1¹/₂ tablespoons capers, drained

Remove tenderloin from refrigerator and trim, if necessary, then pat dry. Melt 1 tablespoon butter and brush over meat. Place on rack in small roasting pan. Bake 35–45 minutes or until meat thermometer registers 135° for medium-rare (or 140° for medium). Remove from oven and cover lightly with foil. Let stand 10–15 minutes before carving.

Meanwhile, melt the remaining 1 tablespoon butter in a medium saucepan and cook 1 tablespoon chopped white part of the onion, until soft. (Thinly slice some of the green part of the onion and set aside for garnish.) Add cream and bring to a boil. Reduce heat and simmer 10–15 minutes or until mixture thickens, stirring occasionally. Remove from heat and add Dijon mustard and capers.

Spoon some of the sauce on each dinner plate and top with a slice of beef tenderloin. Sprinkle with sliced green onion for garnish. Makes 6 servings.

*You must use pasteurized heavy cream or the sauce may not thicken.

Note: Probably the most important thing to remember is to allow time for the meat to stand after roasting. The meat juice will be more evenly distributed, making the tenderloin easier to carve.

Six Ingredients or Less

Over 1,000 dams can be found in Washington.

Stuffed Prime Rib of Beef

1 (10-pound) lip-on rib eye steak
Salt and pepper to taste
5 ounces frozen garlic, minced
16 ounces sun-dried tomatoes in
   olive oil
4 ounces fresh basil
14 ounces shiitake mushrooms
8 ounces Parmigiana Reggiano
   (Parmesan cheese)

Trim lip and excess fat from rib eye. Butterfly open to expose center of steak. Season inside with salt and pepper. Rub inside with garlic. Layer sun-dried tomatoes, basil, mushrooms, more salt and pepper, and shredded Parmigiana. Roll and tie. Season with salt and pepper again to taste. Cook in a preheated oven at 375° for 2–2^1/$_2$ hours until the internal temperature reaches 118° for medium-rare.

Costco Wholesale Employee Association Cookbook

Brajole

1 large boneless round steak
   (about 1^1/$_2$ pounds)
2 tablespoons dry bread crumbs
1 tablespoon dried or fresh
   parsley
1 tablespoon basil
1 tablespoon grated Parmesan
^{1}/$_4$ teaspoon salt
^{1}/$_4$ teaspoon black pepper
1 clove garlic, crushed
3 strips very lean bacon, cut into
   1-inch pieces
Spaghetti sauce
Pasta of choice

Pound steak thin, to about ^{1}/$_4$ inch thick and set aside. Combine all other ingredients and mix well. Spread evenly over meat, staying ^{1}/$_4$ inch from edges.

Individual portion preparation: Roll tightly and tie with heavy string, cutting string and knotting as you go. Then cut meat roll into serving-size sections (2–4 inches wide) and brown on all sides. Simmer for 1^1/$_2$ hours in spaghetti sauce. Serve hot with pasta of your choice.

Entire roll preparation: Wind string in one piece around the entire roll, keeping the roll tight and intact. Brown all sides. Then simmer 1^1/$_2$ hours in spaghetti sauce. Cut roll into serving-size portions. Serve hot with pasta of your choice.

Cooking with Irene!

Round Steak Pasties

1 cup shortening
3 cups flour
1 teaspoon salt
$^1/_2$ teaspoon baking powder
About $^2/_3$ cup cold water
1–1$^1/_2$ pounds round steak,
  cubed

2 cups diced potatoes
2 cups diced carrots
$^1/_2$ cup chopped celery
$^1/_2$ cup chopped onion
Salt and pepper to taste
6 tablespoons water
6 teaspoons butter

Cut shortening into dry ingredients. Add water. Mix. Divide dough into 6 (8-inch) circles (roll). Combine round steak with diced potatoes, carrots, celery, and onion; season to taste. Divide meat and vegetable mixture over the 6 circles. Brush edges of pastry circles with water. Fold into semicircles and seal edges. Cut $^1/_2$-inch slits on top. Place on cookie sheet. Pour about 1 tablespoon of water into each pastie through slit. Also add about 1 teaspoon butter. Bake about 1 hour; bake at 450° for first 10 minutes, reduce heat to 350° to finish. Serve with gravy or ketchup.

Favorite Recipes from Our Best Cooks

One Step Tamale Pie

1 pound ground beef
1 cup chopped onion
2 cloves garlic, minced
1 (12-ounce) can whole-kernel corn, drained
2 (8-ounce) cans tomato sauce
1 cup milk

2 eggs, beaten
Few dashes of Tabasco sauce
$^3/_4$ cup yellow cornmeal
$1^1/_2$–2 teaspoons chili powder
2 teaspoons salt
1 cup grated Cheddar cheese

In large skillet, brown meat, onion, and garlic. Stir in remaining ingredients except cheese. Pour into greased 12x7$^1/_2$x2-inch pan. Bake at 350° for 30 minutes. Add cheese over top. Bake an additional 15 minutes.

Recipes to Remember

Cabbage Rolls

CABBAGE LEAVES:
1 head cabbage

Remove core; steam head in large kettle. Remove leaves as they separate easily from the head; wilt them by further steaming for several minutes. Drain; cool slightly, then place meat mixture on leaf and roll up.

1 cup rice
2$^1/_2$ pounds ground beef
1$^1/_2$ teaspoons salt
$^1/_4$ teaspoon pepper
2$^1/_4$ tablespoons minced onion

1 large can tomato soup, divided
Water
Cabbage Leaves
1 pint sauerkraut

Steam rice according to directions on package. Mix rice with ground beef, salt, pepper, and onion. Add $^1/_2$ can of tomato soup, diluted with equal amount of water. Place $^1/_3$ cup of this mixture on a prepared Cabbage Leaf; roll up tightly and place side-by-side in baking dish. Spread sauerkraut over rolls; pour remaining soup diluted with equal amount of water over rolls and bake for 1$^1/_2$ hours at 350°. Makes 25 Cabbage Rolls.

Unser Tagelich Brot (The Staff of Life III)

Meat Medley Spaghetti Sauce for a Crowd

One of my originals, guaranteed to please. Choose one or all of the meats suggested for a rich, delicious sauce and entrée.

MEATBALLS:

5 pounds lean ground beef	$^1/_2$ teaspoon black pepper
2 cups dry or soft bread crumbs	1 teaspoon fresh or dry basil
$^1/_2$ cup finely chopped fresh parsley	1 teaspoon fresh or dry oregano
	2 tablespoons grated Parmesan
4 eggs, well beaten	3 tablespoons granulated garlic
1 teaspoon salt	

Combine all ingredients and mix well. Shape into $1^1/_2$-inch balls. Brown or boil until fully cooked, then add to Simmering Sauce.

SIMMERING SAUCE:

5 cloves garlic, crushed	$1^1/_2$ teaspoons black pepper
$^3/_4$ cup olive oil	2 teaspoons fresh or dry oregano
3 (32-ounce) cans tomato sauce	
6 (6-ounce) cans tomato paste	4 teaspoons fresh or dry basil
1–$1^1/_2$ cans of water	5 pounds spaghetti or pasta of choice
4 tablespoons salt	

Lightly sauté garlic in oil over medium heat. Add tomato sauce, tomato paste, and water. Stir well and add all seasonings. Bring to simmer over medium heat, stirring often. Add precooked meat and allow to cook for $1^1/_2$ hours. Serve over cooked pasta and top with freshly grated Parmesan.

CHICKEN VARIATION:
Lightly brown 4–6 chicken breast halves before adding to Simmering Sauce.

PEPPERONI VARIATION:
Use large sticks that are about 1 inch in diameter. Cut into 2-inch pieces before adding to Simmering Sauce.

PORK VARIATION:
Small rack ribs cut into 2 bones each, or 4–6 boneless pork chops. Lightly brown before adding to Simmering Sauce.

Cooking with Irene!

Nana's Meatballs

These are the best meatballs I've ever had. My mother-in-law always makes them for me when I'm home or when she visits.

$^1/_2$ pound ground Italian sausage (mild)
$^1/_4$ pound ground veal
$^1/_4$ pound ground pork
1 pound lean ground beef
2 eggs, beaten
$^1/_4$ cup chopped parsley

$^1/_2$ cup Parmesan cheese
1 cup Italian seasoned bread crumbs
Garlic salt and oregano to taste
2 (15$^1/_2$-ounce) jars spaghetti sauce
1 pound pasta, cooked

Mix all ingredients together (with your hands) except pasta. Shape into baseball-sized balls. Put in a large pot and cover with 2 jars of your favorite spaghetti sauce. Bring to a boil and quickly reduce heat to low and simmer for about 4 hours. Check to make sure meatballs aren't sticking to the bottom of the pot. Cook your favorite pasta. Drain and put on a dish. Arrange meatballs around the pasta and pour sauce on top. Sprinkle with some Parmesan cheese. Makes 12 large meatballs.

Recipe by Jamie Moyer, Pitcher, Seattle Mariners
Home Plates

Stuffed Burger Bundles

1 cup herb-seasoned stuffing
  mix
1¹/₂ pounds very lean ground
  beef
¹/₃ cup evaporated milk

1 egg
1 can mushroom soup
1 tablespoon ketchup
2 tablespoons Worcestershire
Salt and pepper to taste

Prepare stuffing mix according to package directions. Set aside. Combine meat, milk, and egg. Make 6 large patties. Put ¹/₆ of stuffing on each meat patty and wrap meat around the stuffing. Place in baking dish. Combine mushroom soup, ketchup, Worcestershire salt, and pepper. Pour over burger bundles. Cover and bake 45 minutes at 350°.

Crime Stoppers: A Community Cookbook

Stuffed Burgers

1¹/₂ pounds lean ground beef

Divide beef into 8 parts and shape into patties (do not squeeze all the juice from the beef).

FILLING:
1 (2¹/₄-ounce) can chopped
  black olives
1 green pepper, chopped
1 cup grated Cheddar cheese

1 small bunch green onions,
  chopped (including tops)
2 tablespoons mayonnaise
Hamburger buns and condiments

In a bowl mix together all ingredients except buns and condiments. Place a generous portion of filling on top of 4 single patties. Cover each with the remaining 4 patties, pressing the edges of each to secure the filling. Grill, barbeque, or broil the burgers to desired doneness.

Serve each Stuffed Burger on large hamburger buns with assorted condiments. Serves 4.

Simply Whidbey

Bar-B-Q Beef

1 pound rump roast or stew meat
1 bottle chili sauce
1 (4-ounce) can mushroom
  slices
1 onion, chopped ($^1/_4$–$^1/_2$ cup)
Salt and pepper to taste
$^1/_2$ teaspoon chili powder
1 dash cayenne pepper

Slice rump roast into 1-inch steaks and cube them. Place meat in a hot skillet to sear and brown. Put browned meat into crockpot together with other ingredients. Deglaze frying pan with $^1/_2$ cup water and add to pot. Cover and cook for 8–10 hours on LOW or 5–6 hours on HIGH. Shred meat before serving. Serve hot on steak buns.

Western Washington Oncology Cook Book

Beef Brisket

Garlic powder
1 (4- to 5-pound) beef brisket
Onion, sliced
1 bottle Heinz Chili Sauce
$^1/_2$ cup cider vinegar
8 tablespoons brown sugar
2 cups water

Sprinkle garlic powder on brisket. Mix remaining ingredients together and pour over roast. Bake at 350° for 3 hours. One hour before roast is done, put in refrigerator for about an hour, then slice. Return slices to pan with juices and cook additional hour.

Crime Stoppers: A Community Cookbook

In 1928, legislators let school children select the state bird, and the meadowlark won hands-down. However, seven other states already had chosen the same bird. Another vote was taken in 1931 by the Washington Federation of Women's Clubs. The goldfinch won. Since there were then two state birds, the Legislature decided to leave the final choice to school children once again. So in 1951, the children voted for the goldfinch, and the Legislature made it unanimous.

Barbecue Pork and Beef Sandwiches

$1^1/_2$ pounds beef for stew
$1^1/_2$ pounds pork cubes
2 cups chopped onions
3 green peppers, chopped
1 (6-ounce) can tomato paste
$1/_2$ cup packed brown sugar
$1/_4$ cup cider vinegar
$1/_4$ teaspoon chili powder
2 teaspoons salt
1 teaspoon dry mustard
2 teaspoons Worcestershire sauce
12 (6-inch-long) hard rolls
Lettuce leaves
Chopped tomato

About $8^1/_2$ hours before serving, in a $3^1/_2$- to 5-quart slow cooker, combine all ingredients, except rolls, lettuce, and tomato. Cover and cook on HIGH 8 hours. With wire whisk, stir mixture until meat is shredded.

To serve, line hard rolls with lettuce leaves; fill with meat mixture. Sprinkle with chopped tomato. Makes 12 sandwiches.

Favorite Recipes, Numerica Credit Union

Garlic Grenadine Pork Roast

3 whole garlic heads
1 teaspoon nutmeg
1 teaspoon thyme
1 (3-pound) boneless pork
   tenderloin roast, tied
2 tablespoons olive oil
1 cup grenadine syrup, divided
$^1/_3$ cup sweet vermouth

$^1/_2$ cup dried cranberries
$^1/_4$ cup orange juice
3 tablespoons minced onions
$^1/_2$ teaspoon ground ginger
2 teaspoons cornstarch
1 teaspoon water
$^1/_2$ cup sour cream (optional)
6–8 sprigs parsley for garnish

Preheat oven to 350°. Cut $^1/_2$ inch from the tops of garlic heads. Combine nutmeg with thyme and rub well into all surfaces of pork roast. Heat olive oil in heavy Dutch oven on stove top. Add pork roast and brown all sides. Place garlic heads evenly around pork roast. Move to preheated oven and bake approximately $1^1/_2$ hours until meat thermometer reads 160°.

Baste frequently during baking with $^1/_2$ cup grenadine. Mix vermouth, cranberries, orange juice, onions, ginger, $^1/_2$ cup grenadine, cornstarch, and water for sauce. When meat is done, remove to serving platter. Squeeze garlic into cooking juice, add sauce mixture (and sour cream, if using), cooking until thick. Slice pork, arrange slices on platter, top with sauce, and garnish with parsley.

Northwest Garlic Festival Cookbook

Each year around 10,000 climbers attempt to climb to the top of Mount Rainier with about 50% success.

Pork Picadillo

This is an ideal recipe for casual entertaining and fun to present. The long list of ingredients just means that it's good! It is very easy to prepare.

3¹/₂ pounds boneless pork shoulder	¹/₂ cup chili sauce
1 large onion, chopped	2 teaspoons salt
2 tablespoons butter	1 teaspoon cinnamon
2 tablespoons oil	¹/₄ teaspoon ground cumin
2 cloves garlic, minced	¹/₂ cup dried currants
2 cups tomato sauce	3 tablespoons cider vinegar
	3 tablespoons brown sugar

Cut pork into ³/₄-inch cubes. In a Dutch oven, sauté onion in butter and oil. When soft, use a slotted spoon to transfer to a large bowl. Brown meat in small batches, setting aside with onion. Return meat and onion to pan, along with remaining ingredients. Cover and simmer 45 minutes, or until meat is tender.

16 flour tortillas	Lime juice
1 bunch green onions, slivered	3 limes, cut in wedges
2 avocados, peeled and sliced	

To serve, warm tortillas in a foil packet in oven. Garnish Pork Picadillo with green onion, and provide a side dish of avocados drizzled with lime juice and surrounded with lime wedges. Placing the tortillas in a napkin-lined basket, instruct your guests to fill each with the Pork Picadillo and avocado, then a squeeze of lime juice. If you wish, provide a pot of refried beans or a platter of steaming corn-on-the-cob and green salad. Serves 8.

The Overlake School Cookbook

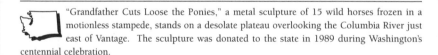

"Grandfather Cuts Loose the Ponies," a metal sculpture of 15 wild horses frozen in a motionless stampede, stands on a desolate plateau overlooking the Columbia River just east of Vantage. The sculpture was donated to the state in 1989 during Washington's centennial celebration.

Mu Shu Pork

MARINADE:
1/4 cup soy sauce
2 tablespoons Marsala wine
2 teaspoons sugar

1 tablespoon dark sesame oil
Salt and pepper to taste

Mix all ingredients in a bowl for Marinade. Toss well. Set aside.

2 tablespoons peanut oil
1/4 cup fresh ginger, cut into
  thin slivers
8 scallions, cut into 2-inch
  lengths and slivered
1 small savoy cabbage, cored
  and cut thin

2 carrots, peeled and grated
10 shiitake mushroom caps,
  sliced thin
8 ounces pork tenderloin,
  trimmed and cut into thin
  strips

Heat peanut oil in large wok over high heat. Add vegetables. Cook about 5 minutes. Stir constantly until vegetables are wilted. Add pork, Marinade, and a little water. Stir constantly. Cook until pork is cooked through. Serve immediately with Asian-style pancakes and plum sauce. Serves 4–6.

Recipe by Rick Griffin, Head Trainer, Seattle Mariners
Home Plates

Sweet 'n Sours

1 1/2–2 pounds pork ribs
Salt and pepper to taste
1/2 cup pineapple tidbits and
  juice
1 cup beef bouillon (2 cubes in
  1 cup hot water)

2 tablespoons soy sauce
1/2 cup white vinegar
1/4 cup sugar
2 1/2 tablespoons cornstarch
1/2 cup cold water

Cut ribs into 1-inch slices. In oven, heat ribs at 350° until cooked and grease is melted out; drain. Season to taste. Mix pineapple, bouillon, soy sauce, vinegar, and sugar together, thicken with cornstarch premixed in cold water; heat thoroughly. Add ribs. Serve over cooked rice and/or with vegetables.

McNamee Family & Friends Cookbook

Sautéed Apples and Pork

$^{1}/_{2}$ cup plus 1 tablespoon flour, unsifted, divided
$^{1}/_{2}$ teaspoon salt, divided
$^{1}/_{2}$ teaspoon ground black pepper, divided
4 (3-ounce) boneless, lean pork steaks
3 tablespoons butter or margarine, divided
2 tablespoons vegetable oil
2 Granny Smith apples, peeled, cored, sliced
2 tablespoons minced onion
1 cup apple juice
$^{1}/_{2}$ cup dry white wine
$^{1}/_{2}$ cup plain yogurt
2 tablespoons Dijon mustard
$^{1}/_{4}$ teaspoon dried thyme leaves

In pie plate or shallow dish, combine $^{1}/_{2}$ cup flour, $^{1}/_{4}$ teaspoon salt, and $^{1}/_{4}$ teaspoon pepper; mix well. Dredge pork steaks in flour mixture to coat lightly. In large skillet, heat 2 tablespoons butter and the oil over medium heat; add pork and cook until brown on both sides and juices run clear. Remove pork to heated platter and reserve.

Add remaining butter to skillet, sauté apples and onions until both are tender. Remove to platter with pork. Add apple juice and wine to skillet; simmer 5 minutes. Combine yogurt, mustard, thyme, and remaining flour, salt and pepper; stir into juice mixture. Simmer 5 minutes, stirring until smooth. Spoon sauce over pork steaks and apples and serve. Serves 4.

Recipe by Washington Apple Commission, Wenatchee
Washington Cook Book

Stuffed Pork Chops

4 pork rib chops (1$^{1}/_{2}$ inches thick)
2 cups soft bread crumbs
1$^{1}/_{2}$ teaspoons poultry seasoning
$^{1}/_{4}$ teaspoon celery salt
$^{1}/_{4}$ teaspoon onion salt
$^{1}/_{3}$ teaspoon salt
2 tablespoons chopped onion
2 tablespoons butter, melted
$^{3}/_{4}$ cup water, divided
2 tablespoons fat

Cut through lean part of each chop to form pocket. Combine bread crumbs, poultry seasoning, celery salt, onion salt, and salt. Sauté onion in melted butter. Add to crumb mixture along with $^{1}/_{4}$ cup water. Stuff each chop and close with toothpicks. Brown chops in hot fat in heavy skillet. Add $^{1}/_{2}$ cup hot water; cover. Bake 1 hour.

Recipes to Remember

Oven Barbecue Pork Chops

$^1/_2$ cup water
$^1/_4$ cup sweet pickle juice or
  vinegar
2 tablespoons sugar
1 tablespoon prepared mustard
$1^1/_2$ teaspoons salt
$^1/_4$ teaspoon pepper

1 cup catsup
2 tablespoons Worcestershire
  sauce
1 teaspoon liquid smoke
6 boneless lean pork chops
6 lemon slices
6 onion slices

Bring water, sweet pickle juice or vinegar, sugar, mustard, salt, and pepper to a boil, simmer for 20 minutes. Add catsup, Worcestershire sauce, and liquid smoke; return to boil. Place pork chops in single layer in a 9x13-inch baking dish. Place lemon and onion slice over each chop. Pour $^1/_2$ of sauce over top. Bake at 325° for $1^1/_2$ hours, basting occasionally with remaining sauce.

Western Washington Oncology Cook Book

Huckleberry Pork Chops

Vegetable cooking spray
6 center-cut loin pork chops
  (about 2 pounds), trimmed
  of fat
Freshly ground black pepper

3 tablespoons huckleberry jam
  or black currant preserves
$1^1/_2$ tablespoons Dijon mustard
$^1/_4$ cup raspberry or white
  wine vinegar

Coat a large frying pan with cooking spray and place over medium-high heat. Sprinkle pork chops generously with pepper, add to pan and brown on both sides, turning once, 8–10 minutes total.

Combine jam and mustard and spoon over chops. Reduce heat to medium-low, cover, and cook an additional 6–8 minutes or until chops are thoroughly cooked but still moist and slightly pink in center. Remove chops to a platter and keep warm.

Add vinegar to pan, increase heat to medium-high, and stir to loosen any browned bits. Bring sauce to a boil and cook, uncovered, until reduced to $^1/_4$ cup, about 2–3 minutes. Spoon sauce over chops and serve immediately. Serves 6.

Gold'n Delicious

Curried Lamb Chops

The following recipe is from Bruce and Heather Hebert, owners and chefs of the Patit Creek Restaurant in Dayton. Their restaurant has received many plaudits and awards and this recipe is a winner! Sheep farms are found throughout the state; several are in southeast Washington.

1 tablespoon olive oil
4–6 loin lamb chops
Salt and pepper
$^1/_2$ teaspoon minced garlic
2 tablespoons brandy
$^1/_2$ cup dry red wine
1 cup beef stock

1 teaspoon curry powder
$^1/_2$ teaspoon dried mint or 2
   teaspoons chopped fresh mint
2 tablespoons butter
Extra chopped fresh mint to
   sprinkle on top (optional)

Heat olive oil in a large frying pan. Add lamb chops and sauté over medium heat until done (about 5 minutes per side for medium). Remove chops from pan, add salt and pepper, and keep warm on heated platter. Cover loosely with foil.

Remove most of the oil from the pan and add garlic. Sauté garlic for a minute over medium heat then add brandy and red wine. Bring to a boil over high heat then add beef stock, curry powder, and mint. Boil until thick and syrupy. Remove pan from heat and whisk in butter. Serve sauce with lamb chops. Sprinkle with minced fresh mint, if desired. Serves 2.

Wandering & Feasting

Lopez Lamb Curry

Lopez Island offers serene, pastoral views of sheep grazing on gently sloping fields. Chicken or prawns can be substitutes for lamb in this aromatic, spicy dish. Serve on scented Jasmine rice for additional flavor.

2 tablespoons extra-virgin
  olive oil
$1/2$ cup chopped onion
2 cloves garlic, minced
1 tablespoon minced fresh
  ginger
1 tablespoon ground coriander
1 teaspoon ground cumin
$1/2$ teaspoon ground cardamom
$1/2$ teaspoon turmeric
$1/4$ teaspoon cayenne pepper
$1^1/2$ pounds lamb shoulder,
  cut into 1-inch pieces

$1^1/2$ cups chicken stock
$1/2$ cup tomato purée
1 cinnamon stick
1 teaspoon salt
$1/4$ teaspoon freshly ground
  pepper
$1/2$ cup yogurt
6 cups cooked Jasmine rice
Toasted coconut, golden
  raisins, chutney, and peanuts
  for condiments

In a large frying pan, heat oil over medium heat. Sauté onion, garlic, and spices until onions are tender, about 5 minutes. Add lamb and sauté until lightly browned on all sides, about 10–15 minutes. Add remaining ingredients, except yogurt, rice, and condiments. Cover pan with lid ajar and simmer curry for 30–40 minutes. While curry is cooking, prepare rice.

Discard cinnamon stick. Just before serving, remove pan from heat and stir in yogurt. Serve curry over rice and offer bowls of condiments at the table. Serves 4.

San Juan Classics II Cookbook

Nearly 100 Orca whales, in three family pods, reside in the water off the San Juan Islands during the summer months

Venison Roast

1 (3- to 4-pound) venison roast
3 tablespoons fat or shortening
1 package dry onion soup mix
1 can cream of mushroom soup
1 bacon strip

$1^1/2$ teaspoons salt
$^1/2$ teaspoon cracked pepper
1 garlic clove, minced
2 cups water

Place venison in large pot or Dutch oven and brown quickly in fat on all sides. Put onion soup, mushroom soup, bacon strip, salt, pepper, and garlic on top of venison. Add water; let cook for 2 hours or until it is tender. Yields 10 servings.

The Wild and Free Cookbook

Roast Venison

1 venison roast
1 clove garlic, sliced
Salt and pepper
$^1/4$ cup water

1 large onion, sliced
1 can mushroom soup, undiluted
1 package onion soup mix

Make slits in meat (top, sides, and bottom). Stuff with garlic slices. Sprinkle with salt and pepper. Put water in roaster with a few slices of onion. Put roast on top of onions and cover with mushroom soup. Sprinkle onion soup mix over top. Add more slices of onion around roast. Cover tightly. Roast at 350° for about $2^1/2$ hours. If liquid boils, turn down to 300°. Check for doneness at about 2 hours, according to the way you like it. This makes its own gravy.

Taste of the Methow

POULTRY

More than 400 bald eagles descend on the upper Skagit River in Northwestern Washington each winter to feast on spawned-out chum salmon, making the area one of the most important winter habitats for eagles in the lower 48 states.

Chicken Breasts Pierre

Serve with pan sauces, crusty French bread and a tossed green salad.

$^1/_4$ cup all-purpose flour
$1^1/_2$ teaspoons salt, divided
1 pinch ground black pepper
6 skinless, boneless chicken
   breast halves
3 tablespoons butter
1 ($14^1/_2$-ounce) can stewed
   tomatoes, with liquid
$^1/_2$ cup water
2 tablespoons brown sugar

2 tablespoons distilled white
   vinegar
2 tablespoons Worcestershire
   sauce
2 teaspoons chili powder
1 teaspoon dry mustard
$^1/_2$ teaspoon celery seed
1 clove garlic, minced
$^1/_8$ teaspoon hot pepper sauce

In a shallow dish or bowl, combine flour, $^1/_2$ teaspoon salt, and ground black pepper. Coat chicken breasts with flour mixture. Melt butter in a large skillet over medium heat, and brown chicken on all sides. Remove from skillet, and drain on paper towels.

In the same skillet, combine tomatoes, water, brown sugar, vinegar, and Worcestershire sauce. Season with salt, chili powder, mustard, celery seed, garlic, and hot pepper sauce. Bring to a boil; reduce heat, and return chicken to skillet. Cover, and simmer for 35–40 minutes, or until chicken is tender, no longer pink, and juices run clear. Makes 6 servings.

Allrecipes Tried & True Favorites

Chicken Breasts Stuffed with Cream Cheese, Crab, Mushrooms, and Sherry

This dish can be made ahead, refrigerated, then baked before serving.

3 tablespoons butter or margarine, divided
2 cups chopped mushrooms, divided
Salt and freshly ground pepper
3 ounces softened cream cheese, regular or light
$^1/_2$ cup crab meat
2 tablespoons sherry
1 teaspoon dried thyme, divided

8 large chicken breast halves, skinned and boned
3 tablespoons all-purpose flour
$^1/_2$ cup chicken stock or canned broth
$^1/_2$ cup milk
$^1/_2$ cup dry white wine
1 cup grated Swiss cheese
2 tablespoons minced parsley

Preheat oven to 325°, unless baking later. Melt 1 tablespoon butter in a medium skillet over medium heat; add $^1/_2$ cup chopped mushrooms and cook until tender. Season with salt and pepper, remove from heat, and combine with cream cheese, crab, sherry, and $^1/_2$ teaspoon thyme; set aside.

Pound each chicken breast half until $^1/_4$ inch thick. (Covering with waxed paper before pounding is helpful.) Season lightly with salt and pepper. Spoon mushroom mixture onto chicken pieces. Wrap chicken around filling and place, seam down, in lightly greased baking dish large enough to hold all rolls. Set aside.

Melt remaining 2 tablespoons butter in skillet over medium heat and sauté remaining $1^1/_2$ cups mushrooms until juices evaporate. Stir in flour and reserved $^1/_2$ teaspoon thyme; blend in stock, milk, and wine. Cook, stirring, until sauce thickens, and season with salt and pepper. Pour sauce over rolled chicken pieces. (Dish may be refrigerated at this time, then taken out about $^1/_2$ hour before baking.) Sprinkle with cheese. Bake, uncovered, for $1^1/_2$ hours. Sprinkle with parsley and serve. Serves 4 with 2 breasts; 8 with 1 breast each.

Wandering & Feasting

Amaretto Chicken

4 large chicken breasts, boned
  and skinned
Italian-seasoned bread crumbs
Butter or margarine
1 cup orange juice

$^1/_2$ cup amaretto liquor
2 teaspoons cornstarch
2 teaspoons brown sugar
Parsley
Orange, thinly sliced

Pound and cut chicken into 2x3-inch pieces. Shake in bread crumbs and brown in butter or margarine. Place in a 9x13-inch baking dish. Mix other ingredients together (except parsley and orange) and pour over chicken. Bake uncovered at 350° for about 45 minutes. Garnish with parsley and thinly sliced orange. Serves 4–6.

Extraordinary Cuisine for Sea & Shore

Chicken Braised in Wine

6 boneless, skinless chicken
  breasts
$^1/_4$ cup all-purpose flour
1 tablespoon butter
1 onion, sliced
4 green onions, finely chopped
1 garlic clove, finely chopped
3 carrots, thinly sliced

1 tablespoon chopped parsley
$^1/_4$ teaspoon thyme
$^1/_4$ teaspoon oregano
$^1/_4$ teaspoon salt (lite)
2 bay leaves
1 cup white wine
1 (4-ounce) can mushrooms,
  drained

Coat chicken thoroughly with flour. Set aside. Combine butter, onions, garlic, and carrots in a 3-quart casserole. Place chicken pieces on top. Sprinkle with parsley, thyme, oregano, and salt. Add bay leaves and wine. Cover and bake 45 minutes at 350°, stirring once. Add mushrooms. Cover and bake for 15 more minutes, until chicken and carrots are tender. Remove bay leaves before serving. Serves 6.

Recipe by Dave Niehaus, Voice of the Mariners, Seattle Mariners
Mariners Mix'n and Fix'n Grand Slam Style

Indian Chicken

$^1/_2$ cup chopped onion	Pinch of freshly ground pepper
6 cloves garlic	$^1/_4$ teaspoon ground cardamom
2 teaspoons grated ginger	1 pound chicken (light meat),
$^1/_2$ teaspoon cumin	skinned and cut into pieces
1 teaspoon chili powder	1 lemon, juiced

In food processor, combine onion, garlic, and spices together. Blend until a smooth paste occurs. Coat chicken with paste. Make small cuts into chicken and squeeze lemon over chicken (if you are a garlic lover, extra garlic can be put into the sliced chicken). Roast chicken at 400° for 30–40 minutes, or until done. Baste often with juice. Yields 4 servings.

Nutritional profile per serving: Calories 217; Prot. 35.7g; Carb. 5.3g; Fat 5.3g; Sat. Fat 1.2g; Chol. 97.3mg; Fiber 0.3g; Sod. 94.5mg.

The Ingredients: Fresh Pacific Northwest Cuisine

Chicken Piccata

4 boneless, skinless split	4 teaspoons oil
chicken breasts	1 tablespoon butter
1 cup flour	1 tablespoon chopped basil
1 teaspoon garlic powder	1 tablespoon lemon juice
$^1/_2$ teaspoon salt	2 teaspoons white wine
$^1/_4$ teaspoon white pepper	

Flatten chicken breasts between 2 sheets of plastic wrap. Coat chicken with flour, garlic powder, salt, and pepper. Sauté each breast in 1 teaspoon oil in nonstick skillet. Keep warm in 200° oven. In same skillet, melt 1 tablespoon butter; add basil. When butter bubbles, splash with lemon juice and wine. Pour over warm chicken breasts. Serve with rice or pasta and a good salad.

Recipes to Remember

Chicken/Mushroom Stroganoff

2 chicken breasts, skinned and
  boned
1 cup diced carrots
1/2 cup chopped onions
2 garlic cloves, minced
2 cups mushrooms
1 tablespoon water

1/2 cup nonfat cottage cheese
2 tablespoons nonfat sour cream
2 tablespoons Dijon mustard
1 tablespoon soy sauce (low
  sodium)
3 cups eggless noodles, cooked
  in water

Wrap chicken, carrots, onions, and garlic in aluminum foil. Place in oven and bake at 375° for 30 minutes. While chicken is cooking, sauté mushrooms in large skillet, using 1 tablespoon of water. Place cottage cheese, sour cream, and mustard in blender and blend until smooth. Cut cooked chicken into strips, and place in large bowl. Add vegetables, cottage cheese mixture, and soy sauce; mix well. Serve over noodles. Makes 4 servings.

From My Heart For Yours

Crispy Parmesan Chicken Strips

1 1/2 cups seasoned croutons,
  crushed
1 1/2 ounces (1/3 cup) fresh
  Parmesan cheese, grated
1 teaspoon dried parsley
1/4 teaspoon garlic salt

2 egg whites
1 tablespoon water
1 pound boneless, skinless
  chicken breast, cut into 1-inch
  pieces
1/4 cup ranch dressing

Preheat oven to 450°. Combine croutons, cheese, parsley, and salt. Whisk egg whites and water. Dip chicken pieces into egg mixture, then into crumb mixture. Place on baking sheet. Bake 14–16 minutes, or until chicken is no longer pink inside. Serve with ranch dressing.

Taste of Balboa

Citrus Cilantro Chicken

A frequent visitor to the Valley introduced me to this low-fat, high-flavor dish.

MARINADE:

1/2 cup fresh lemon juice	4 cloves garlic, minced
1/2 cup fresh lime juice	1 bunch cilantro, chopped
1/2 cup fresh orange juice	1/2 teaspoon fresh-ground
1/4 cup dry white wine	pepper
1/4 cup olive oil	5 bay leaves

Combine and let set for 1/2 hour so flavors blend.

6 chicken breasts, boned and skinned

Place chicken breasts in Marinade, turn to coat, and refrigerate for 2 hours. Preheat oven to 350°. Drain and reserve Marinade. Lay chicken in shallow baking dish. Bake 45 minutes to 1 hour, basting with Marinade at least once to keep chicken juicy. (Or broil chicken, if you prefer.)

Serve with steamed rice and Rhubarb-Mango Chutney, a green salad, and fresh-baked bread.

RHUBARB-MANGO CHUTNEY:

3 cups thinly sliced fresh rhubarb	1 1/2 tablespoons grated fresh ginger
1 large ripe mango, peeled and chopped	3/4 cup dark brown sugar
4 green onions, chopped	1/3 cup chopped blanched almonds
1/2 cup raspberry vinegar	1 cup raisins
1/8 teaspoon cayenne	

Combine first 4 ingredients in saucepan. Bring to a boil and simmer on low heat for 15 minutes. Add cayenne, ginger, sugar, and nuts; simmer for 15 more minutes. Add raisins and continue simmering until chutney has jam-like consistency, about 25 minutes. Serve warm or cold with steamed brown or white rice.

Skagit Valley Fare

Picante Chicken Casserole

4 chicken breast halves

1 can cream of mushroom soup, condensed

1 can cream of chicken soup, condensed

1 can chili without beans

4 ounces picante sauce

1 small onion, chopped

12 corn tortillas, cut into 1-inch pieces

8 ounces Cheddar cheese, shredded

8 ounces Monterey Jack cheese, shredded

Place chicken in deep saucepan and add 2 cups water. Cover pan and simmer about 45 minutes or until chicken is fork-tender. Cool and remove meat from bones. Cut into bite-size pieces. Mix together with soups, chili, picante sauce, and onion. In 3-quart casserole, layer half of the tortillas, sauce, and cheese. Repeat for second layer. Refrigerate overnight to allow for flavors to blend and tortillas to soften.

Cover and bake in a 350° oven for 45 minutes to 1 hour or until bubbly and lightly browned. Let stand for 5 minutes before serving.

Variation: All ingredients can be mixed together in large bowl and then placed into casserole dish. Tortillas soften better this way than in layers. Save some grated cheese to place on top, and you are done.

Harvest Feast

Lemon Chicken in the Crockpot

2–3 whole chicken breasts,
  skinned
$^1/_2$ teaspoon salt
$^1/_4$ teaspoon pepper
$^1/_2$ teaspoon paprika

1 can cream of chicken soup
$^1/_2$ cup white wine
2 tablespoons chopped onion
3 ounces sliced mushrooms
1 teaspoon grated lemon peel

Lay breasts on bottom of pot. Sprinkle with salt, pepper, and paprika. In bowl, combine remaining ingredients and pour over. Cover and cook slowly 5–6 hours.

Heavenly Fare

Chicken Enchiladas

2 cans cream of chicken soup
$^1/_2$ pint sour cream
Pinch garlic powder
Cumin to taste
1 can diced green chiles
Chili powder to taste
1 dozen corn tortillas
2–3 cooked chicken breasts,
  shredded

$^1/_2$ onion, diced
$^1/_4$ pound grated Jack or
  Cheddar cheese (or more)
Chopped parsley for garnish
Chopped green onions for
  garnish

Mix chicken soup, sour cream, garlic powder, cumin, green chiles, and chili powder in bowl. Put some (about $^1/_3$) of soup mixture on bottom of baking pan so the enchiladas won't stick. Fry tortillas, 1 at a time, in hot oil until limp only. Remove excess oil by blotting with paper towels. Fill tortillas with chicken and about 1 tablespoon or so of soup mixture. Add some diced onion and some cheese; roll tortilla. Spread remaining soup mixture over rolled tortillas in baking dish. Sprinkle cheese over enchiladas. Bake $^1/_2$ hour at 350°. You can sprinkle parsley or chopped green onions for extra touch.

Your Favorite Recipes

Chicken Fajitas

$^1/_4$ cup dry white wine
$^1/_4$ cup lime juice
1 clove garlic, minced
2 tablespoons chopped cilantro
1 tablespoon vegetable oil
1 teaspoon chili powder
$^1/_2$ teaspoon salt
$^1/_2$ teaspoon grated lime peel
1 pound boneless, skinless
  chicken breasts
6 flour tortillas

Combine wine, lime juice, garlic, cilantro, oil, chili powder, salt, and lime peel; mix well. Marinate chicken 1–2 hours in covered shallow bowl in refrigerator. Broil or grill chicken until juices run clear. Wrap tortillas in aluminum foil and bake at 300° for 5 minutes or until warm. Thinly slice chicken and wrap in tortillas with choice of Condiments. Makes 6 servings.

CONDIMENTS:

3 cups vertically sliced onion,
  green pepper and red pepper,
  sautéed until tender
1 cup prepared guacamole
1 cup prepared salsa
1 cup dairy sour cream
$^1/_2$ cup minced green onions

Per Serving: Calories 200; Prot. 20g; Fat 4g; Sat. Fat 1g; Carb. 21g; Chol. 44mg; Sod. 368 mg.

The Chicken Cookbook

Chicken Satay with Peanut Sauce

2 whole fryer breasts, skinned
  and boned
1/4 cup soy sauce
1/4 cup dry white wine

1 tablespoon honey
1 tablespoon grated fresh
  gingerroot
Peanut Dipping Sauce

Flatten chicken breasts and slice into strips about 1 inch wide. Thread on skewers and place in shallow pan. Combine soy sauce, wine, honey, and ginger; pour over chicken and marinate 30 minutes, turning occasionally to coat. Drain; broil or grill until chicken is cooked and juices run clear when cut. Serve warm with Peanut Dipping Sauce. Makes 4–6 servings.

PEANUT DIPPING SAUCE:
1/2 cup peanut butter
1/4 cup unsweetened coconut
  milk
2 tablespoons soy sauce
1 tablespoon honey

2 tablespoons minced fresh
  cilantro
1 clove garlic, minced
1/8 teaspoon hot pepper sauce

Combine all ingredients until well blended. Makes about 3/4 cup.

Per serving without sauce: Calories 103; Prot. 15g; Fat 1g; Carb. 7g; Chol. 34mg; Sod. 1094 mg. Sauce per tablespoon: Calories 80; Prot. 3g; Fat 7g; Sat. Fat 2g; Carb. 4g; Chol. 0mg; Sod. 225 mg.

The Chicken Cookbook

Golden Nuggets

3 whole fryer breasts
1 egg, slightly beaten
1/2 cup water
1/4 teaspoon salt

2 teaspoons sesame seeds
1/2 cup flour
1 quart salad oil

Skin and bone chicken and cut into 1x2-inch pieces. Mix egg, water, salt, seeds, and flour. Dip pieces into batter, letting excess drain. Pour oil in frying pan, making sure it is no more than 1/3-full. Heat to medium. Add 4–5 pieces at a time. Fry 3–5 minutes until golden brown.

Recipes to Remember

Eddy's Chicken Kiev

An easier, different approach to this ever-popular entrée . . . so good that it starred in the menu for "Dinner for Ten," an Overlake School auction item.

4 whole chicken breasts, boned
  and skinned
¹/₂ pound butter
¹/₂ cup chopped parsley
¹/₂ cup chopped green onion

4 ounces Monterey Jack cheese
8 thin slices ham
2 eggs, beaten
1¹/₂ cups fine bread crumbs

Preheat oven to 350°. Cut chicken pieces in half and place between 2 sheets of wax paper. Pound with a mallet until uniformly ¹/₄ inch thick. Melt butter over low heat, adding parsley and green onions. Cut cheese into 3x¹/₂-inch sticks. With breasts smooth-side down, top each with a ham slice and piece of cheese. Roll up, tucking in ends, and secure with toothpicks.

Dip breasts in beaten eggs and roll in crumbs. Place, seam-side-down, in ungreased, shallow 8x12-inch casserole. Pour butter mixture over all. Bake, uncovered, at 350° for 45 minutes, basting several times. Serves 4–6.

The Overlake School Cookbook

On November 24, 1971, Dan "D. B." Cooper boarded a flight from Portland to Seattle, hijacked the plane, and demanded a $200,000 ransom. After receiving the money in Seattle, Cooper let all but four of the crew members off the plane before asking the pilot to fly to Mexico City via Reno. Less than 5 minutes into the flight, he jumped from the rear stairway and parachuted into the forest on the border of Clark and Cowlitz counties, near Ariel. He has never been seen again. Years later, some of his loot was discovered in the Columbia River. However, the disappearance of D. B. Cooper is one of the great unsolved mysteries of the 20th century.

Pacific Stir-Fry with Herbed Barley

1¹/₂ pounds Washington-grown chicken parts, skinned and boned
4 tablespoons soy sauce, divided
2 tablespoons sherry wine
1 clove garlic, minced
1 tablespoon cornstarch
1 tablespoon grated fresh gingerroot
4 tablespoons vegetable oil, divided
1 medium onion, sliced
1 medium green or red bell pepper, seeded and sliced
2 ribs celery, sliced diagonally
2 medium carrots, sliced
1 cup sliced zucchini or broccoli
1 cup sliced shiitake or brown mushrooms
¹/₂ cup sliced water chestnuts
Herbed Barley

Slice chicken into strips. Combine 2 tablespoons soy sauce with sherry, garlic, cornstarch and gingerroot. Pour over chicken and marinate 15 minutes. Heat 2 tablespoons oil in wok or deep-sided skillet. Add chicken and stir-fry quickly just until no pink. Remove chicken from pan. Add remaining oil and heat. Add onion, green pepper, celery, carrots, and zucchini. Stir-fry 2–3 minutes. Return chicken to pan along with mushrooms, water chestnuts, and remaining soy sauce. Continue to stir-fry until vegetables are crisp-tender. Serve over Herbed Barley. Makes 4–6 servings.

HERBED BARLEY:
1 cup pearl barley
3 cups seasoned chicken broth
¹/₄ cup minced parsley or 2 tablespoons chopped cilantro

Combine barley with broth. Bring to boil. Cover, reduce heat and simmer 45 minutes or until tender. Toss with minced parsley or cilantro. Makes 3 cups.

Per Serving: Calories 626; Prot. 49g; Fat 21g; Sat. Fat 3g; Carb. 60g; Chol. 120mg; Sod. 1819mg.

The Chicken Cookbook

Salsa Couscous Chicken

3 cups hot cooked couscous or
rice, cooked as package directs
1 tablespoon olive or vegetable
oil
$1/4$–$1/2$ cup coarsely chopped
almonds
2 cloves garlic, minced
8 chicken thighs, skin removed

1 cup salsa
$1/4$ cup water
2 tablespoons dried currants or
raisins
1 tablespoon honey
$3/4$ teaspoon cumin
$1/2$ teaspoon cinnamon

While couscous is cooking, heat oil in large skillet over medium-high
heat until hot. Add almonds; cook 1–2 minutes, or until golden
brown. Remove almonds from skillet with slotted spoon; set aside.
Add garlic to skillet; cook and stir 30 seconds. Add chicken; cook
4–5 minutes, until browned, turning once. In medium bowl, combine salsa and all remaining ingredients; mix well. Add to chicken;
mix well. Reduce heat to medium, cover and cook 20 minutes, or
until chicken is fork-tender and juices run clear, stirring occasionally. Stir in almonds. Serve chicken mixture with couscous.

Your Favorite Recipes

Chicken Supreme

8 chicken thighs or chicken
breasts halves
2 medium onions, sliced very
thin

Salt and pepper to taste
2 ($10^{1}/2$-ounce) cans cream of
mushroom soup
$3/4$ cup dry white wine

Place half of chicken on bottom of 9x13-inch casserole dish. Cover
with half the onions. Season to taste. Blend soup and wine and pour
half over mixture of onions and chicken. Repeat layers as before.
Bake uncovered at 300° for $1^{1}/2$–2 hours. Serve with rice. This will
serve 6 nicely.

Our Burnt Offerings

Comforting Chicken

1 medium onion, sliced
$^1/_2$ cup butter
1 (3- to 4-pound) chicken, cut up
4 medium potatoes, peeled and
  quartered

4 medium carrots, quartered
1 cup whipping cream
1 tablespoon minced parsley
$^1/_2$ teaspoon salt
$^1/_4$ teaspoon pepper

In a large skillet, sauté onion in butter until tender. Remove with a slotted spoon and set aside. In the same pan, brown chicken pieces on all sides. Return onion to pan; add potatoes and carrots. Cover and cook over low heat 30 minutes or until vegetables are tender. Stir in cream, parsley, salt, and pepper. Reduce heat; simmer, uncovered 15 minutes or until slightly thickened. Serves 4.

Western Washington Oncology Cook Book

Chicken Marbella

4 (2$^1/_2$-pound) chickens,
  quartered
1 head garlic, peeled and
  puréed
$^1/_4$ cup dried oregano
Salt and pepper to taste
$^1/_2$ cup red wine vinegar
$^1/_2$ cup olive oil
1 cup pitted prunes

$^1/_2$ cup pitted Spanish green
  olives
$^1/_2$ cup capers with a bit of juice
6 bay leaves
1 cup brown sugar
1 cup white wine
$^1/_4$ cup finely chopped Italian
  parsley or fresh cilantro

In a large bowl, combine chicken quarters, garlic, oregano, salt, pepper, vinegar, olive oil, prunes, olives, capers and juice, and bay leaves. Cover and marinate, refrigerated, overnight.

Preheat oven to 350°. Arrange chicken in a shallow pan and spoon marinade over it evenly. Sprinkle chicken with brown sugar and pour white wine around them. Bake for 50 minutes to 1 hour, basting frequently with juices. Transfer chicken, prunes, olives, and capers to serving platter. Moisten with a few spoonfuls of pan juices and sprinkle generously with parsley or cilantro. Pass the remaining juices around in a sauce boat. Serve over hot rice. Serves 10–12.

Favorite Recipes from Our Best Cooks

Poule Lah-Nee

1 (20-ounce) can pineapple
tidbits, drained, reserve liquid
1 (6-ounce) can pink grapefruit
juice
2 tablespoons cornstarch
1 tablespoon finely shaved fresh
gingerroot
1 tablespoon minced onion
$^1/_2$ cup chopped macadamia
nuts (unsalted)

$^1/_4$ cup flour
$1^1/_2$ teaspoons Accent Flavor
Enhancer
1 teaspoon salt
$^1/_8$ teaspoon white pepper
1 broiler-fryer chicken, cut in
serving pieces
$^1/_4$ cup Mazola corn oil

Stir together pineapple liquid and grapefruit juice in a saucepan.
Stir cornstarch into $^1/_4$ cup of the juice; return to pan over medium
heat, stirring to blend. Add ginger, onion, and nuts. Bring to boil,
stirring constantly, and boil 1 minute or until thickened, then stir in
pineapple.

In plastic bag, mix together flour, Accent, salt, and pepper. Drop
a few pieces of chicken at a time into bag, rotating to coat well. Heat
corn oil in large heavy skillet over medium heat. Add chicken and
brown, turning as needed. Remove pieces as browned and place in
a large baking dish. Pour sauce over chicken. Bake at 325° for 45
minutes or until chicken is done. Makes 4 servings.

Nautical Niceaty's from Spokane Yacht Club

Barbecued Chicken

1 (8-ounce) bottle Russian
dressing
1 envelope dry onion soup mix

1 cup water
1 whole cut-up chicken

Mix dressing, soup mix, and water together and simmer for 10 minutes. Pour over chicken and put in refrigerator for 1 hour or
overnight. Bake at 350° for 40 minutes; turn over and bake 15 more
minutes.

A Taste of Heaven

Basil Tamari Chicken

1 cup wheat-free tamari (or soy sauce)
1 cup white wine
$\frac{1}{2}$ cup ketchup
1 tablespoon dry basil, or $\frac{1}{4}$ cup chopped fresh basil

4 cloves garlic, crushed, or 1 teaspoon powder
2–3 pounds chicken pieces, skinned, fat removed

Mix all ingredients except chicken in a bowl large enough to hold and cover chicken. Place chicken in bowl. Allow to soak for 4–10 hours. Make sure all meat is covered by marinade. Place chicken and marinade in a glass baking dish. Bake at 350° for 45–55 minutes, basting or turning meat several times. Serve with pasta or rice and spinach salad.

Taste of the Methow

Savory Chicken Squares

This is a great luncheon dish.

1 (3-ounce) package cream
  cheese, softened
2 tablespoons milk
2 tablespoons chopped onion
3 tablespoons margarine, melted
2 cups cooked cubed chicken

$^1/_4$ teaspoon garlic salt
$^1/_4$ teaspoon pepper
1 (8-ounce) tube refrigerated
  crescent rolls
Seasoned bread crumbs

Preheat oven to 350°. Blend cream cheese and milk until smooth. Sauté onion in margarine. Mix chicken, seasonings, onion, and cream cheese mixture together; stir well. Separate the dough into 4 rectangles, press perforation to seal. Spoon meat mixture on crescent dough, fold up corners, and seal. Brush tops with remaining melted margarine and sprinkle with seasoned bread crumbs. Bake on ungreased cookie sheet 20–25 minutes, or until golden.

Recipes from Our Friends

Cheesy Chicken Casserole

2 cups milk
2 (8-ounce) packages cream
  cheese
1$^1/_2$ cups Parmesan cheese,
  divided
1 teaspoon salt

1 teaspoon garlic salt
2 (10-ounce) packages broccoli,
  cooked and drained
6 chicken breasts, poached and
  cubed
1 can onion rings

Over medium heat, blend milk, cream cheese, $^3/_4$ cup Parmesan cheese, salt, and garlic salt. In a greased 2-quart casserole, arrange broccoli in the bottom. Pour 1 cup of heated sauce over broccoli. Arrange chicken and onion rings on top. Cover with remaining sauce. Top with remaining Parmesan. Cook at 350° for 30 minutes.

Your Favorite Recipes

White Chili Chicken

2 cups chopped onion
2 cloves garlic, minced
1 tablespoon olive oil
2 (15-ounce) cans white beans, drained
1 (14½-ounce) can chicken broth
2 (4-ounce) cans chopped green chiles

2 tablespoons Italian seasoning
4 cups cooked cubed chicken breasts
Shredded jalapeño Monterey Jack cheese
Salsa
Chopped fresh cilantro

Sauté onion and garlic in oil in 4-quart stockpot until onions are tender. Stir in beans, chicken broth, chiles, and seasoning. Bring to boil; reduce heat and simmer 10 minutes. Stir in chicken. Garnish each serving with cheese, salsa, and cilantro. Makes 6–8 servings.

Per Serving: Calories 437; Prot. 45g; Fat 8g; Sat. Fat 2g; Carb. 47g; Chol. 79mg; Sod. 298mg.

The Chicken Cookbook

Chicken and Broccoli Casserole

1 medium onion, chopped
1 tablespoon butter or margarine
2 cups cooked chicken, diced or shredded
2 cups cooked white rice
1 (10-ounce) package frozen, chopped broccoli

1 cup mayonnaise
Up to 1 teaspoon curry powder
2 teaspoons salt
¼ teaspoon pepper
2 cups grated Cheddar cheese
2 tablespoons lemon juice

Cook broccoli according to package directions; drain. Sauté onion in butter; add the chicken, rice, and cooked broccoli. In a small bowl, stir together the mayonnaise, curry powder, salt, and pepper. Gently but thoroughly, stir this sauce into the chicken and rice mixture. Spread evenly in baking dish. Cook until heated through at 350° for ½ hour. Sprinkle with cheese and lemon juice; cook, uncovered, until melted.

Your Favorite Recipes

Chicken Pot Pies

1 medium onion, chopped
$^1/_4$ cup margarine or butter
$^1/_4$ cup all-purpose flour
1 tablespoon chicken bouillon
$^1/_2$ teaspoon poultry seasoning
$^1/_8$ teaspoon pepper
2 cups milk
3 cups chopped, pre-seasoned
   and cooked chicken or turkey

1 (10-ounce) package frozen
   peas and carrots
1 (4-ounce) can sliced
   mushrooms, drained
$^1/_4$ cup snipped parsley
Salt and pepper to taste
1–2 cans Grands biscuits
1 egg with 1 teaspoon water

In a large saucepan, cook onion in butter until tender but not brown. Stir in flour, bouillon, seasoning, and pepper. Add milk. Cook and whisk until thick and bubbling.

Add chicken or turkey, peas and carrots, mushrooms, and parsley. Stir and cook until bubbling. Season with salt and pepper. Fill individual casserole dishes $^3/_4$-full with mixture. Roll out biscuits, then cover each dish with 1 biscuit. Beat egg and water and brush biscuits. Place casserole dishes on a large cookie sheet. Bake at 450° for 15–20 minutes until crust is golden brown. Makes 8 individual casseroles.

Recipe by Ken Griffey, Jr., Center Fielder, Seattle Mariners
Mariners Mix'n and Fix'n Grand Slam Style

The only father and son to hit back-to-back home runs in a major league baseball game are Ken Griffey, Jr., and his father, Ken Griffey, Sr., both of the Seattle Mariners, in a game against the California Angels on September 14, 1990.

Marvelous Turkey Meatloaf

1¹/₂ medium onions or 2 small onions, thinly sliced

2 tablespoons brown sugar

2 cups sliced and finely chopped fresh mushrooms

3 large cloves garlic, roasted and mashed

2 teaspoons dried basil

1 teaspoon dried oregano

1 tablespoon balsamic vinegar

3 pounds lean ground turkey (extra lean ground beef may be substituted)

1 cup Marlanara (see page 127)

3 large egg whites, lightly beaten

1¹/₂ cups processed onion cracker crumbs

1¹/₂ teaspoons ground black pepper

Cook onions and brown sugar in a small nonstick pan on medium-low heat for about 15 minutes (or more) to caramelize. Add mushrooms, garlic, spices, and balsamic vinegar and cook for a few more minutes. Remove from heat and drain any liquid from pan.

In a large bowl, place ground turkey, Marlanara, egg whites, processed crackers, and pepper. Mix well with hands. Add sautéed onion mixture and mix again. Divide into 2 equal portions, place in 2 sprayed/oiled loaf pans, and bake in preheated 350° oven for about 1 hour or until a meat thermometer reads 165° in the center of the meatloaf. Let cool slightly before slicing. Makes 2 loaves.

Note: If storing for future meals and quesadillas, let cool completely before slicing into ³/₄- to 1-inch slices. I usually wrap and foil 2 slices per portion for freezing so I can thaw smaller amounts as needed.

Good Food for (Mostly) Good People Cookbook

Glazed Turkey Meatballs

1 pound ground turkey
$^1/_2$ cup shredded tart apples
$^3/_4$ teaspoon salt
$^1/_8$ teaspoon garlic powder

2 teaspoons cooking oil
$^1/_2$ cup apple jelly
2 tablespoons spicy brown
   mustard

In a medium bowl, combine turkey, apple, salt, and garlic powder.
Shape into 16 meatballs. Heat oil in large skillet over medium heat.
Add meatballs, cook, and turn until brown (about 8 minutes). In
small bowl, stir together jelly and mustard. Spoon over meatballs;
simmer an additional 8–10 minutes, or until glazed. Turn meatballs
several times. Sauce will thicken as it cools.

Christmas in Washington Cook Book

Southwest Goulash

1 pound ground turkey
1 medium onion, chopped
1 tablespoon Mexican seasoning
1 teaspoon seasoned salt
Pinch pepper
1 (14$^1/_2$-ounce) can diced
   tomatoes

1 (15$^1/_4$-ounce) can whole-kernel
   corn, drained
2 (15-ounce) cans chili beans
1 (13$^1/_2$-ounce) bag Tostitos,
   crushed
2 cups Mexican-blend cheese
Salsa and sour cream

Preheat oven to 350°. Brown turkey with onions. Drain. Add
Mexican seasoning, seasoned salt, and pepper. Put into a 9x13-inch
casserole dish. Add tomatoes, corn, and beans. Mix until everything
is blended. Cover with chips and cheese. Bake for 15 minutes until
cheese is melted. Serve with salsa and sour cream. Serves 6–8.

Recipe by Mark McLemore, Infielder/Outfielder, Seattle Mariners
Home Plates

Goose with Sour Cream and Mushrooms

1 goose	4 tablespoons flour, divided
Garlic salt	$^1/_2$ teaspoon rosemary
Paprika	$^1/_4$ teaspoon thyme
$1^1/_2$ celery stalks, chopped	$1^1/_4$ teaspoons salt
1 carrot, chopped	1 cup sour cream
1 onion, chopped	1 (4-ounce) can mushrooms
4 tablespoons butter	

Preheat oven at 325°. Cut off and reserve neck and wing tips; save giblets. Season goose inside and out with garlic salt and paprika. Place on rack in shallow pan and roast, uncovered, for 1 hour or until browned and fat has cooked off.

Meanwhile, simmer neck, wing tips, and giblets in water to cover for 1 hour. Brown chopped celery, carrot, and onion in butter until soft and golden. Stir in 2 tablespoons flour, then add 1 cup giblet stock. Add rosemary, thyme, and salt. Add remaining flour to sour cream and mix well to keep it from curdling during roasting. Blend sour cream mixture into gravy. Remove goose from first roasting pan and place in deeper one. Pour gravy over goose. Drain mushrooms and add to gravy. Cover and roast for $2^1/_2$ hours or until tender. Makes 4–6 servings.

Duck Soup & Other Fowl Recipes

 In 1946, an Oregon newspaper teased Washington for not having a state tree. The Portland *Oregonian* picked out the western hemlock, but Washington newspapers decided to choose their own and selected the popular western red cedar. State Representative George Adams of Mason County pleaded with the Legislature to adopt the western hemlock. The hemlock, he said, would become "the backbone of this state's forest industry." Adams' bill passed the Legislature and was signed into law in 1947.

Duck in Red Wine

MARINADE:
2 cups red wine	2 teaspoons parsley
1/4 cup brandy	1 teaspoon salt
1 onion, sliced	1/2 teaspoon pepper
2 stalks celery, sliced	Pinch of thyme and marjoram

In a bowl, combine all ingredients for Marinade. Marinate the ducks 2–3 hours; drain, reserving Marinade.

2 ducks, cut into serving pieces	1/2 pound mushrooms, sliced
Butter	and sautéed in butter
Cornstarch	

Brown duck pieces in butter in a skillet. Add Marinade, including the sliced vegetables, and simmer over low heat until tender, about 1 hour. Remove duck pieces to a platter when done. Strain Marinade into a saucepan, thickening with cornstarch mixed in water, and stir until smooth; gently blend in with mushrooms. Makes 4 servings.

Duck Soup & Other Fowl Recipes

Citrus Duck

1 (4- to 6-pound) duck	2 chicken bouillon cubes
1/2 teaspoon salt	1 cup boiling water
Rind of 1 lime, cut into pieces	2 tablespoons fresh orange juice
Rind of 1 lemon, cut into pieces	1 tablespoon fresh lemon juice
Rind of 1 orange, cut into pieces	1 tablespoon fresh lime juice
1/2 cup orange liqueur, divided	1 tablespoon honey
1 onion, quartered	2 teaspoons cornstarch

Rub inside of duck cavity with salt. Preheat oven to 350°. Soak citrus rinds in 1/4 cup orange liqueur for at least 30 minutes. Place citrus rinds and onion and some of liqueur into cavity. Roast about 2 1/2 hours or until tender.

In the meantime, dissolve bouillon in 1 cup boiling water in a saucepan. Add 1/4 cup orange liqueur and remaining ingredients. Heat mixture over low heat until thickened. Brush duck with mixture during last half hour of roasting. Heat extra sauce; serve with duck. Makes 4 servings.

Duck Soup & Other Fowl Recipes

Duck with Apricot-Rice Stuffing

APRICOT-RICE STUFFING:

4 tablespoons diced onion	Salt and pepper
4 tablespoons diced celery	Grating of fresh nutmeg
4 tablespoons butter	1 orange with rind, put through
1¹/₂–2 cups cooked rice	food processor
1 cup chopped dried apricots	¹/₄ cup brandy or white wine

In a skillet, cook onion and celery in melted butter for about 5 minutes without browning. Combine with other ingredients in a mixing bowl and toss lightly but thoroughly to blend.

2 ducks	2 tablespoons butter, melted
Apricot-Rice Stuffing	Cornstarch
¹/₂ cup orange juice	2 tablespoons orange marmalade

Preheat oven to 450°. Stuff ducks with Apricot-Rice Stuffing and truss. Combine orange juice and butter for basting sauce. Roast ducks for ¹/₂ hour, basting frequently. Prepare gravy by boiling up pan juices, stirring to loosen any browned particles, and adding a bit more orange juice if necessary. Thicken slightly with cornstarch mixed with water and stir in orange marmalade. Makes 4 servings.

Duck Soup & Other Fowl Recipes

Pheasant Jubilee

2 pheasants, quartered	¹/₂ cup water
Flour, enough to dredge	¹/₂ cup packed brown sugar
¹/₂ cup margarine	2 tablespoons Worcestershire
1 onion, chopped	sauce
¹/₂ cup raisins	¹/₄ teaspoon garlic powder
1 cup chili sauce	1 cup sherry

Dust pheasants with flour in plastic bag. Melt butter in fry pan; brown birds thoroughly. Place pheasant in casserole. In fry pan, combine remaining ingredients except sherry. Bring to a boil. Scrape bottom and sides of pan and pour over pheasants. Bake covered at 325° for 1 hour. Remove cover, add sherry, and bake 20 minutes longer. Serve with brown or wild rice and a good red wine. Makes 4–6 servings.

Our Burnt Offerings

Cornbread Stuffing

2 cups chopped onion
1 cup chopped celery
$^1/_4$ cup margarine
1 (13$^3/_4$-ounce) can chicken
   broth
1 (17-ounce) can whole-kernel
   corn, drained
1 (7-ounce) can diced green
   chiles

3 tablespoons chopped parsley
$^1/_2$ teaspoon poultry seasoning
$^1/_2$ teaspoon salt
Pepper to taste
$^1/_4$ teaspoon oregano
6 cups crumbled cornbread or
   dry cornbread stuffing mix
$^1/_2$ cup chopped pecans

Heat oven to 350°. In large Dutch oven, sauté onions and celery in margarine until tender. Stir in remaining ingredients except cornbread and pecans, mixing well. Add cornbread and pecans, tossing gently until moistened evenly. Spoon into casserole dish; cover and bake 30 minutes or until heated through.

Christmas in Washington Cook Book

Ko's Wild Rice Dressing

The best dressing with chicken or turkey. You can't stop with one serving.

2 sticks butter
1 apple, chopped
1 cup sliced mushrooms
   (optional)
1 cup chopped celery
1 cup chopped onion

1 cup chopped walnuts
1 cup wild (not marsh) rice
Chicken or vegetable broth
1 package Pepperidge Farms
   Herb Dressing
Salt and pepper to taste

In butter, sauté apple, mushrooms, celery, and onion until soft. Add chopped walnuts.

Wash rice 3 times in cold water. Make sure anything that floats is tossed out. Cook for about 30 minutes (until soft) in chicken or vegetable broth. Add drained wild rice to sautéed mixture along with dressing mix. Add spices to taste along with cooking broth to the consistency you like.

Bounteous Blessings

Oyster Mushroom and Roasted Hazelnut Stuffing

Roasted hazelnuts, oyster mushrooms, and the fresh herb flavor of rosemary and sage blend to wonderful perfection.

1¹/₂ loaves of bread, cut into half-inch cubes
1 pound hazelnuts, roasted and coarsely chopped
1 stick butter
3 medium onions, chopped
1 pound oyster mushrooms, sliced (can also use shiitake)
5 celery stalks, chopped

¹/₂ pound prosciutto or other thin-sliced ham, chopped (optional)
4 tablespoons chopped fresh rosemary
3 tablespoons chopped fresh sage
3–4 cups chicken stock

Dry bread in advance, spread out on sheet pans and bake at 350° for 20 minutes; stir occasionally. Roast hazelnuts on a baking sheet at 350° for 12 minutes. Melt butter in large sauté pan over medium-high heat. Add onions and cook until golden brown. Add mushrooms and cook until they begin to release their juices, about 5 minutes. Add celery and cook a few minutes more. Remove from heat. Stir in prosciutto and mix with dry bread. Add fresh herbs and moisten with chicken stock. Use as you would any dressing or stuffing. Makes about 16 cups dressing.

Washington Farmers' Markets Cookbook and Guide

Oyster Stuffing

$^1/_4$ cup butter
2 small onions, chopped
1 bunch celery, chopped
1 tablespoon chopped garlic
4 cups chicken stock
1 quart shucked oysters, halved
  if large, liquor reserved

$^1/_4$ cup chopped parsley
6–8 cups bread cubes
1 tablespoon ground sage
1 tablespoon dried thyme
Salt and pepper
1 cup grated Parmesan cheese

Heat butter in a large saucepan over medium heat and sauté onions, celery, and garlic for about 5 minutes or until limp. Add chicken stock and oyster liquor. Boil to reduce by $^1/_3$, then add oysters and parsley. Return just to a boil, then immediately take the pan from the heat. Add bread cubes, enough to make a moist dressing but not wet. Add sage, thyme, and salt and pepper to taste, then stir in Parmesan cheese. Put stuffing in a large, buttered baking dish and bake at 350° until heated through and somewhat crusty on top and sides, 15–20 minutes. Makes about 10 cups.

Recipe by Chef Eric Jenkins,
Duncan Law Seafood Consumer Center, Astoria, Oregon
Heaven on the Half Shell

SEAFOOD

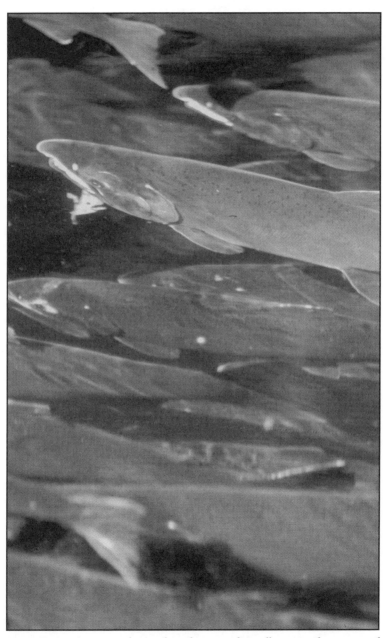

Many Native Americans honor the salmon, traditionally a significant part of Washington cuisine, by holding an annual ceremony for the first catch of the season.

Baked Dijon Salmon

This is a wonderful way to prepare fresh salmon filets in the oven. Be sure to make extra; your family will be begging for more.

$1/4$ cup butter, melted
3 tablespoons prepared Dijon-
  style mustard
$1^1/2$ tablespoons honey
$1/4$ cup dry bread crumbs
$1/4$ cup finely chopped pecans

4 teaspoons chopped fresh
  parsley
4 (4-ounce) salmon fillets
Salt and pepper to taste
1 lemon for garnish

Preheat oven to 400°. In a small bowl, stir together butter, mustard, and honey. Set aside. In another bowl, mix together bread crumbs, pecans, and parsley.

Brush each salmon fillet lightly with honey-mustard mixture, and sprinkle top of filets with bread crumb mixture. Bake salmon in preheated oven until it flakes easily with a fork, approximately 10–15 minutes. Season with salt and pepper, and garnish with a wedge of lemon. Makes 4 servings.

Allrecipes Tried & True Favorites

Herb Baked Salmon

Being from the Northwest, you can't ever have too many recipes for salmon. This is good with chicken, too.

$3/4$ pound salmon fillet
$1/2$ cup fat-free margarine
1 tablespoon poultry seasoning
1 tablespoon sage

1 tablespoon thyme
$1/4$–$1/2$ teaspoon old hickory
  salt

Preheat oven to 400°. Place salmon in a 9x13-inch baking pan sprayed with oil. In a small bowl melt margarine. Stir in seasonings. Spoon herbed butter over fillet. Sprinkle with salt. Bake 15–20 minutes. Serves 2.

Variation: Substitute chicken for salmon. Use sesame seeds for old hickory salt. Bake at 400° in a covered casserole for 35 minutes. Remove cover and bake 10–15 minutes to brown.

Recipe by Howard Lincoln, Chairman and Chief Executive Officer, Seattle Mariners
Home Plates

Baked Salmon with Pesto

Salmon is a perfect choice for easy entertaining. If desired, grill the salmon and serve the pasta as a side dish.

8 ounces fettuccine	1 tablespoon Dijon mustard
4 salmon steaks or a 16-ounce fillet	$^1/_2$ cup pesto, or to taste
1 tablespoon butter, melted	Lemon wedges (optional)

Cook pasta according to package directions; drain. Place salmon in a shallow baking pan sprayed with nonstick cooking spray. Brush with butter and mustard. Bake at 450° for 10 minutes or until a wooden toothpick inserted comes out clean. Toss pasta with the pesto sauce. Place on a serving platter and arrange salmon on top. Garnish with lemon wedges, if desired. Makes 4 servings.

Per serving, Regular version: Calories 652, Prot. 44g; Carb. 47g; Fiber 3g; Fat 31g; Sat. Fat 8g; Chol. 115mg; Sod. 411mg.

Variation: For a lighter version, omit butter on salmon; omit pesto. Toss pasta with 1 tablespoon butter; sprinkle with fresh chopped basil.

Per serving, Lighter version: Calories 497; Prot. 39g; Carb. 45g; Fiber 2g; Fat 17g; Sat. Fat 4g; Chol. 107mg; Sod. 200mg.

Six Ingredients or Less: Pasta & Casseroles

Baked Salmon à la Paul Heald

Artist Paul Heald, longtime summer resident near Hope Island, taught me how to bake salmon this way. Fresh sockeye is best.

SAUCE:

¹/₂ cup butter, melted	¹/₂ teaspoon fresh-ground
¹/₂ cup lite mayonnaise	pepper
¹/₄ cup lite soy sauce	6–8 cloves garlic, crushed

Preheat oven to 400°. Melt butter in a small saucepan. Whisk in mayonnaise, soy sauce, and pepper. Add crushed garlic and combine well. Heat Sauce until just warmed through.

1 large salmon, filleted　　　　**1 large white onion, sliced thin**

Lay salmon fillets on cookie sheets, skin-side-down. Spread thin layer of Sauce over fillets. Arrange sliced onion across top and cover all with more Sauce. Bake until fish flakes—from 20 minutes to 35 minutes, depending on the thickness of the fish. Serves 12.

Skagit Valley Fare

Scotch Salmon

*Even if you don't have fresh spring-run Chinook for this dish, you'll find yourself
sold on this preparation for salmon.*

1 (6- to 7-ounce) salmon fillet
2 tablespoons clarified butter*
Salt and white pepper to taste
1/2 teaspoon minced garlic
1/2 teaspoon minced shallot
1/4 teaspoon Dijon mustard
1/4 teaspoon brown sugar

1 tablespoon raspberry vinegar
Round of Scotch liquor**
1/4 cup orange juice
1/4 cup heavy cream
Round of Drambuie liqueur**
Crème fraîche and candied
   orange zest for garnish

Dust salmon fillet lightly in flour. In a sauté pan, heat butter and
brown fillet slightly on one side. Add salt and white pepper to taste.
Turn fillet over. Add garlic, shallot, mustard, and brown sugar.

   After ingredients cook for a few seconds, add raspberry vinegar.
By now, the second side of the fillet will have browned slightly. With
the fillet still in the pan, deglaze it with a round of Scotch. Add
orange juice. Move pan in a circular motion so ingredients marry.
Reduce sauce till it begins to thicken. Finish with heavy cream and
a round of Drambuie. Garnish with crème fraîche and candied
orange zest. Serves 1.

*See Editors' Extra on page 27 for more information on clarified butter.

**A round is a quick pour around the outside perimeter of the pan, start-
ing and finishing at the handle.

The Best of The Ark and More!

Editors Extra: To make crème fraîche at home, combine 1 cup whipping
cream and 2 tablespoons buttermilk in a glass container. Cover, and let
stand at room temperature from 8–24 hours, or until very thick. Stir well
before covering, and refrigerate for up to 10 days.

 The steelhead trout, Washington's state fish, is an anadromous fish, meaning it returns
to fresh water rivers to spawn. Steelhead trout is one of the most popular fish for recre-
ational fishing, a major industry in Washington State.

Salmon Cakes

1 pound salmon, cooked and
   flaked
1 small onion, finely chopped
2 tablespoons chopped parsley
1 egg, lightly beaten

1 tablespoon flour
Salt and pepper to taste
Dash of Tabasco
5 tablespoons vegetable oil

In a bowl, mix together until smooth the salmon, onion, parsley, egg, flour, salt, pepper, and Tabasco. Shape batter into 12 golf ball-sized rounds, then flatten them slightly. Heat oil in skillet until sizzling. Gently slide salmon cakes into pan. Fry for about 2 minutes on each side. Remove and drain on paper towels. Serve warm or cold with Tarragon Mayonnaise or Pineapple Salsa. Serves 6 as a first course or 4 as a main course.

TARRAGON MAYONNAISE:
2 cups mayonnaise, reduced fat
   or nonfat is okay
1^1/$_2$ teaspoons tarragon
2 tablespoons chopped green
   onions or chives

1 tablespoon malt vinegar
4 tablespoons tomato purée

Combine all ingredients, except tomato purée, in a bowl. Add just enough of the tomato purée to give it a nice pourable consistency. Makes 3 cups sauce.

PINEAPPLE SALSA:
1 medium pineapple, peeled,
   cored and chopped
1 red bell pepper, finely chopped
1 green bell pepper, finely
   chopped
^{1}/$_2$ red onion, diced
2 tablespoons light oil
3 tablespoons coriander

2 tablespoons lime juice
3 tablespoons finely chopped
   parsley
2 hot chiles, diced
Dash of Tabasco
Salt and coarsely ground pepper
   to taste

Mix all ingredients together well. Cover tightly and let set in refrigerator for at least 6 hours. This is a perfect side dish for grilled fish. Makes 4 cups.

20,000 Gallons of Chowder

Ganges Grilled Salmon

This grilled salmon takes its name from the small village of Ganges on Salt Spring Island in the Gulf Island's chain off the west coast of Vancouver, B.C. On a sailing trip, we stumbled across a delicious homemade amaretto apricot preserve in a farmer's market on the Ganges waterfront. It made such a wonderful glaze for grilled salmon, we have been trying to duplicate it ever since!

AMARETTO-APRICOT GLAZE:

6 fresh, ripe small apricots, in season
1/3 cup honey
1/3 cup packed brown sugar
2 tablespoons fresh lemon juice
2 tablespoons unsalted butter
1 tablespoon amaretto liqueur

Purée apricots in a blender. Combine remaining ingredients except amaretto in a saucepan. Cook over medium heat, stirring until thick and smooth, 5–7 minutes. Cool to room temperature and blend in the amaretto.

SOCKEYE SALMON:

1 (4- to 7-pound) sockeye salmon, filleted
1 tablespoon dill (fresh, if available)

Arrange salmon in a dish just large enough to hold it. Top with cooled Amaretto-Apricot Glaze, season with dill, and let stand for 30 minutes. Prepare hot coals for grilling. Place salmon on the grill, skin-side-down. Cook over medium heat, with lid closed, for 12–15 minutes, until fish flakes easily. Lift meat of fish from grill; using a metal spatula and transfer to a platter, leaving the charred skin on the grill, and serve immediately. Makes 8 portions.

Note: Sockeye Salmon, sometimes called blueback, is the best for grilling. The meat, which is deep-red in color, breaks into medium flakes, is firm in texture, and has considerable oil. Since charcoal (or gas) grilling is a dry cooking method, thicker cuts of fish are preferable, as they dry out less during the process than thinner cuts.

Liberty Lake Community Cookbook

The Governor Albert D. Rosellini Bridge at Evergreen Point is the longest floating bridge in the world. At a floating length of 7,578 feet, it beats the runner-up Lacey V. Murrow Bridge by a thousand feet. Both bridges are located on Lake Washington.

Grilled Mahi Mahi with Mango Salsa

MANGO SALSA:
3 tablespoons lime juice
1 tablespoon fish sauce or fish extract
1 teaspoon sugar
2 tablespoons sliced green onions
1½ cups chopped tomatoes
2 ripe but firm mangos, peeled and diced
1 cup chopped Walla Walla or other sweet onions
2 tablespoons chopped fresh cilantro
1 or 2 jalapeño peppers, chopped, or 1 teaspoon crushed red pepper
1 teaspoon minced garlic

Combine lime juice, fish sauce, and sugar in a large bowl. Stir until sugar dissolves. Add remaining salsa ingredients, mix, cover and refrigerate for 30 minutes. Stir well before serving.

FISH:
2 pounds Mahi Mahi

Grill Mahi Mahi over medium-hot coals until fish flakes easily, about 15 minutes. Serve Mango Salsa over fish. Serves 4.

Note: Fish sauce can be found in the International section of many super-markets. Try this recipe with any firm white fish such as halibut, cod, or red snapper.

Gold'n Delicious

Halibut Amontillado

Halibut, being a more expensive fish, should be treated well! The crunchy texture of the hazelnuts is a perfect counterpoint to the smoothness of the mildly flavored cream sauce. Be sure to seek out "Amontillado" sherry as it retains its distinctive flavor even in the cooking.

2 (7-ounce) fresh halibut fillets
$^1/_2$ cup flour
$^1/_2$ cup roasted and finely
   chopped hazelnuts
Salt and pepper to taste

$^1/_4$ cup olive oil
2 tablespoons diced shallots
$^1/_2$ cup Amontillado sherry
3 tablespoons heavy cream
$^1/_4$ pound unsalted butter, cubed

Preheat oven to 375°. In a bowl, combine flour, hazelnuts, salt and pepper. Lightly moisten halibut fillets with cold water and press both sides of each fillet into flour-hazelnut mixture. Heat olive oil in skillet and brown fillets. After browning, transfer fillets to baking dish and bake in preheated oven for 10 minutes. While fillets are baking, prepare butter sauce.

In a small saucepan, combine shallots, sherry, and cream. Cook sauce, stirring constantly, and reduce by half. Remove from heat and whisk in cold butter. Remove fillets from oven, plate up and spoon sauce over halibut and serve. Bon appetit! Serves 2.

Nutritional values per serving: Calories 762; Carb. 32.2g; Prot. 18.1g; Fiber 0.8g; Sugar 31.4g; Fat Cal 548; Total 60.9g; Sat. Fat 20.4g; Chol. 91.9g; Sod. 3523.5mg.

LaConner Palates

 The land mass of the San Juans Archipelago—which includes the Gulf Islands of British Columbia—increases as the tide goes out and decreases as it comes in. When the tide's out, more than 780 island reefs can be seen. When the tide is in, that number drops to less than 460. Only 175 of the islands are named and 65 inhabited.

Orange Broiled Shark

Shark steaks
Undiluted orange juice
  concentrate
Tequila (optional)

Onion rings
Bell pepper, cut into rings
Toasted, sliced almonds

The ingredients aren't given in specific quantities because you adjust to the amount of shark steak you have. Marinate shark steaks in orange juice concentrate overnight in refrigerator, adding tequila (to taste) if desired. A jigger or 2 is plenty. Place marinated shark in baking dish and decorate with rings of onion and bell pepper. Sprinkle with almonds. Broil about 7–9 minutes in preheated oven until meat flakes easily. Watch carefully to avoid burning. Turn and broil about 3 minutes on other side. Serve immediately on bed of rice.

Variation: As an alternate recipe, use a can of frozen piña colada drink concentrate and garnish with toasted coconut.

The Wild and Free Cookbook

Sturgeon Szechwan

There was a brief period in England when King Edward II declared the sturgeon a "royal fish" and a law required that any of the fish caught must be offered to the king. Sturgeon Szechwan lets the modern diner know just what that term "royal fish" means.

1¹/₂ tablespoons sesame oil
4 tablespoons clarified butter*
4 (6-ounce) fillets white
  sturgeon, skin off
Flour
¹/₂ teaspoon minced garlic

¹/₂ teaspoon minced ginger
Pinch of red pepper flakes
¹/₂ lemon
¹/₃ cup sake
³/₄ cup teriyaki sauce
Chopped peanuts

Heat oil and butter until hot. Dust sturgeon fillets lightly with flour. Pan fry until light brown on both sides. Add minced garlic, ginger, and red pepper flakes. Cook until garlic begins to brown. Squeeze juice from lemon over sturgeon and deglaze with sake. Add teriyaki sauce and reduce till caramelized. Garnish with chopped peanuts.

*See Editors' Extra on page 27 for more information on clarified butter.

The Best of The Ark and More!

Fish Cakes

Here's a good way to use up that leftover cooked fish and stale bread.

2 slices bread
1 cup milk
3 cups cooked fish, flaked
1 egg, beaten
$^1/_4$ cup minced parsley

$^1/_2$ teaspoon sea salt
$^1/_4$ teaspoon pepper
$^1/_4$ teaspoon nutmeg
3 tablespoons butter
3 tablespoons oil

Soak bread in milk until soft. Combine with fish, beaten egg, parsley, and seasonings. Form into cakes and brown them on each side in the butter and oil until heated through. Serves 6.

The 99¢ a Meal Cookbook

Keelhauler Tacos

The many versions of this meal originated with the crew team at California Maritime Academy. The contents changed according to how much money we had or what we could recover from the mess hall, but the preparation was always the same. We had a hot plate, a frying pan, and a cutting board, and we used frisbees for plates. The tacos are eaten as they are made; and three or four hungry people can keep one rig busy.

$1^1/_2$–2 cups white fish (ling cod,
   albacore, sea bass, or halibut)
$^1/_4$ cup butter
8–10 whole wheat tortilla shells
$1^1/_2$ cups grated cheese

1 cup salsa
1 cup chopped tomatoes
$^1/_2$ cup chopped green onions
Avocado, chopped (optional)
Sour cream (optional)

Pan-fry fish in butter; flake, then set aside. Warm tortilla shells until soft (fry, or cover with foil, then heat in warm oven). Fill tortilla shells with cheese and salsa and fold once. Add fish, tomatoes, onions, and avocado, and fold up tight. Top with sour cream and enjoy. Serves 8–10.

Extraordinary Cuisine for Sea & Shore

Asian Crab Cakes

2 cups cracker meal, divided
1 pound crabmeat, drained well
1 green onion, finely chopped
$^1/_2$ sweet red pepper, finely
  chopped
1 pound Gruyère cheese,
  grated
$1^1/_2$ teaspoons sesame oil
1 egg white

1 tablespoon sake
1 tablespoon soy sauce
1 tablespoon grated gingerroot
$^1/_2$ teaspoon minced garlic
$^1/_4$ teaspoon black pepper
Peanut oil for frying
2 cups Red Pepper & Ginger
  Mayonnaise
Chive blossoms for garnish

Set $1^1/_2$ cups of cracker meal aside for breading. Combine remaining
$^1/_2$ cup of cracker meal with all remaining ingredients except peanut
oil, mayonnaise, and garnish. Shape into $^1/_2$-ounce patties, carefully
forming the edges, and pat into the reserved cracker meal. Set them
aside.

   Coat bottom of frying pan with a thin layer of peanut oil. Set it
over medium heat and sauté cakes until golden on both sides.

   Pool $^1/_4$ cup Red Pepper & Ginger Mayonnaise on each plate and
top with 2 cakes. Garnish with chive blossoms, bits of red pepper or
green onion strands. Makes 8 servings.

RED PEPPER & GINGER MAYONNAISE:

2 sweet red peppers, roasted,
  peeled, and seeded
1 cup mayonnaise
$2^1/_2$ teaspoons sesame oil
3 tablespoons sake

1 teaspoon soy sauce
1 teaspoon minced garlic
2 tablespoons grated gingerroot
  (or 1 piece, 1 inch in diameter
  by 2 inches long)

Combine all the ingredients and purée in a food processor or blender
until smooth. If you prefer a smoother sauce, pass the mayonnaise
through a fine-mesh strainer. Makes 2 cups.

Note: This mayonnaise sauce is an excellent dip for vegetables or a quick
sauce for fish.

The Shoalwater's Finest Dinners

Crab Broccoli Bake

Enjoy the delicate flavor of crab enhanced with a light cream sauce and fresh broccoli.

1¹/₂ pounds broccoli
¹/₃ cup chopped almonds
¹/₄ cup butter, divided
3 tablespoons flour
¹/₂ teaspoon salt
¹/₈ teaspoon pepper

1 chicken bouillon cube
1¹/₂ cups milk
1 tablespoon lemon juice
12 ounces fresh crab meat
2 tablespoons grated Parmesan
  cheese

Preheat oven to 400°.

Plunge broccoli into a saucepan of salted boiling water. Allow broccoli to cook 1 minute and drain. Arrange broccoli in a shallow 2-quart baking dish.

In a small skillet lightly brown almonds in 1 tablespoon butter over medium heat. Remove from heat and set aside. Melt remaining butter in a small pan over medium heat. Whisk in flour, salt, pepper, and crushed bouillon cube. Gradually stir in milk. Cook, stirring constantly, until the sauce has thickened. Remove sauce from heat and stir in lemon juice. Fold in crab meat. Spoon crab and sauce over broccoli. Sprinkle with toasted almonds and cheese. Bake at 400° for 15 minutes. Serve immediately. Serves 4.

Simply Whidbey

Crab and Shrimp Casserole

2 cups cooked rice
1 cup mayonnaise
¹/₂ cup milk
¹/₂ cup sliced almonds
¹/₄ cup chopped green pepper
¹/₄ cup chopped onion
¹/₂ pound cooked shrimp

¹/₂ pound cooked crab or
  canned crab meat
¹/₂ cup milk
1 cup tomato juice
Salt and pepper to taste
Cracker or bread crumbs

Mix all ingredients except crumbs and top with cracker or bread crumbs. Bake 1 hour in 350° oven in greased, uncovered casserole.

Your Favorite Recipes

Baked Seafood Salad

1 (10- to 12-ounce) package
  frozen shrimp, peeled and
  deveined
1 (6^1/$_2$-ounce) can crab meat
1^1/$_2$ cups chopped celery
^{1}/$_4$ cup finely chopped green
  pepper
^{1}/$_4$ cup finely chopped onion

1 cup mayonnaise
1 teaspoon Worcestershire sauce
^{1}/$_2$ teaspoon salt
1^1/$_2$ cups crushed potato chips
^{1}/$_2$ teaspoon paprika
2 tablespoons butter or
  margarine

Drop shrimp into boiling salted water; cook for 1 minute after water returns to boil, or until pink. If shrimp are large, cut into ^{1}/$_2$-inch pieces. Combine with crab, celery, green pepper, and onion. Mix mayonnaise with Worcestershire sauce and salt; fold in. Spread in 2-quart buttered baking dish or into 6 individual casseroles. Bake at 400° for 10 minutes. Blend potato chips with paprika; sprinkle over mixture. Dot with butter; bake for 10 minutes or until potato chips are brown. Yields 6 servings.

A Taste of Heaven

Shrimp Moses

A family recipe everyone loves.

1 onion, minced
3 garlic cloves, minced
^{1}/$_2$ cup olive oil
1 (28-ounce) can crushed
  tomatoes
1 celery stalk, finely chopped
2 teaspoons chopped parsley

4 ounces white wine
Salt and pepper to taste
1 pound large shrimp, cleaned
  and deveined
^{1}/$_4$ pound goat cheese, crumbled
1 pound linguine, cooked

Brown onion and garlic in olive oil. Add tomatoes and bring to a boil. Lower heat and simmer. Cover for 5–10 minutes. Add celery, parsley, wine, salt, and pepper. Simmer 25 minutes. Add shrimp to sauce. Cook 3 minutes. Turn off heat. Sprinkle cheese over sauce. Cover. Let stand for a few minutes. Serve over cooked linguine. Serves 4–6.

Recipe by John Moses, Coach, Seattle Mariners
Mariners Mix'n and Fix'n Grand Slam Style

Coquilles St. Jacques

1¹/₂ pounds fresh or frozen
  scallops
1 cup dry white wine
1 tablespoon lemon juice
2 sprigs fresh parsley
1 bay leaf
¹/₂ teaspoon salt
1 cup chopped mushrooms
2 tablespoons thinly sliced
  shallots
2 tablespoons butter

2 tablespoons flour
¹/₄ teaspoon salt
¹/₈ teaspoon ground nutmeg
Dash pepper
2 cups milk
2 egg yolks
¹/₂ cup light cream
Bread crumbs
2 tablespoons butter, melted
Gruyère cheese (optional)

Thaw scallops, if frozen. Halve any large scallops. In saucepan, combine scallops, wine, lemon juice, parsley, bay leaf, and ¹/₂ teaspoon salt. Bring to boil, then reduce heat. Cover and simmer for 2–4 minutes or until scallops are opaque. Remove scallops with slotted spoon. Strain wine mixture through cheesecloth; reserve 1 cup.

In skillet cook mushrooms and shallots in 2 tablespoons butter, about 5 minutes. Stir in flour, ¹/₄ teaspoon salt, nutmeg, and pepper. Add reserved 1 cup liquid and milk. Cook and stir until thick. Remove from heat. Combine egg yolks and cream; beat well with wire whisk. Gradually stir about half of the hot mixture into skillet. Add scallops. Heat and stir just until bubbly. Reduce heat, cook, and stir over low heat for 2 minutes.

Place 6 buttered baking dishes in shallow baking pan. Spoon scallop mixture into dishes. Toss together bread crumbs and melted butter; sprinkle over scallop mixture. Bake in 400° oven for 10 minutes or until slightly browned. Can also shred Gruyère cheese and sprinkle. Let melt.

Harvest Feast

Lewis and Clark explored the Columbia River area of what is now Washington in 1805 and 1806. On November 11, 1889, Washington became the 42nd state to enter the Union. It is the only state named for a president.

Shrimp with Ginger

1 cup fresh orange juice
1 cup dry white wine
$^1/_2$ cup honey
$1^1/_2$ teaspoons plus 1 tablespoon grated fresh ginger, divided

6 tablespoons butter, clarified*
12 garlic cloves
36 uncooked medium shrimp
1 cup slivered almonds

Combine orange juice, wine, honey, and $1^1/_2$ teaspoons ginger in small bowl; set aside.

Heat butter with garlic in wok until butter is bubbly. Add shrimp and 1 tablespoon ginger, and sauté briefly. Stir in almonds and continue cooking until almonds are golden brown and shrimp is cooked through. With slotted spoon, remove shrimp, garlic and almonds to heated platter. Pour off excess butter from skillet. Return skillet to burner and heat briefly. Add orange juice mixture and bring to a boil. Reduce heat and simmer 1 minute. Pour over shrimp.

Serve immediately over rice. Serves 6–8.

*See Editors' Extra on page 27 for more information on clarified butter.

Extraordinary Cuisine for Sea & Shore

Oyster Fritters

2 dozen oysters
2 tablespoons lemon juice
4 tablespoons Bisquick or biscuit mix

$^1/_2$ cup water
1 egg white
Cooking oil for frying

Mix oysters with lemon juice and marinate for 15 minutes; then drain. Put biscuit mix in mixing bowl and gradually add water until a smooth batter results. Beat egg white in a separate bowl until peaks form; add egg to batter and blend well. Dip oysters into batter and deep fry until golden brown. Drain on paper towels. Serves 2.

20,000 Gallons of Chowder

Stuffed Olympic Oysters

SHRIMP SAUCE:

1 cup chopped green onion
1/4 cup minced parsley
6 cloves garlic, minced
1/4 cup butter
1/2 cup flour
2 cups half-and-half
1/4 cup sherry

1 teaspoon salt
1 teaspoon freshly ground
  pepper
1/2 teaspoon cayenne
4 egg yolks, beaten
1/2 cup chopped mushrooms
1/2 pound cooked shrimp, diced

Early in the day, cook green onions, parsley, and garlic in butter over low heat for 10 minutes, stirring constantly. Add flour a little at a time. Add half-and-half, stirring until mixture is smooth. Add sherry, salt, pepper, and cayenne. Stir in egg yolks and cook over low heat until mixture thickens. Stir in mushrooms and cook for 2 minutes over low heat. Add shrimp and continue cooking for 3 minutes. At this time the sauce should be quite thick. Pour sauce into a glass bowl and allow to cool at room temperature. Cover with plastic wrap and refrigerate for at least 1 1/2 hours.

TOPPING:

6 tablespoons freshly grated
  Parmesan cheese
4 tablespoons bread crumbs

1/2 teaspoon paprika
1/2 teaspoon salt

Blend all ingredients in an electric blender on high speed.

OYSTERS:

2 dozen oysters on the half shell   9 cups rock salt

Wash and dry the shells; reserve oysters. Spread 3 cups rock salt on each of 3 baking sheets. Preheat oven to 500° at least 45 minutes before you plan to serve the oysters. Place trays of rock salt in oven while it is preheating.

Put an oyster on each shell and place 8 shells on each hot tray of rock salt. Spoon 1 1/2 tablespoons Shrimp Sauce over each oyster. Sprinkle each oyster with 1 teaspoon Topping mixture. Bake at 500° for 15 minutes. Oysters should be well browned on top. Serves 6.

Simply Whidbey

Seafood Marinara

2 pounds fresh fish or seafood
  (halibut, bass, snapper, shrimp
  or scallops)
2 tablespoons olive oil
1 medium onion, chopped
2–3 cloves garlic, pressed
$^3/_4$ teaspoon salt

1 tablespoon soft bread crumbs
1 small tomato, peeled and
  chopped
$^1/_4$–$^1/_2$ cup minced parsley
$^1/_2$ cup dry cooking sherry
$^1/_2$ cup water

Sauté fish in olive oil over medium heat just until delicately browned. As soon as fish starts to brown, add onion, garlic, salt, and bread crumbs; cook for 1 minute. Add tomato and parsley. Lower heat and simmer 3 minutes. Add sherry and water; simmer uncovered 3 more minutes. Serve alone or spoon over hot cooked rice.

Family Favorites Recipes

CAKES

Formerly part of the Great Northern Railroad Station, the 157-foot Clock Tower, located in Spokane's Riverfront Park, is now the signature structure of the park.

Autumn Cheesecake

This is a delicious apple cheesecake that I usually make in the fall.

CRUST:

1 cup graham cracker crumbs	¹/₂ teaspoon ground cinnamon
¹/₂ cup finely chopped pecans	¹/₄ cup unsalted butter, melted
3 tablespoons sugar	

Preheat oven to 350°. In a large bowl, stir together graham cracker crumbs, pecans, sugar, cinnamon, and melted butter; press into bottom of 9-inch springform pan. Bake in preheated oven for 10 minutes.

CREAM CHEESE LAYER:

2 (8-ounce) packages cream cheese, softened	2 eggs
¹/₂ cup sugar	¹/₂ teaspoon vanilla extract

In large bowl, combine cream cheese and sugar. Mix at medium speed until smooth. Beat in eggs 1 at a time, mixing well after each addition. Blend in vanilla; pour filling into baked crust.

APPLE LAYER:

¹/₃ cup sugar	¹/₄ cup chopped pecans
¹/₂ teaspoon ground cinnamon	
4 cups peeled, cored, and thinly sliced apples	

In small bowl, stir together sugar and cinnamon. Toss sugar-cinnamon mixture with apples to coat. Spoon Apple Layer over Cream Cheese Layer and sprinkle with chopped pecans. Bake in preheated oven for 60–70 minutes. With knife, loosen cake from rim of pan. Let cool, then remove rim of pan. Chill cake before serving. Makes 1 (9-inch) cheesecake.

Allrecipes Tried & True Favorites

The Space Needle is fastened to its foundation with 74 bolts, each 32 feet long and four inches in diameter. Built to withstand a wind velocity of 200 miles per hour, the building sways approximately one inch for every 10 mph of wind.

Kahlúa Fantasy Chocolate Cheesecake

CHOCOLATE CRUMB CRUST:

1 1/3 cups chocolate wafer
  crumbs

1/4 cup softened butter
1 tablespoon sugar

Mix and press into springform pan.

CHEESECAKE:

1 1/2 cups semisweet chocolate
  pieces
1/4 cup Kahlúa
2 tablespoons butter
2 eggs, beaten

1/3 cup sugar
1/4 teaspoon salt
1 cup sour cream
2 (8-ounce) packages cream
  cheese, softened

In small saucepan over medium heat, melt chocolate with Kahlua and butter. Stir until smooth. Set aside. In bowl, combine eggs, sugar, and salt. Add sour cream and blend well. Add cream cheese and beat until smooth. Gradually blend in chocolate mixture. Turn into prepared crust. Bake at 350° for 40 minutes or until filling is barely set in center. Remove from oven and let stand at room temperature for 1 hour; then refrigerate several hours or overnight before serving.

Pig Out

Cranberry-Swirl Cheesecake

CRANBERRY PURÉE:

4 cups cranberries

1 cup water

1 cup sugar

Combine cranberries, water, and sugar in a saucepan and bring to a boil. Simmer until the berries pop, about 15 minutes. Allow to cool, then purée in a food processor or blender. You can strain the purée when it is hot, but be careful when you process it—hot liquids explode out of blenders. Strain out skins and seeds, then chill. This sauce keeps well for up to 1 week, refrigerated. Makes 2 cups.

CHEESECAKE:

4 (8-ounce) packages cream
   cheese, softened

1³/4 cups sugar

4 large eggs

4 tablespoons Cranberry Purée,
   divided

Cream together cream cheese and sugar, scraping the bowl well. There should be no lumps. Add eggs 1 at a time, scraping the bowl between additions. Pour ¹/3 of the batter evenly into a buttered and lined 8x3-inch pan and drizzle 2 tablespoons of the Cranberry Purée over the top. Pour another ¹/3 of the batter over the purée, trying not to disturb the pattern, then drizzle 2 more tablespoons Cranberry Purée over the top. Pour in the remaining batter, smoothing carefully.

Place cheesecake in a pan containing enough water to come halfway up the sides of the cheesecake pan. If you are using a spring-form pan, be sure to wrap it in foil so the water doesn't seep in. Bake in a preheated 350° oven until set in center, about 1¹/2 hours.

Cool completely, then turn out onto a serving platter and refrigerate. The cheesecake freezes well at this point. To serve, thaw to refrigerated temperature before glazing.

GLAZE:

4 ounces Callebaut semisweet
   chocolate

¹/4 cup water

¹/4 cup Cranberry Purée

Whipped cream and cranberries
   for garnish

Melt chocolate and water in microwave or over low heat. Whisk in ¹/4 cup of Cranberry Purée until the mixture is smooth and shiny. Allow to cool until thick enough to coat cheesecake. Pour glaze over

(continued)

(continued)

cheesecake, creating a thick layer. Smooth top with flat knife, allowing large, even dribbles to decorate sides of cheesecake.

To serve, thin remaining Cranberry Purée with a little water until you have a sauce. Pool some sauce on each plate and top with a piece of cheesecake. Garnish with cranberries and lightly sweetened whipped cream rosettes. Holly leaves make a nice garnish for the winter holiday season. Send remaining sauce around in a small pitcher. Makes 1 (8-inch) cheesecake.

The Shoalwater's Finest Dinners

Cherry Mini-Cheesecakes

24 vanilla wafers
2 (8-ounce) packages cream
  cheese
3/4 cup sugar

2 eggs
1 teaspoon vanilla
1 can cherry pie filling

Fill 24 muffin cups with cupcake liners; add wafers to liners. Beat cream cheese, sugar, eggs, and vanilla together; fill liners about half full. Bake at 350° for 15 minutes; cool. Add 2 or 3 spoonfuls of cherry pie filling on top. Refrigerate.

Christmas in Washington Cook Book

Bacardi Rum Cake

CAKE:

1 cup chopped pecans or walnuts
1 (18½-ounce) package yellow cake mix
1 (3½-ounce) package vanilla instant pudding and pie filling

4 eggs
½ cup cold water
½ cup oil
½ cup Bacardi dark rum (80 proof)

Preheat oven to 325°. Grease and flour 10-inch tube or 12-cup Bundt pan. Sprinkle nuts over bottom of pan. Mix all cake ingredients together. Pour batter over nuts. Bake 1 hour. Cool. Invert on serving plate. Prick top. Spoon and brush Glaze evenly over top and sides. Allow cake to absorb Glaze. Repeat till Glaze is used up.

GLAZE:

¼ pound butter
¼ cup water
1 cup sugar

½ cup Bacardi dark rum (80 proof)

Melt butter in saucepan. Stir in water and sugar. Boil 5 minutes, stirring constantly. Remove from heat. Stir in rum.

Note: If using cake mix with pudding already in the mix, omit instant pudding. Use 3 eggs instead of 4, and ⅓ cup oil instead of ½. May decorate with border of sugar frosting or whipped cream.

Recipes to Remember

Poppyseed Candlelight Cake

This is an easy, quick version of poppyseed cake that will make people think you have been slaving in the kitchen all afternoon.

CAKE:

1 package yellow or lemon cake mix

1 small package instant vanilla pudding

4 eggs

1 cup sour cream

$^1/_2$ cup salad oil

$^1/_2$ cup cream sherry

$^1/_4$ cup poppy seeds

Preheat oven to 350°. Combine all ingredients in large mixing bowl and beat at medium speed for 2 minutes. Pour into greased 10-inch Bundt pan or angel food cake pan. Bake for 45–50 minutes or until inserted toothpick comes out clean. Cool cake in pan for 15 minutes. Invert and remove from pan and finish cooling on rack.

ORANGE BUTTER GLAZE:

1$^1/_2$ tablespoons milk

1 tablespoon butter

1 tablespoon orange juice

1$^1/_2$ cups powdered sugar

1 teaspoon grated orange peel

Edible flowers for decoration

In a small saucepan, combine milk, butter, and orange juice and stir over medium heat until butter is melted (or combine ingredients in ceramic mixing bowl and microwave). Add powdered sugar and grated orange peel and beat until smooth. Spoon Orange Butter Glaze over cooled cake. Decorate cake top and sides with edible flowers, such as blue borage, before glaze is set.

Skagit Valley Fare

 Over one million visitors attend the Skagit Valley Tulip Festival each April to view 1,200 acres of flowers.

Aunt Lulu's Chocolate Cake

Chocolate cake at zero fat. Unheard of, especially if it's as good as this one. Yummm.

2 cups flour
1 cup sugar
$^1/_2$ cup cocoa
$^3/_4$ cup applesauce

$1^1/_2$ cups nonfat sour cream
1 teaspoon baking soda
1 tablespoon vanilla

Sift flour, sugar, and cocoa together. Work in applesauce like a pie crust (slowly work together with a fork). Add sour cream, baking soda, and vanilla. Mix well. Pour into 8x8-inch baking pan that has been sprayed with vegetable cooking spray. Bake at 375° for 20–25 minutes. Serves 8.

From My Heart For Yours

Scotch Chocolate Cake

1 stick margarine
$^1/_2$ cup shortening
4 tablespoons cocoa
1 cup water
2 cups flour
2 cups sugar

1 teaspoon baking soda
$^1/_2$ cup buttermilk
2 eggs
1 teaspoon cinnamon
Pinch of salt
1 teaspoon vanilla

Bring margarine, shortening, cocoa, and water to a boil and add to flour, sugar, and baking soda while hot. Add and beat buttermilk and eggs. Add cinnamon, a pinch of salt, and vanilla. Batter will be thin. Bake at 350° for 40 minutes in a greased 9x13-inch pan.

ICING:
4 tablespoons milk
$2^2/_3$ teaspoons cocoa
$^1/_3$ cup margarine
1 teaspoon vanilla

$2^2/_3$ cups powdered sugar
Coconut
Chopped nuts

Five minutes before cake is done, bring milk, cocoa, and margarine to a boil. Remove from heat, then add vanilla, sugar, coconut, and nuts and spread on warm cake.

A Taste of Heaven

Butterscotch Heavenly Delight

This cake is as good as it sounds! A rich and satisfying cake with a surprising toffee crunch is great as a party cake for a special celebration or as a wonderful way to end a meal.

1 (9¹/₂-inch) angel food cake
³/₄ pound English toffee
1¹/₂ cups whipping cream

5¹/₂ ounces butterscotch
  topping
¹/₂ teaspoon vanilla extract

Prepare angel food cake from scratch or package mix. Let cake cool. Slice horizontally into 3 layers. In food processor, with the largest blade, crush toffee using pulse setting. Set aside. Using electric mixer, whip cream until it starts to thicken. Slowly add butterscotch topping and vanilla and continue beating until thick. Reserving ¹/₄ cup crushed toffee, fold rest into whipped cream mixture.

Place bottom layer of angel food cake on cake plate and spread butterscotch mixture over top. Repeat with second layer, then third, frosting sides as well. Sprinkle reserved crushed toffee over top of cake. Refrigerate cake for a minimum of 6 hours. Serves 12.

Nutritional values per serving: Calories 244; Carb. 40.5g; Prot. 0.9g; Fiber 0g; Sugar 40.5g; Fat Cal 87; Total Fat 9.7g; Sat. Fat 6.1g; Chol. 31.8g; Sod. 181.8mg.

LaConner Palates

Cream Cake

2 cups flour
3 teaspoons baking powder
1 cup cream, whipped
Pinch salt

1¹/₂ cups sugar
¹/₂ cup cold water
4 egg whites, stiffly beaten
1 teaspoon vanilla

Sift flour 3 times; sift flour and baking powder together. Whip cream stiff, add salt, and slowly add sugar. Add dry ingredients to creamed mixture alternately with water. Fold in stiffly beaten egg whites and vanilla. Bake in 2 greased (8-inch) cake pans or as cupcakes for 25–35 minutes in 350° oven. Good frosted with fudge frosting, if desired.

The Historic Mid-1900's Cookbook

Strawberry Cream Cake

1 white cake mix
1 (8-ounce) package cream
  cheese, softened
2 cups powdered sugar
2 cups Cool Whip

2 cups frozen strawberries (or
  huckleberries, raspberries, etc.)
1/2 cup sugar
3 tablespoons cornstarch

Mix cake mix as directed on package and bake in a 9x13-inch pan.
Cool. Whip cream cheese and powdered sugar; fold in Cool Whip.
Spread over cooled cake. Combine strawberries, 1/2 cup sugar, and
cornstarch in saucepan. Cook until thickened, cool slightly, and
spread over cream mixture. Refrigerate until ready to serve.

Recipes from Our Friends

Huckleberry Dump Cake

1 quart huckleberries
1 cup sugar
2 tablespoons cornstarch
1/4 teaspoon almond extract

1 box white or sour cream cake
  mix
1 stick margarine
1 cup chopped nuts

Put huckleberries in greased 9x13-inch pan. Mix sugar and cornstarch and put over berries. Sprinkle with almond extract. Sprinkle
cake mix on top. Cut margarine in pieces and put on top of cake mix
along with chopped nuts. Bake 40–45 minutes at 350°.

Our Best Home Cooking

Jewish Apple Cake

2$^{1}/_{3}$ cups sugar
1 cup oil
4 eggs
3 cups flour
$^{1}/_{2}$ teaspoon salt
$^{1}/_{3}$ cup orange juice

2$^{1}/_{2}$ teaspoons vanilla
3 teaspoons baking powder
6 medium apples, peeled and
   thinly sliced
1 tablespoon cinnamon
3 tablespoons sugar

Cream together first 3 ingredients. Add flour, salt, orange juice, vanilla, and baking powder. Beat all ingredients until smooth. Batter will be thick. In another bowl, mix sliced apples, cinnamon, and 3 tablespoons sugar; set aside. Grease and flour 10-inch tube pan. Layer batter and apple mixture, starting with batter and ending with apples. Bake at 350° for 1 hour and 45 minutes. Cool 10 minutes and remove from pan.

Liberty Lake Community Cookbook

Apple Cake

4 cups raw apples, peeled and
   cubed
2 eggs
$^{1}/_{2}$ cup oil
1$^{1}/_{2}$ teaspoons vanilla extract
2 cups sugar
1$^{1}/_{2}$ teaspoons cinnamon

1$^{1}/_{2}$ cups chopped dates or
   citron
$^{2}/_{3}$ cup chopped walnuts
2 cups all-purpose flour
1$^{1}/_{2}$ teaspoons baking soda
1 teaspoon salt

Preheat oven to 350°. Place cubed apples in bowl. Break eggs over them and mix well. Add oil, vanilla, sugar, cinnamon, dates, and walnuts and stir together. Sift flour, baking soda, and salt together and add to apple mixture. Mix with wooden spoon until flour mixture is thoroughly blended into apple mixture. Pour batter into greased 9x13-inch baking pan and bake for 45 minutes. Serve warm or cold with Grand Marnier Whipped Cream.

GRAND MARNIER WHIPPED CREAM:
1 cup whipping cream
2 tablespoons Grand Marnier

1 tablespoon powdered sugar or
   to taste

Whip cream in bowl until stiff. Slowly beat in Grand Marnier and powdered sugar until blended.

Skagit Valley Fare

Pineapple Cake

2 cups flour
2 cups sugar
1 (16-ounce) can crushed
  pineapple (in own juice)

$^1/_2$ cup egg substitute
1 tablespoon baking soda

Mix all ingredients together and pour into a 9x9x2-inch baking pan that has been sprayed with vegetable cooking spray. Bake at 350° for 30–35 minutes. Makes 8 servings.

From My Heart For Yours

Pineapple Pound Cake

1 cup oil
3 cups sugar
6 eggs
3 cups flour
1 teaspoon baking powder

Pinch of salt
$^3/_4$ cup crushed pineapple,
  undrained
1 teaspoon vanilla

Combine oil and sugar; mix well. Add eggs, 1 at a time, beating well after each addition. Combine flour, baking powder, and salt. Gradually add to oil mixture, beating well. Stir in pineapple and vanilla. Pour batter into a well-greased and floured 10-inch tube pan. Bake at 350° for 1 hour and 25 minutes. Invert pan and cool 10–15 minutes. Remove from pan and cool completely.

PINEAPPLE GLAZE:
2 tablespoons sugar
1$^1/_2$ teaspoons cornstarch

$^1/_2$ cup pineapple juice

Combine sugar and cornstarch in a heavy saucepan; stir well. Add juice, stirring well. Cook over medium heat until thickened and translucent. Cool slightly, pour over cake.

Liberty Lake Community Cookbook

Banana Nut Cake

This old-fashioned favorite is so easy to make. It is a deliciously moist cake, perfect for backyard picnics.

1/2 cup margarine or butter
1 cup sugar
2 eggs
1 teaspoon vanilla
2 very ripe bananas, sliced
21/4 cups unbleached white
  flour
11/4 teaspoons baking soda

1 teaspoon salt
1/2 cup buttermilk
3/4 cup coarsely chopped
  walnuts
Cream Cheese Frosting
1/4 cup finely chopped walnuts,
  toasted

Preheat oven to 350°. In a large mixing bowl, cream together margarine and sugar. Beat in eggs and vanilla, mixing well. Add bananas and beat again. On low speed, beat in flour, baking soda, and salt to egg mixture. Add buttermilk and mix; stir in 3/4 cup coarsely chopped walnuts.

Pour into a greased and floured 9x13-inch baking pan. Bake for 30–35 minutes or until toothpick inserted in center of cake comes out clean. Remove from oven and place on a wire rack to cool. Prepare Cream Cheese Frosting. When cool, frost cake and sprinkle with toasted walnuts.

CREAM CHEESE FROSTING:
1 (3-ounce) package cream
  cheese
2 tablespoons margarine or
  butter

1 teaspoon vanilla
11/2 cups powdered sugar
1 tablespoon milk, as needed

In a medium bowl, mix together cream cheese, margarine, and vanilla. Gradually beat in sugar until mixture is smooth and easily spread. Add milk to thin, if necessary.

San Juan Classics II Cookbook

Washington leads the nation in production of hydroelectricity, tapping the waters of the Grand Coulee, Chief Joseph and John Day dams, along with additional dams on the Columbia River, the Snake River and other rivers.

Japanese Fruit Cake

FRUIT CAKE:

1 cup margarine or butter	1 teaspoon salt
2 cups sugar	1 box raisins
1 teaspoon vanilla	1 cup chopped nuts
6 eggs	$1/2$ teaspoon cloves
1 cup milk	$1/2$ teaspoon cinnamon
3 cups flour	$1/2$ teaspoon nutmeg
2 teaspoons baking powder	

Cream butter, sugar, and vanilla. Add eggs, beating well. Add milk, a little at a time, with flour, baking powder, and salt; beat well. Divide dough in half. To the first half, add raisins and nuts, mixing well. To the second half, add cloves, cinnamon, and nutmeg, mixing well. Each half will bake 2 layers. Bake first half in 2 cake pans. Bake second half in 2 additional cake pans. Bake at 350° (preheated) for 20 minutes.

FILLING:

2 cups sugar	Juice of 2 oranges
1 cup boiling water	Juice of 1 lemon
2 teaspoons cornstarch	1 cup chopped nuts
1 fresh coconut, grated	Maraschino cherries (optional)

Put sugar, boiling water, and cornstarch in a saucepan; bring to boil. Add coconut, orange and lemon juices; cook until thick. Remove from heat. Add chopped nuts. Frost cake. Can use maraschino cherries to decorate, if desired.

From Our Kitchen to Yours

Washington is number one in the country in the production of apples, lentils, dry edible peas, hops, pears, red raspberries, spearmint oil and sweet cherries.

Classic Sugar-Free Fruit Cake

1 (6-ounce) can orange juice concentrate, thawed
1/2 cup rum
1 cup chopped cranberries
1 (8-ounce) package pitted dates, chopped
1 cup chopped pecans
1 tablespoon grated orange rind
2 eggs, lightly beaten (egg substitute may be used)
1 (8-ounce) can unsweetened pineapple tidbits, drained
2 cups all-purpose flour
1 1/4 teaspoons baking soda
1/2 teaspoon cinnamon
1/2 teaspoon ground nutmeg
1/4 teaspoon allspice
1 tablespoon vanilla extract
1/2 cup orange juice and 1/2 cup rum, for top

Combine orange juice concentrate, 1/2 cup rum, and chopped cranberries and allow to stand for 1 hour. Combine dates, pecans, orange rind, eggs, and pineapple. Add to cranberry mix and stir. Combine flour, baking soda, and spices. Add to fruit mix along with vanilla and stir well.

Spoon batter into Bundt pan that has been sprayed with cooking spray. Bake at 325° for 45 minutes or until cake tests done. Cool for 20 minutes and remove from pan. Combine 1/2 cup orange juice and 1/2 cup rum. Pour over cheesecloth which has been placed over top of cake. Let cake set. Wrap in waxed paper or Saran Wrap, then in foil. Store in cool dry place. May freeze till needed, 1 week or more.

Favorite Recipes from Our Best Cooks

Strawberry Surprise Cake

1 package miniature
  marshmallows
1 white cake mix
2 (10-ounce) packages frozen
  strawberries, thawed

2 (3-ounce) packages strawberry
  Jell-O mix

Butter 9x13-inch cake pan thoroughly. Sprinkle marshmallows on bottom to cover surface. Prepare cake mix as directed. Pour over marshmallows. Pour thawed berries on top of cake mix and then Jell-O mix over that. Bake at temperature directed on cake mix box.

Crime Stoppers: A Community Cookbook

Oatmeal Cake

CAKE:
$1^1/4$ cups boiling water
1 cup quick oats
$^1/2$ cup margarine
1 cup brown sugar
1 cup sugar
2 eggs, beaten
$1^1/2$ cups flour
1 teaspoon baking soda

$^1/2$ teaspoon salt
$^1/2$ teaspoon nutmeg
1 teaspoon cinnamon
1 teaspoon maple flavoring
$^1/2$–$^3/4$ cup ground raisins
  (optional)
$^1/2$–$^3/4$ cups chopped nuts
  (optional)

Pour boiling water over oats and margarine. Let stand 20 minutes. Combine remaining ingredients. Add oat mixture and mix well. Bake in greased and floured 9x13-inch pan at 350° for 35–40 minutes.

TOPPING:
1 cup brown sugar
$^1/4$ cup margarine
$^1/2$ cup chopped nuts

$^1/2$ cup cream
1 cup coconut
$^1/2$ teaspoon vanilla

Combine all ingredients and spread on warm cake. Put under broiler until bubbly and brown.

Taste of the Methow

Carrot Cake

2 cups all-purpose flour
2 cups sugar
1 teaspoon baking powder
1 teaspoon baking soda
1 teaspoon salt

1 teaspoon ground cinnamon
3 cups finely shredded carrots
1 cup oil
4 eggs

Grease and lightly flour a 9x13-inch pan or lightly spray pan with Pam. In a mixing bowl, combine first 6 ingredients. Add next 3 ingredients, beating with electric mixer until combined. Beat on medium speed for 2 minutes. Turn into pan. Bake in a 325° oven for 50–60 minutes or till done. Cool on a rack or in pan. Let the cake cool well before frosting.

CREAM CHEESE FROSTING:
1 (3-ounce) package cream
   cheese
$^1/_4$ cup butter or margarine

1 teaspoon vanilla
2 cups powdered sugar
1 cup chopped nuts (optional)

In a mixing bowl, beat together cream cheese, butter or margarine, and vanilla till light and fluffy. Gradually add powdered sugar, beating until smooth. Spread over cooled cake; sprinkle with chopped nuts, if desired.

Pig Out

Spice Cake

³/₄ cup shortening	³/₄ teaspoon cinnamon
2¹/₄ cups flour	¹/₂ teaspoon ground cloves
1 cup sugar	³/₄ cup brown sugar
1 teaspoon baking powder	1 cup sour milk*
1 teaspoon salt	3 eggs
³/₄ teaspoon baking soda	

Stir shortening to soften. Add all dry ingredients except brown sugar. Add brown sugar and milk. Mix till all flour is dampened. Add eggs and mix till well blended. Bake at 350° in 9x13-inch pan for 30–35 minutes. Let cool.

CREAM CHEESE FROSTING:

2 (3-ounce) packages cream cheese, softened	5 cups powdered sugar
2 tablespoons milk	1¹/₂ teaspoons vanilla

Cream cheese; blend with milk, then stir in sugar and vanilla until all is well blended. Frost cake.

*To make sour milk, add 1 tablespoon vinegar or lemon juice or 1³/₄ teaspoon cream of tartar to 1 cup milk.

Favorite Recipes, Numerica Credit Union

Spicy Bundt Cake
with Honey Roasted Garlic

HONEY ROASTED GARLIC:

5 heads fresh garlic   6 tablespoons honey
6 tablespoons vegetable oil

Cut about ¼ inch off tops of garlic heads, place heads in a small oven-proof pan and drizzle tops with oil and honey. Bake in pre-heated 400° oven for 40–50 minutes or until garlic is soft; cool.

SPICY BUNDT CAKE:

1 cup plain yogurt	3 large eggs
½ cup honey	1 cup vegetable oil
3 cups all-purpose flour	1 cup sugar
½ teaspoon salt	1 cup firmly packed light brown
1 teaspoon baking soda	sugar
2 teaspoons ground cinnamon	1 cup chopped walnuts
1 teaspoon allspice	Powdered sugar, for garnish
½ teaspoon ground ginger	

Preheat oven to 325°. Squeeze Honey Roasted Garlic into a small bowl, adding any liquid in pan; whisk in yogurt and honey until well combined.

Coat a 10-cup Bundt pan with nonstick spray. In a large bowl, whisk together flour, salt, baking soda, cinnamon, allspice, and ginger. In a second bowl, beat eggs; beat in oil and sugars until mixture is creamy. Stir dry ingredients into wet ingredients; stir in garlic mixture to combine. Fold in chopped walnuts. Pour into prepared pan.

Bake 55–60 minutes, until a tester inserted in center comes out clean. Cool in pan on rack 10 minutes, then turn out of pan and cool completely. Dust cooled cake with powdered sugar, if desired.

Northwest Garlic Festival Cookbook

Marlea's Pumpkin Roll

3 eggs
1 cup sugar
$^2/_3$ cup pumpkin
1 teaspoon lemon juice
$^3/_4$ cup flour

1 teaspoon baking powder
2 teaspoons cinnamon
1 teaspoon ginger
$^1/_2$ teaspoon nutmeg
$^1/_2$ teaspoon salt

Preheat oven to 375°. Line 10x15x1-inch pan with foil and spray with cooking spray. Mix eggs and sugar. Add pumpkin and lemon juice. In separate bowl, combine flour, baking powder, cinnamon, ginger, nutmeg, and salt. Add to pumpkin mixture. Pour batter into pan and bake 12–15 minutes. When done, turn out onto a dish towel covered with powdered sugar and roll up. Chill in freezer approximately $^1/_2$ hour and then unroll.

FILLING:
1 cup powdered sugar
1 (8-ounce) package cream
   cheese, softened

4 tablespoons margarine,
   softened
$^1/_2$ teaspoon vanilla

Mix ingredients until fluffy and smooth. Spread on pumpkin cake and roll up again. Can be frozen for 1–2 months.

Pig Out

214

COOKIES *and* CANDIES

Washington's coast includes the rugged and rocky Olympic Peninsula, encompassing the longest stretch of wild coastline outside Alaska.

Frost Bites

Orange spiced oatmeal cookies dipped in white chocolate.

3 tablespoons orange juice
3/4 cup raisins
1/2 cup margarine, at room
  temperature
3/4 cup sugar
1 large egg
2 teaspoons grated orange peel

1 cup flour
1 teaspoon baking soda
1 1/2 cups rolled oats
9 ounces (1 1/2 boxes) Nestle Toll
  House Premier White Baking
  Bars

In a small bowl, combine orange juice and raisins. Let stand several hours or overnight. In a large bowl, beat margarine and sugar until fluffy. Beat in egg and orange peel. In another bowl, combine flour and baking soda; stir into butter mixture. Add raisins, any soaking liquid that may be left in bowl, and oats. Mix well.

Drop dough by rounded teaspoonfuls onto ungreased baking sheets, spacing 2 inches apart; flatten slightly. Bake at 350° for 10–12 minutes. Transfer to racks and cool completely.

Follow melting directions on box of white chocolate, using either microwave or double boiler method. When cookies are completely cool, dip 1/3 of cookie in white chocolate. Set on waxed paper-lined baking sheets. Chill until chocolate is firm. Yields about 3 dozen.

Sharing Our Best

 Washington contains more glaciers than the other 47 contiguous states combined.

Oatmeal Cookies

1 cup butter
³/₄ cup sugar
³/₄ cup brown sugar
2 eggs
1 teaspoon vanilla
¹/₂ teaspoon salt
1 teaspoon baking soda
1¹/₂ cups flour

2 cups oats
1 (6-ounce) package chocolate chips
1 cup peanut butter (optional)
1 cup coconut (optional)
1 cup chopped nuts (optional)
1 cup raisins (optional)

Cream butter, sugars, eggs, and vanilla. Add dry ingredients, chocolate chips, and optional ingredients (if desired); mix well. Drop on greased baking sheet and bake at 375° for 10–12 minutes.

Note: Honey may be substituted for sugar, but use ¹/₂ the amount. These cookies are especially good with all ingredients.

Tastes of Country

No-Bake Oatmeal Chocolate Cookies

Great recipe for those who don't have an oven.

1 cup sugar
¹/₂ cup butter
¹/₃ cup milk
¹/₂ cup pecans, chopped
¹/₂ cup coconut

2 tablespoons grated lemon or orange peel
2 cups oatmeal
1 cup chocolate chips
2 tablespoons orange juice

Put sugar, butter, and milk in a food processor. Process until smooth. Add pecans, coconut, peel, oatmeal, chocolate chips, and orange juice. Process until just mixed. Line 2 cookie sheets with waxed paper. Drop mixture by teaspoonfuls onto waxed paper. Refrigerate 1 hour and store in airtight container. Keep refrigerated. Makes 36.

Recipe by Mariners Moose, Mascot, Seattle Mariners
Mariners Mix'n and Fix'n Grand Slam Style

Peanut Butter-Chocolate Chip Cookies

1 cup creamy peanut butter   2 large eggs
1 cup sugar   1 cup semisweet chocolate chips

It's no mistake—there's no flour or butter in these cookies. Heat oven to 350°; mix peanut butter, sugar, and eggs in a medium bowl with a wooden spoon until blended. Stir in chocolate chips. Drop rounded teaspoonfuls 2 inches apart on ungreased cookie sheet. Bake 10–12 minutes or until bottom of cookies are lightly browned. Cool on cookie sheet 2 minutes before removing to a wire rack to cool completely. Makes approximately 2 dozen. You may substitute raisins or coarsely chopped peanuts for some of the chocolate chips.

A Taste of Heaven

Mrs. Overlake's Cookies

The secret is to overdose on chocolate chips and nuts, then underbake for a chewy, moist, scrumptious cookie.

1 cup butter, melted   1 teaspoon baking soda
3/4 cup sugar   1 teaspoon salt
3/4 cup brown sugar   3–4 cups (18–24 ounces)
2 eggs   chocolate chips
1 overflowing teaspoon vanilla   2 cups chopped pecans
2 1/2 cups unsifted flour

Preheat oven to 325°. In a large bowl, cream together butter and sugars, then beat in eggs and vanilla. Sift together flour, baking soda, and salt. Stir into butter mixture, forming a stiff batter. Add chips and nuts.

Use an ice cream scoop to drop batter on ungreased cookie sheet, averaging 9 cookies per sheet. Bake at 325° for 15–18 minutes, checking periodically to see that they are not overbaked. Yields 27 big cookies!

The Overlake School Cookbook

Banana Drop Cookies

A family favorite. This recipe comes from my sister-in-law and is so good. Banana flavored cookies are hard to find.

2 cups all-purpose flour
1 teaspoon baking powder
1/2 teaspoon ground cinnamon
1/4 teaspoon baking soda
1/4 teaspoon salt
1/4 teaspoon ground cloves

1/2 cup butter
1 cup sugar
2 eggs
1/2 teaspoon vanilla
2 medium bananas

In a bowl mix flour, baking powder, cinnamon, baking soda, salt, and cloves. Set aside. In mixing bowl beat butter for 30 seconds. Add sugar and beat until fluffy. Add eggs and vanilla. Beat well. Add dry ingredients and 1 banana at a time. Drop from teaspoon 2 inches apart. Bake at 350° for 10–12 minutes. Remove from cookie sheet immediately. Cool. Frost. Makes 3 dozen.

FROSTING:
2 cups powdered sugar, sifted
1/4 cup mashed banana

2 tablespoons butter, softened
1/2 teaspoon vanilla
2 tablespoons milk

In a bowl, mix all ingredients well. Frost cookies as desired.

Recipe by Gil Meche, Pitcher, Seattle Mariners
Starters & Closers

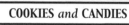

Rice Krispies Cookies

1 cup shortening	1 teaspoon baking soda
$^1/_3$ cup butter or margarine	$^1/_2$ teaspoon baking powder
1 cup sugar	$^1/_2$ teaspoon salt
1 cup brown sugar	2 cups oatmeal
2 eggs	1 cup coconut
1 teaspoon vanilla	2 cups Rice Krispies
2 cups flour	

Cream shortening, butter or margarine, and sugars; add eggs and vanilla. Add dry ingredients including oatmeal and coconut. Add Rice Krispies last. Drop onto greased cookie sheet and press down with a fork. Bake at 350° for 10–12 minutes or until lightly browned.

Favorite Recipes from Our Best Cooks

Butterfinger Cookies

These great cookies never last long.

$^1/_2$ cup butter, softened	1 cup all-purpose flour
$^3/_4$ cup sugar	$^1/_2$ teaspoon baking soda
$^2/_3$ cup brown sugar	$^1/_4$ teaspoon salt
2 egg whites	5 (2.1-ounce) Butterfinger candy
$1^1/_4$ cups chunky peanut butter	bars, chopped
$1^1/_2$ teaspoons vanilla	

Preheat oven to 350°. In a mixing bowl, cream butter and sugars. Add egg whites. Beat well. Blend in peanut butter and vanilla. Combine flour, baking soda, and salt and add to cream mixture. Mix well. Stir in candy bars. Shape into $1^1/_2$-inch balls and place on greased cookie sheet. Bake for 10–12 minutes or until golden brown. Cool on wire racks. Makes 4 dozen.

Recipe by Bryan Price, Pitching Coach, Seattle Mariners
Home Plates

Corn Flake Macaroons

2 egg whites
¹/₂ teaspoon vanilla
³/₄ cup sugar

2 cups cornflakes
¹/₂ cup chopped nuts
³/₄ cup shredded coconut

Beat egg whites and vanilla until foamy; gradually add sugar while beating. Continue to beat until stiff and glossy. Fold in cornflakes, nuts, and coconut. Drop by level tablespoon onto well-greased cookie sheet. Bake at 350° about 12 minutes or until lightly browned. Remove from baking sheets immediately and cool on wire rack. Yields about 2¹/₂ dozen macaroons.

Our Best Home Cooking

Molasses Crinkles

²/₃ cup oil
1 egg
¹/₄ cup molasses
¹/₂ cup sugar
¹/₂ cup brown sugar
2 cups flour

1 teaspoon baking soda
1 teaspoon baking powder
¹/₄ teaspoon salt
¹/₂ teaspoon cloves
1 teaspoon cinnamon
1 teaspoon ginger

Preheat oven to 375°. Mix wet and dry ingredients separately. Blend them together and chill. Roll into balls then roll in sugar. Bake for 10–12 minutes.

Taste of Balboa

 In 1974, Spokane became the smallest city in size to host a World's Fair.

Grandma Lizzie's Ginger Cookies

'Member the day of the cookie jar? Is the spicy fragrance of ginger or molasses cookies only a faded memory? These are more than cookies as they will rekindle your memories of your grandmother.

1 cup sugar	1 teaspoon ginger
1 cup butter (no substitute)	1 teaspoon baking soda
1 cup molasses	A little hot water
1 egg	4 cups flour
1 tablespoon vinegar	

Mix all ingredients together and chill. Roll out to your own desired thickness and cut to shapes for the occasion. Bake at 375° for 7–10 minutes.

Sleigh Bells and Sugarplums

Big Soft Ginger Cookies

These are just what they say—big, soft, gingerbread cookies. They stay soft, too.

2¹/₄ cups all-purpose flour	³/₄ cup margarine, softened
2 teaspoons ground ginger	1 cup plus 2 tablespoons sugar,
1 teaspoon baking soda	divided
³/₄ teaspoon ground cinnamon	1 egg
¹/₂ teaspoon ground cloves	1 tablespoon water
¹/₄ teaspoon salt	¹/₄ cup molasses

Preheat oven to 350°. Sift together flour, ginger, baking soda, cinnamon, cloves, and salt. Set aside.

In large bowl, cream together margarine and 1 cup sugar until light and fluffy. Beat in egg, then stir in water and molasses. Gradually stir sifted ingredients into molasses mixture. Shape dough into walnut-size balls and roll them in remaining 2 tablespoons sugar. Place cookies 2 inches apart onto an ungreased cookie sheet and flatten slightly.

Bake for 8–10 minutes in preheated oven. Allow cookies to cool on baking sheet for 5 minutes before removing to wire rack to cool completely. Store in an airtight container. Makes 2 dozen.

Allrecipes Tried & True Favorites

Chocolate Marshmallow Cookies

¹/₂ cup butter, softened
1 cup sugar
1 egg
1 teaspoon vanilla
¹/₄ cup milk
1³/₄ cups sifted flour
¹/₂ teaspoon salt
¹/₂ teaspoon baking soda

¹/₂ cup cocoa
18–24 marshmallows, cut in half
2 cups sifted powdered sugar
5 tablespoons cocoa
¹/₈ teaspoon salt
3 tablespoons butter
4–5 tablespoons cream
¹/₂ cup pecan halves

Cream butter and sugar. Add egg, vanilla, and milk; beat well. Sift together the flour, salt, baking soda, and cocoa; add to creamed mixture and blend well. Drop by teaspoon onto cookie sheet. Bake at 350° for 8 minutes; don't overbake. Remove from oven and press ¹/₂ of a marshmallow, cut-side-down, onto each cookie. Bake 2 minutes longer. Cool. Combine powdered sugar, cocoa, salt, butter, and cream; cream together well. Frost tops of cookies and top with pecan halves. Store in airtight container to keep marshmallows soft.

Sleigh Bells and Sugarplums

Kruste
(Italian Honey Cookies)

¹/₂ cup butter-flavored Crisco, melted
¹/₂ cup vegetable oil
1 ounce bourbon
1 dozen large eggs

¹/₂ cup sugar
6–7 cups flour (depending on size of eggs, you may need more or less flour)
Oil for deep frying

Use blender to blend all ingredients together, except flour and oil. Blend well. Pour the mixture into a very large bowl. Add flour slowly using a wooden spoon. Dough will reach a bread dough consistency. Be careful not to add so much flour that the dough is dry. Divide dough into 3 portions. On floured surface, roll dough no thicker than ¹/₄ inch. Cut into 2x2-inch squares. Cut a slit in the center of each square. Deep-fry in at least 3 inches of oil only until a golden color on each side. Cool and set aside.

2 quarts honey
1 cup shelled crushed walnuts
3 tablespoons sugar

1 tablespoon cinnamon
Zest from 3 large oranges

Dip cookie into simmering honey. If desired, sprinkle with finely crushed walnuts and mixture of sugar, cinnamon, and zest.

Cooking with Irene!

Safeco Field, Seattle's newest ballpark for the Mariners baseball team, opened on July 15, 1999. (The former ballpark, the Kingdome, was imploded on March 26, 2000.) Safeco Field's retractable roof covers the ballpark, but does not enclose it. Like a big umbrella, the nine-acre roof covers the field and seating areas. The roof is 275 feet high, weighs 22 million pounds, and contains enough steel to build a 55-story skyscraper. Opening and closing with the push of a button, it uses less power than it takes to operate a car. Roof sections move about six miles per hour, resting on steel wheels that roll along steel rails.

Almond Bars

This cookie has been a favorite in our family for over 30 years. When our daughter was married at the Seattle Yacht Club, these bars were requested in lieu of a cake.

CRUST:
3/4 cup butter
1/2 cup sugar
1 egg

1 teaspoon vanilla
2 1/4 cups flour
1/2 teaspoon salt

Cream butter and sugar. Stir in the other ingredients. Press into a greased 9x13-inch pan.

ALMOND LAYER:
2 eggs
1/2 cup sugar
2 teaspoons butter

1 (8-ounce) can almond paste
1 teaspoon almond extract
3/4 cup chopped almonds

Beat eggs with sugar; slowly add butter, almond paste, and almond extract. Pour over Crust and spread with nuts. Bake at 325° for 25–35 minutes or until a toothpick in center comes out clean. Cool. Cut into bars.

Extraordinary Cuisine for Sea & Shore

Mike's Babe Ruth Bars

1 cup sugar
1 cup light corn syrup
1 cup chunky peanut butter
6 cups Special K Cereal

1 (6-ounce) package chocolate chips
1 (6-ounce) package butterscotch chips

Combine sugar and corn syrup in saucepan. Place over medium heat and bring to a boil, stirring occasionally. Remove from heat. Add peanut butter and mix well. Stir in cereal until evenly coated. Press mixture into a buttered 9x13-inch pan. Cool. Melt chips. Spread over cooled mixture. Cool; cut into bars.

Recipes from Our Friends

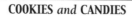

German Chocolate Bars

1 package German chocolate
  cake mix
$^2/_3$ cup butter

1 cup chocolate chips
1 container pecan frosting
$^1/_2$ cup milk

Mix cake mix together with butter. Divide it in half and spread half in a 9x13-inch pan; bake at 350° for 10 minutes. Remove from oven; sprinkle with chocolate chips. Drop frosting by teaspoonfuls on top of chocolate chips. Combine milk with reserved batter and drop on top of frosting by teaspoonfuls. Bake at 350° for 30–35 minutes, or until top appears dry. Cool completely before cutting.

Western Washington Oncology Cook Book

Peanut Butter Brittle

It's a two-person job at the end, but well worth the trouble. It melts in your mouth.

2 cups peanut butter
$1^1/_2$ cups sugar
$1^1/_2$ cups light corn syrup
$^1/_4$ cup water
2 tablespoons butter

2 cups dry-roasted, unsalted
  peanuts
1 teaspoon baking soda,
  dissolved in 2 teaspoons water
1 teaspoon vanilla

Place peanut butter in double boiler to warm while syrup cooks. In a saucepan, cook sugar, syrup, and water until candy thermometer reaches 275°. Remove thermometer. Lower heat to medium. Add butter; stir until dissolved. Add peanuts. Stir 5 minutes over medium heat. Continue to cook until candy starts turning brown (300° on candy thermometer). Remove from heat. Add baking soda and water mixture and vanilla. Fold in peanut butter as lightly as possible, peanut butter should be warm by this time. Pour on well-greased slab or table, or use 2 (11x17-inch) cookie sheets. Candy should be spread as thin as possible. It should be golden brown and flaky.

Harvest Feast

Velveeta Fudge

1 cup butter
8 ounces Velveeta cheese
1 1/2 teaspoons vanilla

2 pounds powdered sugar
1/2 cup cocoa
Chopped pecans (optional)

Melt butter and cheese in saucepan over low heat, stirring constantly. Mix in vanilla. Pour over mixture of powdered sugar and cocoa in bowl; mix quickly until well blended. Spread in buttered 9x13-inch dish. Pat pecans over top, if desired. Let stand until set. Cut into squares. Yields 3 pounds fudge.

Favorite Recipes, Numerica Credit Union

Never Fail Fudge

4 1/2 cups sugar
1 large can evaporated milk
4 tablespoons butter
1/4 teaspoon salt
1 (12-ounce) package chocolate
  chips

12 ounces plain sweet chocolate
  bars
1 pint marshmallow creme
2 cups broken walnuts
1 teaspoon vanilla

Boil first 4 ingredients for 10 minutes. Remove from heat. Add remaining ingredients. Stir until smooth. Pour into a greased 9x13-inch pan. Cut after mixture has set. Store in tightly covered container. Yields 5 pounds. Freezes well.

Heavenly Fare

Roca

1 pound walnuts
30 (1.55-ounce) Hershey's bars
1 pound butter (no substitute)

1 pound light brown sugar
1 pound raw cashews (broken
 pieces work fine)

Crush walnuts. Put half of walnuts in bottom of a jellyroll pan (18x12x1 inches). Cover with 15 unwrapped Hershey's bars. Melt butter in a heavy kettle. (A pressure saucepan works well.) Add brown sugar. Stir until dissolved. Cook to 284°, stirring constantly to prevent burning. Remove from heat and add cashews. Pour over prepared pan. Spread syrup to all corners of jellyroll pan. Cover with remaining Hershey's bars and quickly spread out evenly. Top with remaining walnuts. Let set overnight. Using a chef's knife, cut into irregular-size pieces. Store in an airtight container. The crumbs left on the pan can be saved for use as ice cream topping.

Sharing Our Best

Chocolate Ball Candy

1 can condensed milk
1 cup butter
2 pounds powdered sugar, sifted
14 ounces flaked coconut

1 cup chopped nuts
1 (12-ounce) package chocolate
 chips
1 block paraffin

Heat milk and butter, stirring constantly, until butter melts. Remove from heat and slowly add sifted powdered sugar, coconut, and nuts. Cool. Roll into balls. Let stand until cold.

Melt chocolate chips and paraffin. Dip balls into chocolate and set on cookie sheet. Freezes well.

From Our Kitchen to Yours

Films and television shows that have made Washington famous include: "Sleepless in Seattle," "Snow Falling on Cedars," "The Egg and I," "Singles," "Fabulous Baker Boys," "Assassins," "An Officer and a Gentleman," "Lassie Come Home," "War of the Roses," "Frasier," "Twin Peaks" and "Northern Exposure."

Granny's Divinity Nut Rolls

2 cups sugar
$^1/_2$ cup water
1 cup white Karo syrup, divided
2 egg whites

1 teaspoon vanilla
1 can sweetened condensed milk
$^1/_4$ teaspoon salt
3 cups chopped walnuts

Combine sugar, water, and $^1/_2$ cup Karo syrup; stir well. Stir over low heat until sugar is dissolved. Cover pan; bring to boil for 1 minute. Remove cover; continue cooking over medium heat until mixture reaches 265° on candy thermometer.

Meanwhile in large bowl, beat egg whites until stiff, then pour sugar mixture (gradually) over egg whites, beating until stiff; add vanilla. Let stand at room temperature until stiff (like dough). With buttered hands, form into about 25 small rolls. Let set at least 3 hours. Combine condensed milk, salt, and remaining $^1/_2$ cup Karo syrup, and cook over low heat about 20 minutes or until at soft-ball stage. Stir often. Drop rolls in mixture 1 at a time, turning to coat log. Remove with fork, then roll logs in nuts. Let stand until firm, then slice.

From Our Kitchen to Yours

White Chocolate Clusters

Kids love to help make these cereal treats.

$1^1/_4$ pounds vanilla-flavored
   candy coating or almond bark,
   cut up
$1^1/_2$ cups mini marshmallows

$1^1/_2$ cups peanut butter cereal
$1^1/_2$ cups crisp rice cereal
$1^1/_2$ cups chopped mixed nuts

In a heavy 2-quart saucepan, over low heat, melt candy coating; stir constantly. Remove from heat. In a large bowl, combine marshmallows, cereals, and nuts. Pour melted coating over mixture; stir to coat. Drop mixture by rounded teaspoons onto baking sheets lined with wax paper. Cool. Makes about 40 clusters.

Recipe by Charles Gipson, Outfielder, Seattle Mariners
Starters & Closers

Stix 'n Stones

These were one of the sweet treat favorites in our home when our children were growing up. Actually, Dad enjoyed them the most.

1 (12-ounce) package
  butterscotch chips
2–3 cups Kix cereal

1 cup dry (oriental) noodles
1–1¹/₂ cups miniature
  marshmallows

Melt chips on low-medium burner or in the microwave. They will hold their shape until stirred, so test often or they may scorch. Add remaining 3 ingredients to melted chips, stir gently to coat well. Drop by large spoonfuls onto waxed paper; let cool.

We have added other cereals, other chips, and melted some of the marshmallow with the chips. Also try adding raisins, coconut, granola, nuts or M&M'S. Any flavor chip works well and cereals, too.

McNamee Family & Friends Cookbook

PIES *and* OTHER DESSERTS

Mount St. Helens is the only volcano to erupt in recent history on the continental United States. When the volcano erupted in 1980, it devastated 230 square miles of southwest Washington.

Northwest Huckleberry Pie

Native huckleberries are a summer treat for hikers throughout the timberline areas of the Pacific Northwest. These small, firm berries are a favorite of cooks and bears alike. If you are unable to find them, blueberries are a reasonable alternative.

1 (9-inch) pie crust, unbaked

FILLING:
$3/4$ cup sugar
$1/4$ cup all-purpose flour
$1/2$ teaspoon nutmeg
$1/2$ teaspoon cinnamon

5 cups peeled, cored, and thinly sliced tart apples
1 cup huckleberries or blueberries

TOPPING:
1 cup all-purpose flour
$1/2$ cup butter, cut into pieces

$1/2$ cup brown sugar

Press pie crust into a 9-inch pie plate and flute edges. Combine Filling ingredients and place in pie crust. Combine Topping ingredients and mix until crumbly. Sprinkle over pie filling. Bake at 375° for 50 minutes. Cover with aluminum foil for the last 10 minutes if top browns too quickly. Serves 8.

Gold'n Delicious

Huckleberry Pie

$3/4$ cup sugar
$2^{1/2}$ tablespoons cornstarch
$1/4$ teaspoon salt
$2/3$ cup water
3 cups huckleberries (fresh or frozen), divided

2 tablespoons butter
$1^{1/2}$ tablespoons lemon juice
1 cup whipped cream
2 tablespoons powdered sugar
$1/2$ teaspoon vanilla
1 (9-inch) pie shell, baked

Combine first 4 ingredients and 1 cup huckleberries; boil until thick. Add butter and lemon juice, then cool. Fold in remaining berries and chill. Whip cream with powdered sugar and vanilla and spread half in baked pie shell. Add filling and top with remaining whipped cream.

Favorite Recipes from Our Best Cooks

Elderberry Pie

4 cups elderberries
1 pint water
3 tablespoons lemon juice
1 pinch salt

2 cups sugar
3 tablespoons flour
1/4 teaspoon cinnamon
Pastry for 2 crusts

Combine berries, water, and lemon juice then add the dry ingredients and mix well. Pour into unbaked pie crust and top with second crust. Pinch edges and trim excess. Slit top in 4 places. Bake at 425° for 25–35 minutes or until done.

The Wild and Free Cookbook

My Secret Apple Pie

1 1/4 cups sugar
1 1/4 teaspoons cinnamon
1/2 teaspoon nutmeg
1/2 teaspoon salt
1/3 cup cornstarch

2 (9-inch) pie crusts, unbaked
6–7 cups sliced apples
1/4 cup orange juice
1/4 cup honey or maple syrup

Mix all dry ingredients in 1 gallon plastic bag. Line pan with crust. Add sliced apples to the plastic bag. Shake quickly to coat apples and dump immediately into crust. Mix orange juice and honey. Spread juice mixture over apples and seal on top crust. Sprinkle drops of water on crust and then a little sugar on the set spots. Cut a few vent holes in top and bake with edge of crust protected. Uncover edge for the final 10–15 minutes of baking. Bake at 425° for 70–75 minutes. The secret is out!

Taste of the Methow

 Washington is the nation's top apple-producing state, so it is appropriate that the apple was named the state fruit.

Ann's Lemon Pie

FILLING:

1 1/4 cups sugar	1/3 cup lemon juice
6 tablespoons cornstarch	1/2 teaspoon lemon extract
2 cups water	2 teaspoons vinegar
3 egg yolks (reserve whites	3 tablespoons butter
for Meringue)	1 (9-inch) pie shell, baked

Mix sugar and cornstarch; add water. Combine egg yolks with lemon juice; beat. Add to sugar mixture. Cook in double boiler for 25 minutes, until thick. Add lemon extract, vinegar, and butter. Pour into pie shell.

MERINGUE:

1 tablespoon cornstarch	3 tablespoons sugar
2 tablespoons cold water	1 teaspoon vanilla
1/2 cup hot water	1/8 teaspoon salt
3 egg whites	

Mix cornstarch with cold water. Add hot water and boil until thick. Cool. Beat egg whites until foamy. Stir in sugar, vanilla, and salt. Add cornstarch mixture and beat on high speed to blend. Put on Filling and bake at 350° for 10 minutes.

Our Best Home Cooking

Hawaiian Chess Pie

1 cup sugar	1 heaping teaspoon cornmeal
4 eggs, beaten	2 cups coconut
1/2 cup butter or margarine, melted	1 cup crushed pineapple, drained
1 heaping teaspoon flour	1 (9-inch) unbaked pie shell

Mix sugar and eggs. Add butter, flour, cornmeal, coconut, and pineapple. Mix well. Pour into unbaked pie shell. Bake at 350° for 1 hour. Good with a dollop of whipped cream.

Crime Stoppers: A Community Cookbook

Cream Pie

1 cup milk	1/2 teaspoon salt
1 cup light cream	2 egg yolks
3 tablespoons flour	1 teaspoon vanilla
1 tablespoon cornstarch	1 pie shell, baked
1/2 cup sugar	Meringue

Scald milk and cream in double boiler. Combine flour, cornstarch, sugar, and salt. Mix together thoroughly. Add to scalded milk and cook 15 minutes, stirring constantly. Pour slowly over slightly beaten egg yolks and return to double boiler. Cook 1 minute. Cool and add vanilla. Pour into pie shell and top with meringue.

Tastes of Country

In 1792 Captain George Vancouver of Britain became the first European to complete a detailed survey of the Washington coast and the inland waters. Vancouver named many Washington landmarks, including Mount Rainier, Mount Baker, and many of the San Juan Islands. Vancouver named Puget Sound after the officer who first sighted it, Peter Puget.

Washington Nut Pie

1 (9-inch) pie pastry
3 eggs
1/2 cup sugar
4 tablespoons butter, melted

1 cup dark Karo syrup
1/4 teaspoon salt
1 teaspoon vanilla
1 cup chopped pecans

Line a 9-inch pie plate with pastry. Beat eggs; add sugar, butter, syrup, salt, and vanilla. Fold in nuts. Bake at 450° for 15 minutes, then reduce to 375° for 25–30 minutes. Be careful not to overbake—should be like a custard.

Unser Tagelich Brot (The Staff of Life III)

Peanut Butter Fudge Pie

1 (8-ounce) package cream
  cheese
1/2 cup peanut butter
1 cup powdered sugar, sifted
2 tablespoons milk
1 teaspoon vanilla

4 ounces frozen whipped
  topping, thawed
1 graham cracker pie shell
3/4 cup fudge ice cream topping,
  divided
Chopped peanuts for garnish

Soften cream cheese, add peanut butter, and beat with mixer until combined. Add sugar, milk, and vanilla, and beat until combined. Fold in whipped topping. Spoon half the cream cheese mixture into pie shell, and spread with 1/2 cup fudge topping. Place remaining mixture in crust; cover and freeze at least 6 hours. Let pie stand at room temperature 15 minutes before serving. Drizzle with remaining topping and sprinkle with chopped peanuts.

Washington Cook Book

Huckleberry Cream Tart

Wild huckleberries are full of flavor and combine well with cream cheese.

TART SHELL:

$^1/_3$ cup butter	1 egg yolk
$^1/_4$ cup sugar	1 cup all-purpose flour

Preheat oven to 375°. Make tart shell by beating butter with sugar until light and fluffy. Add egg yolk and combine. Gradually beat in flour until just blended. Form dough into ball and press into bottom and sides of an ungreased 9- to 10-inch tart pan with removable bottom. Bake in oven for 10–12 minutes. Cool on rack.

FILLING:

3 cups huckleberries (fresh or frozen)	1 (3-ounce) package cream cheese, regular or light
1 cup sugar mixed with $^1/_4$ cup all-purpose flour	$^1/_2$ cup powdered sugar
1 tablespoon lemon juice	$^1/_2$ teaspoon vanilla
	$^1/_2$ cup heavy (whipping) cream

Combine huckleberries, sugar-flour mixture, and lemon juice in a medium saucepan and cook over medium or medium-high heat just long enough to thicken, 12–15 minutes, stirring frequently. (Turn down heat if mixture boils rapidly.) Berries should remain nearly whole. Let cool.

Beat the cream cheese, powdered sugar, and vanilla in a medium bowl until light. Whip cream stiff in separate bowl and fold into cream cheese mixture. Spread evenly into baked Tart Shell and top with cooled huckleberry mixture. Chill in refrigerator for 2 hours or longer before serving. Serves 6–8.

Wandering & Feasting

 The square dance is the official Washington state dance. When the pioneers came west, they brought with them a dance called the quadrille, which means square in French. The pioneers liked the simpler term and so the square dance was born.

Wild Blackberry Tart

CRUST:

1 cup flour

Pinch of salt

8 tablespoons butter

3 ounces cream cheese

Combine flour and salt in food processor. Cut butter and cream cheese into small pieces and distribute over flour. Process till dough just begins to come together. (Do not overwork dough.) Form into ball by hand. Wrap in plastic and refrigerate for $1/2$ hour.

Roll out on lightly floured surface. Carefully lay in 9- or 10-inch lightly greased tart pan. (Do not stretch dough. Patch rather than re-roll. Do not overwork.) Trim edges leaving $1/2$-inch finished edge. Freeze for 1 hour. Partially bake for 15 minutes at 350° to set crust. Pierce any bubbles that start to form while baking.

FILLING:

12 ounces cream cheese,
  softened

$1/2$ cup sugar

2 eggs

1 teaspoon grated lemon rind

$1/2$ teaspoon vanilla

Whip cream cheese thoroughly till all lumps are gone. Scrape sides of bowl often. Put mixer on low; add sugar slowly, scraping bowl often. Add eggs, 1 at a time. Mix in lemon rind and vanilla.

Pour Filling into Crust; bake about 30 minutes in 350° oven till lightly puffed and set—just beginning to take on a light golden hue—do not overcook. Cool at room temperature, about $1/2$ hour.

BLACKBERRY TOPPING:

4 cups wild blackberries,
  divided

3 tablespoons cornstarch

1 cup sugar

1 teaspoon freshly squeezed
  lemon juice

Mash 1 cup blackberries; strain; reserve pulp. Add cornstarch to blackberry juice; mix thoroughly. Add sugar. Place in saucepan over medium heat; stir until translucent and thickened—about 2 minutes. Boil until thickened and slightly reduced. Remove from heat. Add reserved pulp, 3 cups wild blackberries, and lemon juice. Stir. Spread gently over tart. Rest at room temperature 30 minutes; refrigerate till firm. Serves 10–12.

Note: Cut with clean, hot, dry serrated knife to keep the dark berry color separate from the rich white cream filling.

The Best of The Ark and More!

Apple Blackberry Crisp

FILLING:

6 Golden Delicious apples
2 cups blackberries (fresh or frozen)

¹/₂ cup sugar
2 tablespoons flour

Preheat oven to 350°. Butter a 9x13-inch baking dish. Peel and core apples. Cut into thin slices. Place apples in prepared dish. Top with blackberries. (If using frozen berries, do not thaw first.) Sprinkle with sugar and flour.

TOPPING:

¹/₂ cup rolled oats
¹/₂ cup flour
¹/₂ cup chopped nuts (optional)

¹/₃ cup butter, melted
¹/₃ cup brown sugar
1 teaspoon cinnamon

Combine oats, flour, nuts, butter, sugar, and cinnamon in a bowl till crumbly. Sprinkle Topping evenly over Filling. Bake till fruit is soft and bubbly and Topping is browned, 35– 40 minutes. Serve warm, topped with ice cream or whipped cream. Serves 6.

Favorite Recipes from Our Best Cooks

Raspberry Almond Crisp

Serve warm with a dollop of good-quality vanilla ice cream.

FILLING:

3 (12-ounce) packages frozen raspberries, thawed, or 6 cups fresh

$^1/_2$ cup sugar
1 teaspoon almond extract
$^1/_2$ cup flour

Preheat oven to 375°. Butter an 8x8-inch baking pan. If using frozen raspberries, drain them. In a medium bowl, gently mix raspberries, sugar, and almond extract. Sprinkle flour over mixture and gently mix well. Spoon mixture into pan.

TOPPING:

1 cup packed brown sugar
1 cup flour
$^3/_4$ cup regular or quick rolled oats
1 teaspoon ground cinnamon

1 stick ($^1/_2$ cup) unsalted butter, room temperature, cut into pieces
$^1/_2$ cup sliced almonds

Combine brown sugar, flour, rolled oats, and cinnamon in a medium bowl. Using a pastry blender, work butter into the mixture. (It will be crumbly.) Add almonds and mix well. Sprinkle Topping evenly over Filling. Bake 30 minutes, or until fruit is bubbling and the top is golden. Serve with whipped cream or vanilla ice cream. Yields 6–9 servings.

Good Times at Green Lake

Strawberry-Apple Crisp

6–8 large tart apples (Granny
   Smiths are good)
1½–2 cups fresh strawberries or
   frozen, thawed with juice
2 tablespoons apple juice

1 tablespoon lemon juice
1 tablespoon all-purpose white
   flour
2 teaspoons cinnamon

Peel and core apples. Thinly slice apples lengthwise and place in a
9x13-inch baking dish. Add strawberries with juice, apple juice,
and lemon juice. Sprinkle with flour and cinnamon and lightly toss
in the baking dish.

TOPPING:
1½ cups old-fashioned rolled
   oats
¼ cup wheat germ, toasted
⅓ cup finely chopped pecans
Pinch of salt
1 teaspoon cinnamon

½ teaspoon nutmeg
2 tablespoons honey
¼ cup brown sugar
3 tablespoons melted butter or
   olive oil

In a medium bowl, combine all Topping ingredients and sprinkle
evenly on top of apples and strawberries. Bake at 375° for 35–40
minutes, until apples are soft. Serve warm with non-fat frozen
yogurt or ice cream. Mmm!

Note: Blackberries, raspberries, or peaches may be substituted for strawberries.

Good Food for (Mostly) Good People Cookbook

Monsignor Chapel sits high atop the hillside of Red Willow Vineyard in Woodinville.
Inspired by the historic chapels in the great vineyards of France, it was built from stones
that were cleared from the land.

Old-Fashioned Berry Cobbler

This recipe is unbeatable and so attractive.

FRUIT:

4 cups frozen raspberries, blackberries, or loganberries

$^1/_2$ cup seedless raspberry jam

2 tablespoons quick-cooking tapioca

2 tablespoons sugar

2 tablespoons butter

Heat oven to 425°. Grease 10x6-inch baking dish or 1$^1/_2$-quart casserole. In large bowl, combine berries, jam, tapioca, and sugar; mix gently. Spread in greased dish. Dot with butter. Bake at 425° for 15–20 minutes or until berries begin to bubble; stir.

TOPPING:

1 cup flour

2 tablespoons sugar

2 teaspoons baking powder

$^1/_4$ teaspoon salt

$^1/_4$ cup butter

2–4 tablespoons milk

1 egg

$^1/_2$ teaspoon sugar

Lightly spoon flour into measuring cup; level off. In large bowl, combine flour, sugar, baking powder, and salt; mix well. With pastry blender or fork, cut in butter until crumbly. In small bowl, beat 2 tablespoons milk and egg until blended, adding to flour mixture with additional milk if necessary, to form stiff dough. On lightly floured surface, roll out dough to $^1/_2$-inch thickness. With 2-inch cookie cutter, cut out hearts, stars, circles, or diamonds. Place on top of hot fruit mixture; sprinkle with $^1/_2$ teaspoon sugar. Bake at 425° for 15–25 minutes or until fruit bubbles around edges and biscuits are light golden brown. Serve warm with cream or ice cream.

Bounteous Blessings

Cobbler in a Shake

6–8 apples
$^1/_4$ cup sugar, divided
1 teaspoon cinnamon
$^1/_3$ cup raisins (optional)

$^1/_2$ cup biscuit mix
2 eggs, beaten
1 cup milk

Butter a deep-dish pie plate and fill it with peeled, thinly sliced apples. Sprinkle with a mixture of $^1/_8$ cup sugar and cinnamon. Scatter the raisins. In a quart jar, shake together biscuit mix, eggs, milk, and remaining sugar until they are evenly blended, and pour over apples. Bake at 375° for 35–45 minutes or until apples are tender.

A Taste of Heaven

Quick and Easy Blackberry Cobbler

2 quarts blackberries
$^1/_2$ cup lemon juice
4 cups sugar

1 tablespoon butter
2 packages canned biscuits

Mash berries and add lemon juice, sugar, and butter. Bring to a boil and reduce heat. Simmer for 10 minutes or until berries change color and mixture thickens. Pour into buttered baking dish or a thin pie crust. Top hot berries with canned biscuits, just touching, and bake, following package directions for biscuits. This is usually about 8–12 minutes at 400°–425°. Serve hot with whipped cream or vanilla ice cream.

The Wild and Free Cookbook

Teapot Dome Service Station, located on Old State Highway 12 in Zillah, Washington, was built in 1922 and is the oldest operating gas station in the United States.

Apple Strudel

DOUGH:

1 large egg	⅛ teaspoon salt
1 tablespoon sugar	¼ cup warm water
1 tablespoon butter, melted	1+ cups flour

Mix egg, sugar, butter, salt, and warm water in large bowl. Add 1 cup flour, a little at a time. (May need from ⅛ to ¼ cup more flour for desired consistency.) Work Dough until satin-like. Place on floured cloth and cover with a bowl which has been warmed with hot water. (Pour water out of bowl, but do not dry.) Turn bowl upside down over dough for 1 hour.

FILLING:

1½ cups sugar	¾ cup plus 4 tablespoons
2 teaspoons cinnamon	melted butter, divided
1½ cups bread crumbs	6 cups finely chopped apples

Mix sugar, cinnamon, bread crumbs, and ¾ cup melted butter for Filling; set aside.

Roll Dough into small circle and butter well with melted butter. Let set ½ hour. With Dough on a tablecloth, roll paper thin. Spread with chopped apples out to edges. Sprinkle Filling mixture over apples and by lifting 1 edge of cloth, roll-up like a jellyroll. Place on greased cookie sheet and brush with melted butter. Bake at 425° for 15 minutes, then turn oven to 350° and bake another 30 minutes. Lightly baste a time or two with melted butter while baking. Cool and dust with powdered sugar.

Unser Tagelich Brot (The Staff of Life III)

Fresh Peach Summer Surprise

4 ounces cream cheese
16 ounces Cool Whip, divided
Graham cracker crust
6 fresh peaches

1 (5.1-ounce) package vanilla
instant pudding, (prepared as
directed on package)

Mix well cream cheese and 8 ounces Cool Whip. Spread over graham cracker crust. Spread a single layer of sliced fresh peaches. Mix vanilla pudding; pour over peaches. Top off with remaining Cool Whip. Chill for about an hour.

Note: You may substitute your choice of fresh fruit.

Costco Wholesale Employee Association Cookbook

Blackberry Pizza

CRUST:
1 cup flour
$^{1}/_{2}$ cup powdered sugar

1 stick margarine, softened

Mix together crust ingredients to make crumb mixture. Pat into a 13-inch pizza pan. Bake at 350° for 6–10 minutes, until lightly brown.

SAUCE:
1 (8-ounce) package cream
  cheese, softened

$^{1}/_{2}$ cup sugar

Mix thoroughly. When Crust is cool, spread Sauce mixture over Crust.

GLAZE:
1 cup berry juice
$^{1}/_{4}$ cup sugar
1 tablespoon cornstarch

2 cups blackberries
Cool Whip
Fresh blackberries for garnish

Cook berry juice, sugar, and cornstarch until thick and clear. Mix in berries and pour over Sauce mixture. When cool, top with dollops of Cool Whip and garnish with fresh berries.

From Our Kitchen to Yours

Fruit Pizza

1¹/₂ cups margarine or butter,
  softened
1 cup powdered sugar
3 cups flour
1 (8-ounce) package cream
  cheese, softened
1¹/₄ cups sugar, divided
1 teaspoon vanilla

1 teaspoon lemon juice
1 cup pineapple juice or other
  fruit juice
2 tablespoons cornstarch
Fruit: blueberries, sliced
  pineapple, oranges, kiwi,
  peaches, apples, bananas,
  halved strawberries, grapes etc.

In a large mixing bowl, beat margarine on medium speed of an electric mixer till softened. Beat in powdered sugar. Slowly beat in flour till well combined. Spread or pat dough into bottom of a 12-inch pizza pan. Bake in a 325° oven for about 30 minutes or till edges are lightly browned. Cool.

In a small mixing bowl, beat together cream cheese, ¹/₂ cup sugar, vanilla, and lemon juice till creamy. Spread over cooled crust. In a small saucepan, combine juice, cornstarch, and the remaining ³/₄ cup sugar. Cook and stir over medium heat till thickened and bubbly. Cook and stir 1 minute more. Remove from heat and cool slightly. Top pizza with desired fruit. Spoon glaze over fruit. Refrigerate till well chilled. Makes 12–16 servings.

Recipes from Our Friends

Rhubarb Dream Dessert

1 cup flour
¹/₂ cup margarine
5 tablespoons powdered sugar
1¹/₂ cups sugar

¹/₄ cup flour
³/₄ teaspoon salt
2 eggs, beaten
2 cups finely chopped rhubarb

Blend flour, margarine, and powdered sugar for crust; press into a greased 7x11x1-inch pan. Bake at 350° for 15 minutes.

Mix sugar, flour, and salt; add eggs and rhubarb. Spoon into crust. Bake at 350° for 35 minutes. Serve warm with whipped cream.

Heavenly Fare

1-2-3 Layer Dessert

NUT CRUST:

^{1}/$_2$ cup margarine   1^1/$_4$ cups flour
1 cup chopped nuts

Mix and press into a greased 9x13-inch pan. Bake until light brown, about 15 minutes.

LAYER #1:

1 cup powdered sugar ^{1}/$_2$ carton Cool Whip
1 (8-ounce) package cream
  cheese, softened

Mix together and put into cooled crust.

LAYER #2:

1 (3-ounce) package butterscotch   1^1/$_2$ cups milk
  instant pudding

Prepare pudding according to package instructions, using only 1^1/$_2$ cups milk. Put on top of Layer #1.

LAYER #3:

1 (3-ounce) package chocolate ^{1}/$_2$ carton CoolWhip
  instant pudding   Nuts
1^1/$_2$ cups milk

Prepare pudding according to package instructions, using only 1^1/$_2$ cups milk. Put on top of Layer #2.

  On top, spread rest of Cool Whip. Sprinkle with nuts.

Tastes of Country

Easy Banana Cream Dessert

This dessert is similar to banana cream pie, but much faster because there is no pie crust to make. Little helpers can squish the pudding, break and arrange the graham crackers, cut bananas with a plastic knife, and sprinkle on the crumbs.

1 small box vanilla instant pudding mix

2 cups milk, 2% or whole milk works best

1 resealable freezer bag, gallon size

2 cups frozen whipped topping, thawed or 1 package prepared nondairy whipped topping, divided

8 whole graham crackers (16 squares)

3 bananas

1 tablespoon graham cracker crumbs (1 cracker square)

1 tablespoon wheat germ (optional)

Put pudding mix and milk into plastic bag. Be sure bag is well sealed. Squeeze and shake the bag until pudding is thoroughly mixed and thickened. Add 1 cup whipped topping to pudding in bag and reseal it. Squeeze bag until topping and pudding are well mixed.

Cover bottom of an 8x8-inch pan with 1 layer of graham crackers, breaking crackers as needed. Add layer of sliced bananas. Cut diagonally across 1 corner of bag and squeeze half of the pudding out onto the layer of bananas. Spread evenly over bananas. Repeat with additional layers of graham crackers, bananas, and the second half of the pudding. Top with remaining whipped topping.

Mix cracker crumbs and wheat germ and sprinkle on top. Refrigerate for about 2 hours to soften crackers and chill dessert, then cut into squares and serve.

Food for Tots

Washington contains more than 20 Native American reservations, including one of the largest in the country, belonging to the Yakama peoples.

Cream Puffs

¹/₂ cup butter	1 cup flour
1 cup water	4 eggs

In medium saucepan, bring butter and water to rolling boil. Add flour and stir vigorously over low heat until mixture forms a ball, about 1 minute. Remove from heat. Add eggs, 1 at a time, beating thoroughly. Drop from spoon onto ungreased baking sheet, about 3 inches apart. Bake at 400°. For large puffs bake 45–50 minutes; for small puffs bake 30 minutes or until puffs are lightly browned and dry. Allow to cool. Cut off tops; remove soft dough and fill with desired filling. Makes 10–12 large or 35–40 small puffs.

Note: Leave whole and frost with powdered sugar glaze, or fill with whipped cream, pudding or ice cream. Tiny cream puffs can also be filled with assorted meat fillings and served as appetizers.

McNamee Family & Friends Cookbook

Clafouti
(A French Flan)

1¹/₄ cups 2% milk	²/₃ cup flour, divided
²/₃ cup sugar, divided	1¹/₂ cups bing cherries, pitted
3 eggs	Powdered sugar
2 teaspoons vanilla extract	

Place greased pie pan on stove top burner set at medium heat. In a food processor, mix milk, ¹/₃ cup sugar, eggs, and vanilla, and beat 1 minute. Add half the flour and blend 30 seconds. Add remaining flour and blend another 30 seconds. Pour ¹/₄ inch batter into heated pie pan. Keep pan on burner for 2 minutes or until a film of batter has set on bottom of pan. Remove from heat and spread cherries over batter. Sprinkle with remaining ¹/₃ cup sugar. Pour rest of batter over cherries and bake at 350° for 1 hour. Cool a few minutes and then cut into 6 pie shaped servings. Good with a sprinkle of powdered sugar and served on breakfast plate with a light meat such as thin-sliced, cold, smoked turkey.

Recipe from Moon and Sixpence Bed & Breakfast, Friday Harbor
Washington Cook Book

Carrot Custard

The humble carrot makes a delicious dessert.

2 cups sliced cooked carrots
2 cups milk
3 eggs

4 tablespoons honey
¹/₄ teaspoon nutmeg
¹/₄ teaspoon allspice

Whirl all ingredients in a blender and pour the mixture into oiled custard cups. Set the cups in a pan of hot water and bake at 325° for 50 minutes or until set. Serves 6.

The 99¢ a Meal Cookbook

Swedish Baked Rice Pudding

$\frac{1}{2}$ cup uncooked regular
   long-grain rice
2 tablespoons sugar
2 cups milk
1 tablespoon margarine or
   butter
6 eggs

1 cup sugar
1 teaspoon cinnamon
$\frac{1}{2}$ teaspoon salt
$\frac{1}{2}$ teaspoon nutmeg
$\frac{1}{2}$ cup raisins
2 cups milk
1 teaspoon vanilla

In medium pan (nonstick), combine rice, sugar, milk and butter. Bring to a boil. Reduce heat to low; cook 20–25 minutes or until thickened and creamy, stirring so as not to stick. Remove from heat and cool slightly. Grease an 8-inch-square baking dish.

In large bowl, beat eggs; stir in remaining pudding ingredients and rice mixture. Pour into greased pan. Bake at 350° for 55–60 minutes, until set. Serve warm with cream over each serving.

Note: May plump raisins by soaking in warm amaretto or water.

Nautical Niceaty's from Spokane Yacht Club

 Washington's capitol building was the last state capitol building to be built with a rotunda.

Ann's Bread Pudding

This dessert has been the only constant on The Shoalwater's dessert tray since the restaurant opened.

7 cups day-old French bread, torn into 1-inch pieces
$^{1}/_{2}$ cup currants or raisins
3 eggs
4 egg yolks
$^{1}/_{2}$ cup sugar

2 cups half-and-half
1 cup heavy cream
1 tablespoon Myers dark rum
$^{1}/_{2}$ teaspoon vanilla
Crème Anglaise, for topping

Place bread pieces in an 8x8-inch baking dish. Sprinkle currants over the top. Whisk together eggs, egg yolks, and sugar in a medium mixing bowl. Add half-and-half, cream, rum, and vanilla. Mix well. Pour custard over bread. With the back of a spoon, press bread down into custard until all bread is wet.

Cover the pan with foil, sealing edges well. Set pan in a water bath coming halfway up sides of pan and bake in preheated 350° oven until set, about 45 minutes. Cool. Serve topped with Crème Anglaise. Makes 6–8 servings.

CRÈME ANGLAISE:
2 cups half-and-half
3 egg yolks
$^{1}/_{4}$ cup sugar

1 tablespoon dark rum or Frangelico liqueur
$^{1}/_{4}$ teaspoon vanilla

Heat half-and-half in a saucepan until just before it boils. Beat egg yolks and sugar in a mixing bowl until they become pale yellow and begin to thicken. With mixer on low, add the hot half-and-half in a slow stream.

Return the mixture to the saucepan and cook over low heat, stirring constantly for several minutes, until the Crème Anglaise begins to thicken and coat a spoon. When it begins to thicken, remove it from heat and add rum and vanilla.

Crème Anglaise may be served warm or cold. Makes 2 cups.

Note: This basic dessert sauce is a quick and easy way to dress up many desserts. Try it with apple pie (flavored with a little cinnamon schnapps), poached pears (flavored with Poire Williams) or under a slice of rich, dark cake.

The Shoalwater's Finest Dinners

Chocolate Bread Pudding with Kahlúa Ganache Sauce

Says Chef Main, "This is a cross between a chocolate soufflé and a custard pudding. The reassuring thing about this recipe is that it is forgiving of most mistakes, and it will not fall as you present it!"

CHOCOLATE BREAD PUDDING:

4 cups day-old French bread
  cubes
$3^1/2$ cups half-and-half
2 teaspoons vanilla
1 tablespoon Kahlúa
Pinch of salt
2 ounces unsweetened chocolate

$^1/2$ cup strong coffee
1 tablespoon butter
3 egg yolks
1 cup sugar
$^1/4$ teaspoon grated lemon zest
Pinch of cinnamon

Soak bread cubes in half-and-half, vanilla, Kahlúa, and salt for 2 hours at room temperature. Melt together in a small saucepan chocolate, coffee, and butter. Stir into bread cube mixture.

Using an electric mixer, whip egg yolks till light. Gradually add sugar, scraping the sides of the bowl as needed. Continue beating the egg mixture. Strain 2 cups of the cream mixture from the bread cubes and add it to the egg mixture, scraping the bowl several times. Stir remaining bread and cream mixture into egg and cream mixture with lemon zest and cinnamon.

Grease a 9x13-inch baking pan; fill with pudding mixture. Cover it with foil, and set in a larger pan with enough water to reach $^2/3$ up the sides of the inner one. Bake at 350° for 35–45 minutes or till pudding is set like custard. It will shake slightly in the center. Let it rest at least 15 minutes to set more firmly before serving. To serve, fill dessert dishes with about 1 cup Chocolate Bread Pudding; pour Kahlúa Ganache Sauce over each. Pipe Whipped Cream on top and garnish with chocolate shavings. Yields 8 servings.

KAHLÚA GANACHE SAUCE:

$^3/4$ cup heavy cream
1 tablespoon unsalted butter
1 tablespoon sugar
$^1/4$ pound shredded semisweet
  chocolate

2 tablespoons Kahlúa
$^1/2$ cup coarsely chopped black
  walnuts

(continued)

(continued)

Stir and bring to a simmer in a heavy-bottomed saucepan heavy cream, butter, and sugar. Stir in semisweet chocolate, Kahlúa, and chopped black walnuts. Yields 1½ cups sauce.

WHIPPED CREAM:

1 cup chilled heavy cream   Chocolate shavings for garnish
1 teaspoon vanilla

Whip cream with vanilla, and use a pastry bag with a star tip to pipe this over the Kahlúa Ganache Sauce. Top with chocolate shavings.

The Best of The Ark and More!

Hot Fudge Pudding

A favorite at our home for years. Rich pudding on bottom of cake makes this popular. Spoon into bowls and serve with whipped cream or ice cream.

1 cup flour   ½ cup milk
2 teaspoons baking powder   2 tablespoons margarine
¼ teaspoon salt   1 cup chopped nuts
¾ cup sugar   1¾ cups hot water
2 tablespoons cocoa

Mix sifted dry ingredients with milk and melted margarine. Add nuts. Pour into greased 9-inch-square pan. Sprinkle with Topping. Lastly, pour hot water over entire cake (do not stir). Bake at 350° about 45 minutes.

TOPPING:

1 cup brown sugar   ¼ cup cocoa

Mix together and sprinkle on top of cake.

Tastes of Country

Washington's Grand Coulee Dam on the Columbia River is four times larger than the Great Pyramid of Giza, one of the original seven wonders of the world. It is second only to the Great Wall of China as the largest man-made structure in the world.

Orange Mousse

3$^{1}/_{2}$ cups skim milk
3 large eggs
3 egg whites
1 cup sugar
$^{2}/_{3}$ cup cornstarch
$^{1}/_{4}$ teaspoon salt

$^{1}/_{2}$ cup orange juice
1 tablespoon grated orange peel
1 tablespoon unsalted butter
4 teaspoons vanilla extract
2 cups light frozen nondairy
  whipped topping, thawed

In a large saucepan, heat milk over medium heat just until bubbles form around edges. Meanwhile, using electric mixer set on high speed, beat eggs, egg whites, sugar, cornstarch, and salt until light and fluffy, about 3 minutes. Beat in orange juice and peeling. Beat 1 cup hot milk into egg mixture. Whisk egg mixture into pan with remaining milk. Bring orange mixture to a boil, whisking and boiling until thickened, about 2 minutes. Remove from heat; whisk in butter and vanilla. Pour orange mixture into bowl. Cool slightly, cover with plastic wrap, and chill until cold, about 2 hours. Fold whipped topping into cold orange mixture. Spoon into dishes and refrigerate until ready to serve. May garnish with orange segments.

Harvest Feast

Old-Fashioned Strawberry Shortcake at its Best

Serve in large individual bowls and enjoy!

1¹/₂–2 quarts fresh
  strawberries
¹/₂ cup sugar

2 tablespoons Grand Marnier (or
  orange juice)
¹/₂ teaspoon vanilla

Rinse berries and let dry. Hull and set aside 6 large ones. In food processor or blender, purée half of remaining berries with sugar, Grand Marnier, and vanilla. Slice remaining berries and stir into purée. Cover and let stand 20 minutes, or make ahead and refrigerate for no more than 6 hours. If refrigerated, let warm to room temperature before serving.

SHORTCAKE:
2¹/₄ cups all-purpose flour
6 tablespoons sugar
1¹/₂ teaspoons baking powder
³/₄ teaspoon baking soda
¹/₈ teaspoon salt
1¹/₂ teaspoons grated orange
  zest (peel)

¹/₂ cup chilled butter or
  margarine, cut in pieces
³/₄ cup buttermilk
Extra sugar for sprinkling on
  top
1 cup heavy (whipping) cream

Preheat oven to 400°. Combine flour, sugar, baking powder, baking soda, salt, and orange zest together in large bowl. Cut in chilled butter with pastry blender (or forks) until mixture resembles coarse crumbs. Add buttermilk, tossing with fork, until mixture can be gathered into a ball.

Roll dough out on a floured surface to about 1-inch thickness. The dough may then be cut into 6 rounds with large cookie cutter, or cut into squares. Sprinkle with sugar, place on lightly greased cookie sheet, and bake for 20–23 minutes or until done. (These may be made ahead and reheated for a few minutes in a 250° oven.) Cool shortcakes slightly; split them.

Whip cream. Spoon strawberries over bottoms, replace tops, and spoon more berries over. Serve with whipped cream and reserved whole berries. This dessert is best served in large individual bowls. Serves 6.

Wandering & Feasting

Angel Lemon Delight

A pudding-cake, this is refreshing and different and easy. In fact, it's just plain wonderful. Pretty served in shallow, glass bowls with stem strawberries on the side.

1½ cups sugar, divided
½ cup flour
¼ teaspoon salt
3 egg yolks
Juice and grated rind of 2 large
   lemons

2 tablespoons butter, melted
1½ cups milk
3 egg whites

Preheat oven to 375°. Mix 1 cup sugar, flour, salt, egg yolks, juice and rind, butter, and milk together in order given. Beat until very smooth and creamy. Beat egg whites until stiff. Add ½ cup sugar and beat again. Fold into first set of ingredients. Pour into ungreased, shallow, 8x12-inch, glass baking dish. Set in a shallow roasting pan in 1 inch hot water. Bake, uncovered, for 40 minutes. Serve warm or cold. Serves 6–8.

The Overlake School Cookbook

Lemon Heaven Ice with Berries

This ice does not require an ice cream maker.

4 cups cold water
1¹/₂ cups sugar
1¹/₂ cups fresh lemon juice
  (about 8 medium lemons)

2 tablespoons white table wine
  (optional)
1 cup fresh strawberries or other
  seasonal berries

Bring water and sugar to a boil in medium saucepan. Stir until sugar has dissolved. Remove from heat and cool. (To cool faster, pour mixture into another large heat-proof pan or bowl.) Add lemon juice and white wine to sugar syrup; stir well. Pour mixture into a large shallow noncorrosive baking pan and carefully place in freezer. When almost frozen (about 4 hours), remove and break up into small pieces.

Process the mixture in a blender or food processor until the texture is like grainy snow. Spoon into a covered container and freeze. Serve in individual bowls with strawberries or other seasonal fruit. Yields 1¹/₂ quarts.

Good Times at Green Lake

Easy Frozen Yogurt

What a fun way to eat fruit! A healthy alternative to ice cream.

2 cups frozen whole
  strawberries

¹/₃ cup plain yogurt
3 tablespoons powdered sugar

Assemble food processor with metal blade. Put strawberries, yogurt, and powdered sugar into the processor bowl. Process until smooth, stopping as needed and stirring with spoon to evenly distribute fruit. Serve immediately. Yields 1¹/₂ cups.

Variations: Frozen raspberries, sweet cherries, peaches, or blueberries may be substituted. Add ¹/₂ banana for milder flavor.

Note: To freeze berries, put 1 layer washed fruit on a cookie sheet lined with waxed paper. Freeze until solid, then put fruit in resealable freezer bags for longer storage.

Food for Tots

Victorian Amaretto Cheese Dip

Serve this dip with seasonal fresh fruit as a sweet alternative to a heavy dessert.

2 (8-ounce) packages cream
   cheese
4 egg yolks

$^1/_2$ cup sugar
$^1/_4$ cup amaretto liqueur

Combine all ingredients and cream together until smooth. Serve the dip in the middle of a platter of mixed fresh fruit. Yields $1^1/_2$ cups.

Simply Whidbey

Baked Bananas in Orange Juice

We love bananas. It's an old family recipe.

6 medium firm bananas
1 medium orange
2 tablespoons orange juice
2 tablespoons lemon juice

$^1/_3$ cup sugar
Dash of ground cinnamon
Dash of ground nutmeg

Preheat oven to 350°. Peel bananas. Peel and chop orange. Arrange bananas and orange pieces in an 8x8-inch baking dish. In a small bowl combine juices, sugar, cinnamon, and nutmeg. Pour over fruit. Bake for 25–30 minutes until bananas are golden and tender. Serve hot with ice cream. Serves 6.

Recipe by Jay Buhner, Outfielder, Seattle Mariners
Starters & Closers

CATALOG *of* CONTRIBUTING COOKBOOKS

The Hood Canal, an inlet of Puget Sound, extends deep into the foothills of the Olympic Mountains.

CATALOG *of*
CONTRIBUTING COOKBOOKS

All recipes in this book have been selected from the cookbooks shown on the following pages. Individuals who wish to obtain a copy of any particular book may do so by sending a check or money order to the address listed by each cookbook. Please note the postage and handling charges that are required. State residents add tax only when requested. Prices and addresses are subject to change, and the books may sell out and become unavailable. Retailers are invited to call or write to same address for discount information.

ALLRECIPES TRIED & TRUE FAVORITES

Allrecipes   Phone 206-292-3990
524 Dexter Avenue North   Fax 206-292-1793
Seattle, WA 98109   tnt@allrecipes.com

Unlike most present-day cookbooks that focus on celebrity chefs and expensive restaurants, the recipes within *Allrecipes Tried and True Favorites* cookbook are easy to make, utilize familiar ingredients, and in most cases, are ready to serve in under an hour.

$17.95 Retail price
 $1.57 Tax for Washington residents
 $1.78 Postage and handling
Make check payable to Allrecipes, Inc.   ISBN 0-9711723-0-7

ANOTHER TASTE OF WASHINGTON STATE

Washington State Bed & Breakfast Guild
Winters Publishing   Phone 812-663-4948
P. O. Box 501
Greensburg, IN 47240   tmwinters@juno.com

Enjoy over 280 tempting recipes in this 224-page cookbook! Featuring favorite recipes from the finest bed and breakfasts in the state of Washington—from Mt. Rainier Snowball Cookies to Smoked Salmon Hash. Detailed inn information will help you find the perfect location for your Washington getaway.

$15.95 Retail price
 $2.00 Postage and handling
Make check payable to Winters Publishing   ISBN 1-883651-15-8

THE BEST OF THE ARK AND MORE!

by Nanci Main & Jimella Lucas
The Ark Restaurant   Phone 360-665-4133
P. O. Box 95   Fax 360-665-5043
Nahcotta, WA 98637   ark@willapabay.org

Nanci Main & Jimella Lucas, owners/chefs of The Ark Restaurant for 20 years, are pioneers in their commitment to creative cuisine using both fresh and local products. Their prestigious careers include features in *Newsweek, New York Times, Boston Globe, Oregonian, Sunset Magazine, Food & Wine,* as well as hundreds of TV and personal appearances.

$24.95 Retail price
 $4.50 Postage and handling
Make check payable to The Ark Restaurant   ISBN 1-55868-595-2

BOUNTEOUS BLESSINGS

by Frances A. Gillette
P. O. Box 351
Yacolt, WA 98675

Phone 360-686-3420
Fax 360-686-3054
eathappy@aol.com

This book will kindle your spirit and give you pride to be an American. Do you appreciate where you live and all that our flag stands for? A patriotic American cookbook full of facts and treasured recipes. Wishing you a heart full of beats "for the red, white, and blue!"

$19.95 Retail price
$1.77 Tax for Washington residents
$3.00 Postage and handling

Make check payable to Fran Gillette   ISBN 0-9636066-3-8

THE CHICKEN COOKBOOK

The Washington Fryer Commission
2003 Maple Valley Highway 212
Renton, WA 98055

Phone 425-226-6125
Fax 425-226-8238
contact@cluckcluck.org

This cookbook is a celebration of some of Washington's finest foods, since Washington-grown chicken is best enjoyed with other locally grown products. It features 28 contemporary recipes, but also provides basic cooking methods, nutritional information and food safety information. 40 pages, including colorful photos.

$3.50 Retail price

Make check payable to Washington Fryer Commission

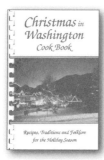

CHRISTMAS IN WASHINGTON COOK BOOK

by Janet Walker
Golden West Publishers
4113 North Longview Avenue
Phoenix, AZ 85014-4949

Phone 800-658-5830
Fax 602-279-6901
goldwest1@mindspring.com

Christmas dinner Washington style. Holiday traditions include families and friends gathering for sumptuous feasts and festivals of lights. *Christmas in Washington* includes recipes from innkeepers, homemakers and professional chefs. Try these recipes and create new Christmas traditions in your home.

$9.95 Retail price
$3.00 Postage and handling

Make check payable to Golden West Publishers   ISBN 1-885590-07-5

THE COLOPHON CAFE BEST RECIPES

by Ray Dunn & Taimi Dunn Gorman
Mama Colophon, Inc./Village Books
1206 11th Street
Bellingham, WA 98225

Phone 800-392-BOOK

Best recipes of the legendary Colophon Cafe in historic Fairhaven. 48 pages, spiralbound, 29 recipes.

$8.95 Retail price
$.70 Tax for Washington residents
$3.00 Postage and handling

Make check payable to Village Books

THE COLOPHON CAFE BEST SOUPS
by Ray Dunn & Taimi Dunn Gorman
Mama Colophon Inc./Village Books   Phone 800-392-BOOK
1206 11th Street
Bellingham, WA 98225

Best soups of the legendary Colophon Cafe in historic Fairhaven. 75 pages, spiralbound, 48 recipes serving 4–6 people.

   $9.95   Retail price
    $.78   Tax for Washington residents
   $3.00   Postage and handling

Make check payable to Village Books   ISBN 0-9667283-0-0

THE COLOPHON CAFE BEST VEGETARIAN RECIPES
by Ray Dunn & Taimi Dunn Gorman
Mama Colophon, Inc./Village Books   Phone 800-392-BOOK
1206 11th Street
Bellingham, WA 98225

Best vegetarian recipes of the legendary Colophon Cafe in historic Fairhaven. 81 pages, spiralbound, 56 recipes.

   $9.95   Retail price
    $.78   Tax for Washington residents
   $3.00   Postage and handling

Make check payable to Village Books   ISBN 0-9667283-2-7

COOKING WITH IRENE!
ITALIAN AND OTHER DELICIOUS ORIGINALS
by Irene Schmidt
City Graphics   Phone 509-534-4302
4011 East 19th   Fax 509-535-5468
Spokane, WA 99223   charlie.schmidt@att.net

Italian, Polish and other originals mostly learned from Irene's mother and mother-in-law. They immigrated in the early 1900s from Italy and Poland to America. One of the main ingredients in Irene's experience and recipes is love. Enjoy!

  $19.99   Retail price
   $1.62   Tax for Washington residents

Make check payable to Irene Schmidt

COSTCO WHOLESALE EMPLOYEE ASSOCIATION COOKBOOK
Costco Employee Association   Phone 509-737-8861
8505 W. Gage Blvd.   Fax 509-737-8862
Kennewick, WA 99336   smwelch@urx.com

The cookbook represents a sharing of recipes between employees, family members and executive members of Costco Wholesale. The cookbook has 72 pages of recipes in all categories, including several recipes from our favorite local restaurants.

  $7.50   Retail price
   $.60   Tax for Washington residents
  $1.50   Postage and handling

Make check payable to Costco Employee Association

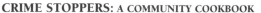

CRIME STOPPERS: A COMMUNITY COOKBOOK

Thurston County Crime Stoppers
P. O. Box 3400
Lacey, WA 98509

Phone 360-438-2658
dschuder@ci.lacey.wa.us

A compilation of recipes by members of law enforcement, local businesses and community members who support the Crime Stoppers Program. Crime Stoppers pays cash rewards for anonymous tips that lead to arrests and charges filed on any crime.

$5.00   Retail price
$.40   Tax for Washington residents
$2.00   Postage and handling

Make check payable to Thurston County Crime Stoppers

DUCK SOUP & OTHER FOWL RECIPES

by Lyndia Vold
12605 E. Valleyford Ave
Valleyford, WA 99036

Phone 509-926-8554
Fax 509-926-8554
lvold@spokanecounty.org

Duck Soup and Other Fowl Recipes, a wild bird cookbook, contains over 100 duck recipes, 25 goose recipes, and many marinades, sauces, and stuffings to go with the bird preparation. The cookbook includes how to prepare wild birds for the best flavor, all within 105 pages.

$9.95   Retail price
$.81   Tax for Washington residents
$3.00   Postage and handling

Make check payable to Lyndia Vold   ISBN 0-9643140-0-2

EXTRAORDINARY CUISINE FOR SEA & SHORE

Seattle Yacht Club
1807 East Hamlin
Seattle, WA 98112

Phone 206-325-1000
Fax 206-324-8784
sycadmin@seattleyachtclub.org

The purpose of this book was that by sharing our recipes for boating and entertaining with others, we could raise funds to support non-profit boating organizations in the community. The recipes are not limited to boating but are planned to enhance enjoyment of boating and entertaining on board our boats.

$12.95   Retail price
$1.13   Tax for Washington residents
$2.50   Postage and handling

Make check payable to Seattle Yacht Club   ISBN 0-89716-354-0

FAMILY FAVORITES RECIPES

Women's Ministries
First Church of the Open Bible
224 W. Hoerner
Spokane, WA 99218-2122

Phone 509-446-1255

Our ladies needed a fund raiser and thought this would be a fun way to do it—by putting together a cookbook of favorite recipes. Our 133-page, 322-recipe cookbook is a great success! Enjoy.

$8.00   Retail price
$2.00   Postage and handling

Make check payable to Women's Ministries

FAVORITE RECIPES FROM OUR BEST COOKS

St. John Vianney Altar Society
10413 E. DeSmet Avenue   Phone 509-926-0487
Spokane, WA 99206

Favorite Recipes from our Best Cooks has 180 pages of delicious recipes—all have been tried and only the best were included. There are over 500 recipes. The cover has been popular also, for its beautiful design. The print is for very easy reading.

$10.00   Retail price
  $3.00   Postage and handling

Make check payable to St. John Vianney

FAVORITE RECIPES FROM THE EMPLOYEES, FAMILY, AND FRIENDS OF NUMERICA CREDIT UNION

Numerica Credit Union   Phone 509-535-7613
P. O. Box 6011   Fax 509-536-6119
Spokane, WA 99202   NCUMemberService@numericacu.com

Over 180 recipes loved by employees, families, and friends of Numerica Credit Union. Proceeds benefit Credit Unions for Kids which raises funds for local children's hospitals. Our employees love to cook—and to eat—and our cookbook is filled with tempting treats. Please help us help the kids and purchase our book today!

$10.00   Retail price
  $2.00   Postage and handling

Make check payable to Numerica Credit Union

FOOD FOR TOTS
THE COMPLETE GUIDE TO FEEDING PRESCHOOLERS

by Jennifer Pugmire and Janice Woolley, M.D.
Food for Tots Publishing   Phone 1-866-foodfortots
P. O. Box 871463   Fax 206-374-2864
Vancouver, WA 98687-1463   info@foodfortots.com

Food for Tots contains more than 100 kid-tested recipes that please even the pickiest eater. It also includes information about nutrition, food allergies, food safety, and how to handle eating problems. Informative reading for both new and experienced parents of young children. 288 pages

$16.95   Retail price
  $1.61   Tax for Washington residents
  $4.00   Postage and handling

Make check payable to Food for Tots   ISBN 1-890908-01-0

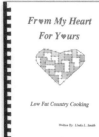

FROM MY HEART FOR YOURS

by Linda L. Smith
2219 194th Avenue KPS   Phone 253-884-2225
Lake Bay, WA 98349   nliten@att.net

Delicious low-fat, heart-healthy, country recipes from breakfast through dinner including yummy desserts. 171 pages, laminated cover.

$12.95   Retail price
  $1.06   Tax for Washington residents
  $3.00   Postage and handling

Make check payable to Linda L. Smith   ISBN 1-889494-06-2

FROM OUR KITCHEN TO YOURS
COOKING WITH JEWELL & JEANETTE

by Jewell and Jeanette   Phone 360-295-3594
P. O. Box 113
Vader, WA 98593

We have a collection of recipes we wanted to share. At Christmas and all through the year, people would call us for recipes; we thought it would be easier to do the book. It's for a good cause, a scholarship at our local high school.

$10.00   Retail price
 $3.00   Postage and handling

Make check payable to Jewell Hancock

GOLD'N DELICIOUS

The Junior League of Spokane   Phone 509-328-2801
315 W. Mission Avenue, Suite 10   Fax 509-328-1827
Spokane, WA 99201

These 261 recipes are hand-picked, hand-tested, and handed down by the Junior League of Spokane. The 239-page collection, including Golden Harvest Bread, Huckleberry Pork Chops, Walla Walla Sweet Squares, and Holiday Cheesecake, embraces the land we live in and celebrates the gold of community and the delicious warmth of gathering.

$11.95   Retail price
 $3.00   Postage and handling

Make check payable to Junior League of Spokane   ISBN 0-9646784-0-3

GOOD FOOD FOR (MOSTLY) GOOD PEOPLE COOKBOOK

by Marla Emde
Delectable Deeds   Phone 509-326-6983
P. O. Box 9688   Fax 509-326-4901
Spokane, WA 99209-9688   emde3m@msn.com

Simple recipes . . . great food! This book selects fresh ingredients and uses whole grains, fresh fruits, and vegetables throughout. Many recipes are designed to be prepared in large quantities—to enjoy right away or frozen for future convenience. A mix and match concept for quick easy meals, anytime!

$12.95   Retail price
 $1.05   Tax for Washington residents
 $3.00   Postage and handling

Make check payable to Delectable Deeds

GOOD TIMES AT GREEN LAKE
RECIPES FOR SEATTLE'S FAVORITE PARK

by Susan Banks and Carol Orr
Washington State University Press   Phone 800-354-7360
P. O. Box 745910   Fax 509-335-8568
Pullman, WA 99164-5910   wsupress@wsu.edu

Over 50 enticing recipes reflect the authors' love of ethnic foods but don't require exotic ingredients. Embellished with photographs and vignettes depicting the delightful community of Green Lake. 128 pages. Paperback.

$16.95   Retail price
 $1.29   Tax for Washington residents
 $4.00   Postage and handling

Make check payable to WSU Press   ISBN 0-87422-235-4

HARVEST FEAST

Christ Church Women's Group
Puyallup, WA

Favorite recipes of our parish family compiled by the Women's Group of Christ Episcopal Church. Some have been handed down for generations and have treasured memories attached. As you share these dishes, we hope that as the food nourishes the body, God's blessings will nourish your soul. This book is currently out of print.

HEAVEN ON THE HALF SHELL

by David Gordon, Nancy Blanton, Terry Nosho
Washington Sea Grant Program   Phone 206-543-6600
3716 Brooklyn Avenue N.E.   Fax 206-685-0380
Seattle, WA 98105-6716   seagrant@u.washington.edu

The story of oyster farming in the Pacific Northwest. Entertaining text and photos present the efforts of pioneering aquaculturists, scientists, field technicians, oyster connoisseurs, and others who have shaped this unique industry. Eighteen oyster recipes round out this lively portrait of the bivalve we love best.

$21.95   Retail price
 $1.93   Tax for Washington residents
 $3.00   Postage and handling
Make check payable to Univ. of Washington   ISBN 1-55868-550-2

HEAVENLY FARE

Presbyterian Women of Montesano Presbyterian Church
P. O. Box 110
Montesano, WA 98563

Heavenly Fare is a 99-page cookbook crammed with 325 favorite recipes of members and friends of the Montesano Presbyterian Church. It even includes a recipe for Winter Bird Pudding and one for a solution that really gets windows clean.

$6.00   Retail price
 $.49   Tax for Washington residents
$1.75   Postage and handling
Make check payable to Presbyterian Women of Montesano

THE HISTORIC MID-1900'S COOKBOOK

Tunk Valley Grange #1019   Phone 509-826-2658
51 Mullens Way
Riverside, WA 98849

First published by the Tunk Valley Grange of Okanogan County in the early 1950s, this 240-page, 286-recipe book is a real treasure. Many of the original contributors are still around and hope you enjoy their book with "pinches," "dashes," and "small package" instructions.

$15.00   Retail price
 $2.00   Postage and handling
Make check payable to Tunk Valley Grange #1019

HOME PLATES

Seattle Mariners Wives and Mariners Care
Seattle Mariners Merchandise Department
P. O. Box 4100   Phone 1-800-MY MARINERS
Seattle, WA 98104

During the 2000 baseball season, wives of Mariners players, coaches, and staff compiled *Home Plates*, featuring fun photos, tidbits of information, and favorite recipes of their husbands. This cookbook raised over $220,000 for the Fred Hutchinson Cancer Research Center's Pediatric Oncology Department.

$10.00 Retail price
 $5.95 Postage and handling

Make check payable to Seattle Mariners Merchandise Department

THE INGREDIENTS: FRESH PACIFIC NORTHWEST CUISINE

Tools for Life/IA Publications   Phone 877-492-1957
P. O. Box 53028   Fax 425-644-9840
Bellevue, WA 98015-3028   tflia@msn.com

This recipe book features over 100 healthy, gourmet recipes that are quick and easy to prepare. There are recipes for great side dishes, spreads, sauces, salads, main dishes, soups, and delicious desserts. Nutritional breakdowns, yield and serving sizes, as well as health tips are included for each recipe.

$14.95 Retail price
 $1.32 Tax for Washington residents
 $5.95 Postage and handling

Make check payable to Tools for Life   ISBN 1-888-561-03-3

LaCONNER PALATES: AN ILLUSTRATED COOKBOOK

by Patricia Flynn and Patricia McClane
Bookends Publishing   Phone 360-675-6244
3064 Ironwood Lane   Fax 360-675-2033
Oak Harbor, WA 98277   jhflynn@whidbey.net

An eclectic collection of recipes from restaurants, merchants and B&B's in and around the area of LaConner. Illustrations and descriptive copy about each contributor is included. Spiralbound with easel for ease of reference.

$21.95 Retail price
 $1.82 Tax for Washington residents
 $3.00 Postage and handling

Make check payable to Bookends Publishing   ISBN 0-9659303-0-0

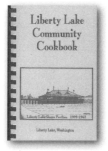

LIBERTY LAKE COMMUNITY COOKBOOK

The Friends of Pavilion Park
P. O. Box 325
Liberty Lake, WA 99019-0325

Liberty Lake Community Cookbook, consisting of 194 pages and 346 recipes, is a collection of favorite recipes ranging from down-home to gourmet cuisine. A cookbook for all ages, this cookbook was sponsored by The Friends of Pavilion Park as a fund raiser for the building of our community park.

$10.00 Retail price
 $2.50 Postage and handling

Make check payable to The Friends of Pavilion Park

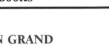

MARINERS MIX'N AND FIX'N GRAND SLAM STYLE

Seattle Mariners Wives and Mariners Care
Seattle Mariners Merchandise Department
P. O. Box 4100   Phone 1-800-MY MARINERS
Seattle, WA 98104

During the 1998 Mariners baseball season, wives of Mariners players, coaches, and executive staff compiled fun photos, tidbits of information, and favorite recipes of their husbands. With this cookbook, over $100,000 was raised for the Fred Hutchinson Cancer Research Center's Pediatric Oncology Dept.

$10.00   Retail price
$5.95   Postage and handling

Make check payable to Seattle Mariners Merchandise Department

McNAMEE FAMILY & FRIENDS COOKBOOK

by Terri L. McNamee-Snyder
452 Meadow Court   Phone 509-684-2230
Colville, WA 99114

These heirloom specials have been passed on to us by our loved ones and friends. Many have been adapted, revised or given a personal touch with special "notes" and comments. Helpful charts and hints are included with these 700 recipes in over 300 pages.

$9.95   Retail price
$2.50   Postage and handling ($4.95 for rush delivery)

Make check payable to McNamee Family c/o Terri Snyder

NAUTICAL NICEATY'S FROM SPOKANE YACHT CLUB

Spokane Yacht Club
c/o Betty Feltman   Phone 509-928-6538
9016 E. Frederick Avenue   feltmansyc120@msh.com
Spokane, WA 99212

This book has 150 pages with approximately 430 recipes from club members, friends and family. Our Main Dish and Desserts categories seem to be the most popular. The Miscellaneous section is very interesting with recipes ranging from Hot Cakes to Holding Tank Treatment.

$10.00   Retail price
$.80   Tax for Washington residents
$2.00   Postage and handling

Make check payable to Spokane Yacht Club

THE 99¢ A MEAL COOKBOOK

by Bill and Ruth Kaysing
Breakout Productions/Loompanics Unlimited   Phone 800-380-2230
P. O. Box 1197   Fax 360-385-7785
Port Townsend, WA 98368   service@loompanics.com

This 230-page cookbook shows that cooking with fresh rather than processed foods is far less expensive and healthier. These delicious low-cost recipes rely heavily on grains, fresh vegetables and fruits, legumes, and herbs. The reader is led through pantry stocking to shopping in season.

$14.95   Retail price
$1.23   Tax for Washington residents
$5.95   Postage and handling

Make check payable to Loompanics Unlimited   ISBN 1-55950-140-5

NORTHWEST GARLIC FESTIVAL COOKBOOK, VOLUME 3

Ocean Park Area Chamber of Commerce   Phone 888-751-9354
P. O. Box 403   Fax 360-665-2938
Ocean Park, WA 98640   opchamber@willapabay.org

Northwest Garlic Festival Cookbook pays homage to the "stinking rose" with over 200 recipes in 220 pages. Garlic is more versatile than you would think; you'll find recipes from entrées to desserts.

  $10.00 Retail price
    $3.20 Postage and handling for 1-3 books

Make check payable to Ocean Park Area Chamber of Commerce

OUR BEST HOME COOKING

Pend Oreille County Historical Society   Phone 509-447-2770
P. O. Box 1409
Newport, WA 99156

A collection of favorite recipes from members and friends of the historical society. Some represent locally grown items, most are well used and appreciated by our contributors. 94 pages, 235 recipes.

  $5.58 Retail price
   $.42 Tax for Washington residents
  $2.50 Postage and handling

Make check payable to Pend Oreille County Historical Society

OUR BURNT OFFERINGS

Presbyterian Women-First Presbyterian Church   Phone 360-573-5188
4300 Main Street
Vancouver, WA 98663

This 332-page cookbook is full of delectable recipes collected by the women of First Presbyterian Church. Some of our men cooks submitted their recipes to this collection also. Cross indexed for easy use. You are sure to find something to suite your taste buds.

  $10.00 Retail price
   $2.00 Postage and handling

Make check payable to Presbyterian Women-First Presbyterian Church

THE OVERLAKE SCHOOL COOKBOOK

by Edited by Bonnie Stewart Mickelson
Pickle Point, Inc.   Phone 425-641-7424
P. O. Box 4107   Fax 425-641-7148
Bellevue, WA 98009

This "little blue book of great recipes," contains 180 quick and easy favorites for casual menus or party fare. Pretty and inviting, it is hardbound to lie flat when open. 182 pages. It's the book you'll go to first for meal planning.

  $13.95 Retail price
   $1.15 Tax for Washington residents
  $2.50 Postage and handling

Make check payable to Pickle Point, Inc.   ISBN 0-9622412-6-1

PIG OUT

Skamania County Law Enforcement
P. O. Box 790
Stevenson, WA 98648

Phone 509-427-9490
Fax 509-427-4369
cindyh@co.skamania.wa.us

A 2001 Special Olympics fundraising campaign; 48 pages of favorite recipes submitted by sheriff's office deputies . Everything from appetizers to desserts. Includes a guide to healthy cooking and eating.

$7.00 Retail price
$2.00 Postage and handling

Make check payable to SCLEA

RECIPES FROM OUR FRIENDS

Friends of Whitman County Library
102 South Main Street
Colfax, WA 99111

Phone 877-733-3375
Fax 509-397-6156
brianp@colfax.com

This hardcover, spiralbound volume contains 693 treasured recipes from county friends. *Recipes from our Friends* is the largest fundraising project ever for the Friends of Whitman County Library in southeastern Washington. The cookbook is dedicated to rural children with proceeds to benefit children's library projects throughout the county.

$10.00 Retail price
$2.00 Postage and handling

Make check payable to Friends of Whitman County Library

RECIPES TO REMEMBER

St. Joseph Hospital & Long Term Care
Staff, Family, Residents, & Volunteers
St. Joseph Auxiliary
P. O. Box 69
Chewelah, WA 99109

Phone 509-935-5276

Our cookbook includes more than 500 recipes collected over a 30-year span. Contributors include residents, patients, staff, family, friends, and volunteers who have become family as they walked through our door. This cookbook is a meaningful legacy of the history we share and family we've become.

$10.00 Retail price
$2.00 Postage and handling

Make check payable to St. Joseph's Hospital Auxiliary

SAN JUAN CLASSICS II COOKBOOK

by Dawn Ashbach and Janice Veal
Northwest Island Associates
5538 Guemes Island Road
Anacortes, WA 98221

Phone 360-293-3721

Celebrates the abundance of the Pacific Northwest island area. The authors' second book featuring new cooking styles, new restaurants, and chefs of the region. An eclectic collection of more than 250 recipes from quick and healthy to complex and decadent. 284 pages.

$19.95 Retail price
$3.00 Postage and handling

Make check payable to Northwest Island Associates
ISBN 0-9629778-1-0

SHARING OUR BEST
A COLLECTION OF FAMILY FAVORITES FROM DIANNE BERST
by Dianne Berst
15020 Dubuque Road
Snohomish, WA 98290

Sharing Our Best is a collection of approximately 200 family favorite recipes collected as a Christmas gift for the author's daughter, Julie. With her husband Bill's encouragement, Dianne made the cookbook available for sale. Readers praise the recipes for being easy and not requiring unusual ingredients.

$8.00   Retail price
$.62   Tax for Washington residents
$2.00   Postage and handling
Make check payable to Dianne Berst

THE SHOALWATER'S FINEST DINNERS
Shoalwater Restaurant
Harris & Friedrich   Phone 360-642-2595
P. O. Box A   winedine@willapabay.org
Seaview, WA 98644

The Shoalwater's Finest Dinners showcases nine Northwestern winemaker's dinner menus, and features recipes, appropriate wine accompaniments and commentary on both the wine selections and the recipes themselves by the restaurant's owners. 200 pages, 6 four-color food photos, 110 recipes.

$19.95   Retail price
$1.56   Tax for Washington residents
$3.49   Postage and handling

Make check payable to Shoalwater Restaurant   ISBN 1-880166-01-1

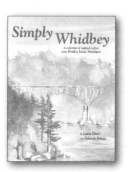

SIMPLY WHIDBEY
by Deborah Skinner and Laura Moore
Saratoga Publishers   Phone 360-675-9592
1581 W. Links Way   Fax 360-679-9131
Oak Harbor, WA 98277

Sample the "flavor of the Northwest" when you prepare Smoked Salmon and Onion Cheesecake, Stuffed Penn Cove Mussels, or Whidbey's Loganberry Champagne Spume—just a few of the "simply delightful" recipes from local innkeepers, cooks, and island residents within this 226-page cookbook.

$18.95   Retail price
$1.55   Tax for Washington residents
$3.00   Postage and handling

Make check payable to Saratoga Publishers   ISBN 0-9628766-0-7

SIX INGREDIENTS OR LESS
by Carlean Johnson
CJ Books   Phone 800-423-7184
P. O. Box 922   Fax 253-265-8537
Gig Harbor, WA 98335   www.sixingredientsorless.com

Life's best recipes are sometimes the simplest. *Six Ingredients or Less* will get you in and out of the kitchen fast with a minimum of fuss and a maximum of flavor. Quick and easy recipes using common ingredients. Over 1 million copies of our books have been sold. 352 pages.

$16.95   Retail price
$1.44   Tax for Washington residents
$3.25   Postage and handling

Make check payable to CJ Books   ISBN 0-942878-05-1

SIX INGREDIENTS OR LESS
COOKING LIGHT & HEALTHY
by Carlean Johnson
CJ Books   Phone 800-423-7184
P. O. Box 922   Fax 253-265-8537
Gig Harbor, WA 98335   www.sixingredientsorless.com

Now you can have it all, quick and easy recipes lower in fat and cholesterol designed to fit today's busy lifestyles—all without sacrificing taste or quality. Nutritional analysis included. Enjoy such recipes as Oriental Shrimp Soup, Chicken Fajitas, Lasagna Rolls, and Apple-Cranberry Crisp. 224 pages.

$12.95   Retail price
  $1.05   Tax for Washington residents
  $2.75   Postage and handling

Make check payable to CJ Books   ISBN 0-942878-03-5

SIX INGREDIENTS OR LESS: PASTA & CASSEROLES
by Carlean Johnson
CJ Books   Phone 800-423-7184
P. O. Box 922   Fax 253-265-8537
Gig Harbor, WA 98335   www.sixingredientsorless.com

This exciting book offers a wide variety of ways to prepare pasta—from simple, everyday recipes to sophisticated fare for company meals—all using six ingredients or less. A must-have for every cook, each recipe contains the regular version plus a low-fat version and a nutritional analysis. 224 pages.

$14.95   Retail price
  $1.21   Tax for Washington residents
  $2.75   Postage and handling

Make check payable to CJ Books   ISBN 0-942878-04-3

SKAGIT VALLEY FARE: A COOKBOOK CELEBRATING BEAUTY AND BOUNTY IN THE PACIFIC NORTHWEST
Lavone Newell   Phone 360-445-2091
18598 Skagit City Road
Mount Vernon, WA 98273

Skagit Valley Fare is filled with recipes collected by the author over a period of 50 years. The book includes recipes from fellow artists, family, immigrants, innkeepers, and pioneers. It is a celebration of a place, its history, its artistry, and of all those who love to cook the Valley's bountiful harvest.

$19.95   Retail price
  $1.60   Tax for Washington residents
  $2.50   Postage and handling

Make check payable to Lavone M. Newell   ISBN 0-9615580-5-9

SLEIGH BELLS AND SUGARPLUMS
by Frances A. Gillette   Phone 360-686-3420
P. O. Box 351   Fax 360-686-3054
Yacolt, WA 98675   eathappy@aol.com

Old-fashioned sentiments, country background and faith inspired this tribute to Christmases past. You will use this treasured book all year long; at Christmas you will read the stories and know that without the Christ child, born so humbly Christmas Day, we would have no purpose.

$14.95   Retail price
  $1.18   Tax for Washington residents
  $2.50   Postage and handling

Make check payable to Frances A. Gillette

STARTERS & CLOSERS

Seattle Mariners Wives and Mariners Care
Seattle Mariners Merchandise Department
P. O. Box 4100   Phone 1-800-MY MARINERS
Seattle, WA 98104

During the 2001 baseball season, wives of Mariners players, coaches, and executive staff compiled fun photos, tidbits of information, and favorite appetizer and dessert recipes of their husbands. This cookbook raised $300,000 for the Fred Hutchinson Cancer Research Center's Pediatric Oncology Dept.

$10.00   Retail price
  $5.95   Postage and handling

Make check payable to Seattle Mariners Merchandise Department

TASTE OF BALBOA

Balboa Elementary Parent Teacher Group
Attn: Atania Gilmore   Phone 509-234-2338
6920 N. Cochran Street   a.t.graphics@mindspring.com
Spokane, WA 99208

Taste of Balboa was produced by the Parent Teacher Group of Balboa Elementary in Spokane, Washington. There are over 200 recipes in eight categories. These recipes are all family favorites, so it should come as no surprise that the dessert section is 62 pages long!

$8.00   Retail price
$3.00   Postage and handling

Make check payable to Balboa PTG

A TASTE OF HEAVEN

Grand Coulee United Methodist Women   Phone 509-633-1962
3025 Rd. "W" N.E.
Mansfield, WA 98830

The Grand Coulee United Methodist Women's hard cover spiralbound cookbook represents 200 of our cook's best recipes.

$9.00   Retail price
$2.50   Postage and handling

Make check payable to Grand Coulee United Methodist Women

TASTE OF THE METHOW

Methow Valley United Methodist Women   Phone 509-997-9292
193 Old Twisp Highway   Fax 509-997-9290
Twisp, WA 98856   jtonseth@methow.com

Taste of the Methow contains 114 pages with 295 recipes from the Methow Valley United Methodist Women, family and friends. Profits from the book sales are used to help support our work and mission activities locally and worldwide.

$7.00   Retail price
$2.50   Postage and handling

Make check payable to Methow Valley United Methodist Women

TASTES OF COUNTRY
by Frances A. Gillette   Phone 360-686-3420
P. O. Box 351   Fax 360-686-3054
Yacolt, WA 98675   eathappy@aol.com

Capture incredible old-fashioned taste, with most ingredients for each recipe in your cupboard. A fantastic book for beginning cooks, newlyweds, and anyone who wishes to receive rave reviews! Are you older or younger than the Hostess Twinkie? This book will tell you this and many interesting thoughts. Illustrated. 222 pages.

$14.95   Retail price
  $1.18   Tax for Washington residents
  $2.50   Postage and handling

Make check payable to Frances A. Gillette

20,000 GALLONS OF CHOWDER
by Ray Dunn
Omar Publishing/Village Books   Phone 360-647-0092
1206 11th Street
Bellingham, WA 98225

The best clam chowder and other recipes for the semi-adventurous! The sailboat dwelling founder of the legendary Colophon Cafe shares unique recipes for the boat person and landlubber along with great sailing tales.

$12.95   Retail price
  $1.01   Tax for Washington residents
  $3.00   Postage and handling

Make check payable to Village Books   ISBN 0-9967283-3-5

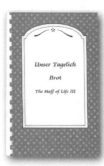

UNSER TAGELICH BROT (THE STAFF OF LIFE III)
Odessa Memorial Hospital Auxiliary
Attn: Laura Estes   Phone 590-982-2908
P. O. Box 151
Odessa, WA 99159-0151

This is the seventh cookbook Odessa Memorial Hospital Auxiliary has published. It is a compilation of all the German recipes plus many favorites from the previous six books, in addition to many newly contributed recipes. There are 466 recipes on 183 pages, from Apple Strudel to Zwetschen Kuchen.

$9.00   Retail price
$3.00   Postage and handling

Make check payable to Odessa Memorial Hospital Auxiliary

WANDERING & FEASTING
A WASHINGTON COOKBOOK
by Mary Houser Caditz
Washington State University Press   Phone 800-354-7360
P. O. Box 645910   Fax 509-335-8568
Pullman, WA 99164-5910   wsupress@wsu.edu

Filled with more than 200 recipes celebrating Washington's bounty, *Wandering & Feasting* takes readers on a culinary journey through the state, highlighting each region's history and foods in delicious recipes. 352 pages. Spiralbound.

$22.95   Retail price
  $1.74   Tax for Washington residents
  $4.00   Postage and handling

Make check payable to WSU Press   ISBN 0-87422-138-2

WASHINGTON COOK BOOK

by Janet Walker
Golden West Publishers, Inc.
4113 N. Longview Avenue
Phoenix, AZ 85014-4949

Phone 800-658-5830
Fax 602-279-6901
goldwest1@mindspring.com

More than 175 tasty recipes! Featuring favorite recipes from the Evergreen State's finest restaurants, bed and breakfasts, homemakers, dignitaries and chefs—including Graham Kerr.

$6.95   Retail price
$3.00   Postage and handling

Make check payable to Golden West Publishers   ISBN 0-914846-97-3

WASHINGTON FARMERS' MARKETS COOKBOOK AND GUIDE

by Kris Wetherbee
Maverick Publications, Inc.
4290 Rice Valley Road
Oakland, OR 97462

Phone 541-849-2838
kwether@jeffnet.org

A handsomely designed and illustrated, 216-page oversize softcover book filled with a collection of over 200 recipes, along with a treasury of valuable cooking and shopping tips, helpful gardening advice, and interesting tidbits.

$14.95   Retail price
$2.00   Postage and handling

Make check payable to Kris Wetherbee   ISBN 0-89288-278-6

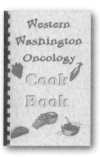

WESTERN WASHINGTON ONCOLOGY COOK BOOK

by Diane Fisher
Western Washington Oncology
Olympia, WA

This book was created from recipes submitted to us by patients and employees to raise money for the American Cancer Society's relay for life. This book is currently out of print.

THE WILD AND FREE COOKBOOK

by Tom Squier
Breakout Productions/Loompanics Unlimited
P. O. Box 1197
Port Townsend, WA 98368

Phone 800-380-2230
Fax 360-385-7785
service@loompanics.com

Written by a former Green Beret who taught survival techniques; you'll find some unusual yet tasty recipes in this 280-page tome. There's Christmas Tree Jelly, Dandelion Wine, and Yellowjacket Soup. Luckily, the author includes techniques for gathering and preparation and sound nutritional information.

$19.95   Retail price
$1.64   Tax for Washington residents
$5.95   Postage and handling

Make check payable to Loompanics Unlimited   ISBN 1-55950-128-6

YOUR FAVORITE RECIPES

Mukilteo Presbyterian Church
822 Third Street
Mukilteo, WA 98275

Phone 425-355-2802
Fax 425-513-2752
Mukbeth@aol.com

Into the new millennium...with hospitality and love presented in 425 recipes by members of our congregation and the larger community. Easy, good, fast food for small and large families, including recipes for and by soccer moms, bachelors, and grandmas; and just plain good reading—especially the many "old world" recipes.

$15.00   Retail price
 $3.00   Postage and handling

Make check payable to Mukilteo Presbyterian Church

INDEX

Put your hands on the oars of a graceful pulling boat or the tiller of a tradition-al wooden catboat and go back in time at the Center for Wooden Boats on Seattle's Lake Union.

Special Discount Offers!

The Best Club *Enjoy the grand flavors of America all at once!*

- You receive the entire 35-volume BEST OF THE BEST STATE COOKBOOK SERIES.
- The cost is only $445.00—a 25% discount off the retail price of $593.25.
- The UPS shipping cost is only $10.00 for addresses anywhere in the United States.
- You receive advance notice of each new edition to the series and have the first opportunity to purchase copies at a 25% discount with no obligation.

The Best of the Month Club

Experience the taste of our nation, one state at a time!

- You receive a different BEST cookbook each month or, if you prefer, every other month.
- You enjoy a 20% discount off the price of each book ($16.95 discounted to $13.56).
- You automatically become a member of the BEST CLUB once you receive all available volumes, which entitles you to a 25% discount on future volumes.
- No minimum purchase required; cancel at anytime.
- Members say: "My BEST books are my very favorite cookbooks."
  "I usually buy more than one copy—they have a way of disappearing."
  "Most of my other cookbooks are on the shelf—my BEST books stay on the kitchen counter."

Join today! 1-800-343-1583

Speak directly to one of our friendly customer service representatives, or
visit our website at **www.quailridge.com** to order online.

Recipe Hall of Fame Collection

The extensive recipe database of Quail Ridge Press' acclaimed BEST OF THE BEST STATE COOKBOOK SERIES is the inspiration behind the RECIPE HALL OF FAME COLLECTION. These Hall-of-Fame recipes have achieved extra distinction for consistently producing superb dishes. *The Recipe Hall of Fame Cookbook* features over 400 choice dishes for a variety of meals. The *Recipe Hall of Fame Dessert Cookbook* consists entirely of extraordinary desserts. The *Recipe Hall of Fame Quick & Easy Cookbook* contains over 500 recipes that require minimum effort but produce maximum enjoyment. Appetizers to desserts, quick dishes to masterpiece presentations, the RECIPE HALL OF FAME COLLECTION has it all.

All books: Paperbound • 7x10 • Illustrations • Index
The Recipe Hall of Fame Cookbook • 304 pages • $19.95
Recipe Hall of Fame Dessert Cookbook • 240 pages • $16.95
Recipe Hall of Fame Quick & Easy Cookbook • 304 pages • $19.95

NOTE: All three HALL OF FAME cookbooks can be ordered as a set for $39.90
(plus $4.00 shipping), a 30% discount off the total list price of $56.85.
Over 1,300 HALL OF FAME recipes for about 3¢ each—an incredible value!

Preserving America's Food Heritage

Best of the Best State Cookbook Series

Best of the Best from
ALABAMA
288 pages, $16.95

Best of the Best from
ARIZONA
288 pages, $16.95

Best of the Best from
ARKANSAS
288 pages, $16.95

Best of the Best from
CALIFORNIA
384 pages, $16.95

Best of the Best from
COLORADO
288 pages, $16.95

Best of the Best from
FLORIDA
288 pages, $16.95

Best of the Best from
GEORGIA
336 pages, $16.95

Best of the Best from the
GREAT PLAINS
288 pages, $16.95

Best of the Best from
ILLINOIS
288 pages, $16.95

Best of the Best from
INDIANA
288 pages, $16.95

Best of the Best from
IOWA
288 pages, $16.95

Best of the Best from
KENTUCKY
288 pages, $16.95

Best of the Best from
LOUISIANA
288 pages, $16.95

Best of the Best from
LOUISIANA II
288 pages, $16.95

Best of the Best from
MICHIGAN
288 pages, $16.95

Best of the Best from the
MID-ATLANTIC
288 pages, $16.95

Best of the Best from
MINNESOTA
288 pages, $16.95

Best of the Best from
MISSISSIPPI
288 pages, $16.95

Best of the Best from
MISSOURI
304 pages, $16.95

Best of the Best from
NEW ENGLAND
368 pages, $16.95

Best of the Best from
NEW MEXICO
288 pages, $16.95

Best of the Best from
NEW YORK
288 pages, $16.95

Best of the Best from
NO. CAROLINA
288 pages, $16.95

Best of the Best from
OHIO
352 pages, $16.95

Best of the Best from
OKLAHOMA
288 pages, $16.95

Best of the Best from
OREGON
288 pages, $16.95

Best of the Best from
PENNSYLVANIA
320 pages, $16.95

Best of the Best from
SO. CAROLINA
288 pages, $16.95

Best of the Best from
TENNESSEE
288 pages, $16.95

Best of the Best from
TEXAS
352 pages, $16.95

Best of the Best from
TEXAS II
352 pages, $16.95

Best of the Best from
VIRGINIA
320 pages, $16.95

Best of the Best from
WASHINGTON
288 pages, $16.95

Best of the Best from
WEST VIRGINIA
288 pages, $16.95

Best of the Best from
WISCONSIN
288 pages, $16.95

Cookbooks listed above have been completed as of December 31, 2002. All cookbooks are ringbound except California, which is paperbound.
Note: Great Plains consists of North Dakota, South Dakota, Nebraska, and Kansas; Mid-Atlantic includes Maryland, Delaware, New Jersey, and Washington, D.C.; New England is comprised of Rhode Island, Connecticut, Massachusetts, Vermont, New Hampshire, and Maine.

Special discount offers available!

(See previous page for details.)

To order by credit card, call toll-free **1-800-343-1583** or visit our website at **www.quailridge.com** to order online. Use the form below to send check or money order.

Order form

Use this form for sending check or money order to:
QUAIL RIDGE PRESS • P. O. Box 123 • Brandon, MS 39043

❏ Check enclosed

Charge to: ❏ Visa ❏ MC ❏ AmEx ❏ Disc

Card #_____

Expiration Date _____

Signature _____

Name _____

Address _____

City/State/Zip_____

Phone # _____

Email Address _____

Qty.	Title of Book (State) or Set	Total

Subtotal _____

7% Tax for MS residents _____

Postage ($4.00 any number of books) + 4.00

Total _____